MW01230878

Seeing Heaven in the Face of Black Men

Tod M. Ewing

Copyright © 2009 by Tod M. Ewing

ISBN 0-7414-5268-5

Book Cover design by Mr. Tyrone V. Parker.
Mr. Parker is an artist living in Newport News, Virginia.
He can be reached via email at tyroneParker39@yahoo.com.
He would love to hear from you.

Published by:

PUBLISHING.COM

1094 New DeHaven Street, Suite 100
West Conshohocken, PA 19428-2713
Info@buybooksontheweb.com
www.buybooksontheweb.com
Toll-free (877) BUY BOOK
Local Phone (610) 941-9999
Fax (610) 941-9959

Printed in the United States of America
Published August 2009

Contents

Acknowledgments

I want to appreciate so many people and because I worked on this book on and off for seven plus years, I will no doubt forget someone. Please forgive me and for those I have remembered, please know my heart is more grateful than I can convey in a sentence or two.

To Nancy Songer who for years kept saying, "Tod you have to write a book." I kept saying "I can't," and she kept saying, "Yes, you can!" Thanks to Barry Magnus and Hughia Magnus who gave me the perspective, early on, of a White man and a Black woman. It was invaluable and a few years later Hughia read the book again providing me with more encouragement. To Barbara Talley who is a prolific author and whose indefatigable work on her own books and constant advice and encouragement were priceless. To yet another friend and editor, Stacia Stribling, whose editing, perspectives and encouragement were a great gift. To the final editor, Yvonne Richter who found all that stuff I would have rather not dealt with but knew I needed to. To Tony Joy, who was working on his own book at the same time and, by simply being Tony, provided constant support. To Fiyah Rootz, for her excellent creation of the blog site for this book. To Faith Holmes, who reminded me how important it is I share both the joy and pride in being African American as well as the challenges. To my, just like a brother friend, Carroll Coley who is what a friend should be. To Lisa Puzon for her many artistic contributions and thought-provoking insights. To Chuck Egerton for his input on the two spiritual oaths on the website.

I give thanks to two of my Professors, Dr. Clem Gifford and Dr. Eunice Gifford, who co-founded the *Institute for Self Transcendence,* now located in Atlanta, Georgia. Through the classes they conducted in the field of Spiritual Psychology,

I've come to know myself more profoundly as a spiritual being. Consequently I have come to realize more deeply than ever the possibilities for humankind.

To my dear precious wife, who exhibited infinite patience with my ups and downs in writing two books at the same time and over an eight-year period. Her faith in me has been unwavering.

To my daughter Angela, son-in-law Karim, granddaughters Ananda, Satiya, and Zaynab for their sweet and *powerful* examples of love and fortitude and to my (our) precious but deceased daughter Talia Carmel Ewing, who lived love and unity (she passed at age 19).

To my sister, who by her own independence, sheer motivation and indefatigable pursuit of excellence has always inspired me, as has her ever-available tender love.

To my brother Geoff Ewing, whose life has inspired me for years, and who had the fortitude to read two separate drafts of this book and give me frank and incredibly helpful advice as only he could.

To my dear sister-in-law, Nancy Nelson Ewing, who provided much needed early advice.

To my mom and dad, who are heroes and always have been and yet don't know it. They have, by their example, been racial unity trailblazers all of their adult lives.

Finally in a category of its own, I would like to honor God for inspiring me to take my best shot. Most importantly, He guided me to the Bahá'í Faith, whose tenets are most timely and call for the world to embrace unity.

I dedicate this book to my daughters Angela Ewing Boyd and Talia Carmel Ewing.

Preface

It is in the spirit of both the pain and hope of my early years of life and subsequent experiences, that I share this book with you. It is in that spirit I offer my post high school perspective on "a day in the life" of this fifty something male, waking up (Black) in the US of America and seeing heaven in the face of black men.

What is it about? It's about why so few Whites and so few Blacks *expect* to see heaven (beauty, strength, dignity spirituality) in the face of black men. It's about what I see, think I see and feel about race as it crops up and pops up on a daily basis. It's about my inner struggles, inner dialogues and daily experiences trying to make sense of it all and understand it. It's about my hard-gained understanding that the only way toward racial unity and justice in this country, or any country, is to recognize the essentially spiritual nature of the problem/disease of racism and to apply spiritual, yet practical, solutions. I call it the practicality of spirituality.

Because religion and spirituality are sensitive subjects, let me explain what I mean by spirituality and the practicality of spirituality. In a broad sense, spirituality is motivated by the core or common purpose of all major religions of the world. It is the desire and willingness to think and act in a noble, honorable and spiritual or what some call transpersonal (beyond personality) manner. However, choosing to live life from a spiritual or transpersonal frame of reference does not require that individuals claim allegiance to one or the other of these religions. Spirituality is defined as that quality and depth of consciousness that realizes an interconnectedness with all humanity. When drawn upon, it impels us to act and react from our noble and better selves and live in integrity, even in the face of seemingly insurmountable challenges. We each have within us, access to a quality of consciousness that, when chosen, allows us to sense and be guided by our highest and noblest self and to be conscious of the sacredness of our life's purpose; specifically how we are intended to act toward and react to others. Spirituality has more to do with the quality of principled responses, first in thought and then in action, than it is does with any material, emotional or physical outcome. In short it is about the ability to conquer our lower nature with our higher nature and thus to sacrifice our baser egocentric needs and responses, to a higher and more profound self; a self that believes, as succinctly stated by Dr. Eunice Gifford, co-director for the Institute of Self Transcendence in Atlanta, Georgia, "when deep speaks to deep, deep responds."

It is spirituality that, in the heat of our daily challenges and inner struggles with race, provides us with a transformative way of responding, lifting us through, out and above our emotional and protective impulses. It can lift us through the emotional pain and anger associated with race and transform it into motivation, will and strength to build unity and justice. All too often we admire that demonstration of character in others, yet fail to choose it for ourselves. Spirituality then has more to do with how we live our faith than it does with what we call ourselves.

That, however imperfectly stated, is my understanding of spirituality. Each and every one of us can tap that spiritual or transpersonal (beyond personality) self. It is the practicality of spirituality that will lift us from the pain of racial antagonism to the glory of racial unity and justice.

So this book then is about the battle that confronts me as I try to manage and balance my anger and frustration about racism and prejudice and tap that transpersonal spiritual self that has faith and hope that good will conquer evil if I persevere with the right spirit. (Barack Obama's run for presidency is one major, but not the only, reason for that hope.*) It's about the battle to stick to spiritual principles and to avoid responding, or acting, based on ego and anger. It's about the effort it takes to stay focused on the positive and not let the hypocrisy and double standards I see consume me. It's about the struggle to avoid putting excessive blame on White folk for so many of the challenges in some African American communities. It's about the struggle to balance empathy for the cumulative and crippling impact of racism in so many Black communities and neighborhoods with the need to hold those same communities accountable.

It's about figuring out which of the battles to fight and which to let go, how hard to push and how to maintain the right spirit during the push. It's about the struggle to call upon my higher self to transform my pain into spiritual strength. As important as anything else, it's about my hope that Black folk, with all the challenges in some of our communities, will continue to stand tall and see the beauty and strength in ourselves. And from that vantage point, continue to overcome the impact of racism and related challenges in our communities and in the nation at large.

Similarly it's about my hope, that White folk, with all the strengths and challenges in their cultures and communities, will manifest a fuller measure of their beauty and continue to fight racism within themselves, their communities and the nation at large.

In the spirit of the spirituality that has sustained so many of us in our lives, I ask my Black brothers and sisters to fight the fight for family and for our legacy. Realize deep down that, like our nation and our own community, the world needs the latent and manifest gifts we have gained through culture, creativity and crucifixion. I ask that we realize without resentment that we can learn from our White brothers and sisters and that we have much to share with them as well. I ask that we realize that sharing, Black to White and White to Black can only happen at an intersection in our lives where we can create a sacred, new reality, on fresh ground.

In that same spirit I ask my White brothers and sisters to realize that, though you may not have created the problem of race prejudice, you inherited it just like we did and are *equally* responsible to help correct it. I ask that you come to see Black folk not as helpless victims who cannot, do not and will not help themselves. I ask that you focus more on the many of us who help ourselves and contribute fully to society instead of solely on the ones who do not. I ask that you take a closer look at those low income communities you consider so terrible, see the rich potential in so many of the people and then find ways, *as equal partners*, to foster the realization of that potential. I ask you to realize that, in many respects, your communities are no different than ours. You too have persons who contribute to society and those who don't, the moral ones and the immoral ones, the ones who wreak havoc and the ones who don't. We, Black and White, just happen to do our respective stuff in different ways. I ask that you realize and internalize this perspective in your hearts so that you can finally accept us as fully human, fully capable and fully necessary to your existence.

I ask my White brothers and sisters to acknowledge that you have not and do not have to deal with the impact of color prejudice and accept that it makes a difference. Individually you have problems and struggles too and some of them very painful, but for the most part you've never had the added layer of color. That is a blessing and a privilege you have long enjoyed. I ask that you acknowledge that advantage and take the next step which is to reach up, reach down and reach out to make sure everyone gets the same blessings.

Though not a simplistic task, it's really just that simple. So with this, I ask my White brothers and sisters to reach out, and not to continue expecting Black folk to come to your space; to be willing to move to that space in the intersection that belongs to no one—that place of creative new possibilities.

What I'm also asking is for the two *races* to meet each other halfway at the intersection, realizing that we are each responsible for our respective pieces of the puzzle. Both of us have to take higher ground to build greater justice and peace.

Why do I see this as critical for our nation at this time? Because on every level, unity is life and disunity is death and right now we could go either way. Because in a nation founded on equity and justice, our glaring racial injustices, not withstanding significant progress, have held us back for far too long. We cannot play a leadership role in the world that has any moral credibility until we remove the remaining vestiges of our still debilitating form of racism. Only together can we set the kind of example for the world that true equality, true democracy and true freedom are possible. The world needs that example, at this time, more than ever because as a people we are literally, figuratively, biologically and spiritually "one." We cannot survive until that consciousness is attained by both Black and White. That's why. And if those reasons aren't good enough, it's worth taking note that any problem, disease or dysfunction that goes untreated, partially treated or ill treated will only get worse for everyone. Ask yourself if you think our nation can survive that.

Before I go on, let me say that more and more credible research indicates that genetically, all human beings share almost the same identical make-up. Additionally, quantum physics indicates that life forms and matter in general are simply energy vibrating at higher and lower rates of frequency, giving the impression of being mass. Particles of energy are what the universe and we as human beings are composed of. So in fact, if we are just energy then we are all truly *one,* simply appearing as different forms of expression. I say that because I believe the concept of separate and distinct races is outdated and merely a social construct. I simply use the terms Black, White and race(s) for ease of reference and because of the historical relationship. I believe, however, we are one race biologically and if we are all energy, we are one in that regard too. I will not say any more on this subject, but the sciences are continually offering evidence to prove the reality of our *underlying oneness.*

To my point then: it is at the intersection of our lives, as Blacks and Whites, where hope lives and new possibilities exist. In his book entitled, *The Medici Effect,* Frans Johansson discusses what can happen if seemingly opposite concepts, ideas, realities or fields of study can connect and intersect. There is a remarkable chance for a creative explosion. The outcome of that connection is what he refers to as intersectional innovations or intersectional ideas. His fundamental premise is that diversity breeds innovation. Johansson offers an intriguing example. An architect was asked to design a building for an extremely hot climate that would maintain a constant temperature of around seventy-five degrees. The trick was that the building could not have air conditioning. Eventually the architect studied the mounds built by termites and found these mounds maintained a constant temperature of eighty-seven degrees on extremely hot days and cold nights. He went on to design the building based on the structure of termite mounds. Initially a sum of $3,500,000 was saved by not having air conditioning. The building uses only ten percent of the energy of similar structures. Two seemingly opposite realities and fields created something truly innovative (Johansson, 2006, p. 3–4).

Such intersecting and connecting can happen for Blacks and Whites if we so choose. We have existed, in a sense, as polar opposites from the beginning. Our relationship is a lightening rod for prejudice in the US of America. If we bring our spiritual selves to the intersection, with our common yet very different life experiences, we can create a community unlike anything we have seen; an innovative explosion based on unity in diversity.

So I write this book not with a pie-in-the-sky hope, but rather from the vantage point of understanding the "practicality of spirituality" in my own life. I believe it is *spiritually possible and perhaps emotionally impossible* to transcend our limited and preconceived notions, hurts, pains and fears. What does that mean? There is a largely untapped "spirit" quality that is a part of true human nature and that, when engaged, creates its own miracles. There are so many deeply rooted emotional wounds, bruises, scars and other related complexities involved in race issues that there has to be a way to transcend them; not ignore or negate them, but transcend them. Spirit allows us to transform emotional confusion and pain into constructive energy. That is what I mean by the practicality of spirituality. It makes practical sense to draw on that capacity. What might start out as a rational discussion or effort quickly moves into emotional no win warfare, if the spirit is not engaged as the sustaining element. It is that spirit force that can lead us together out of the despair of racism and into the life of new possibilities based on unity and justice.

A passage from a publication and statement entitled *The Promise of World Peace* (The Universal House of Justice, 1985) says it better than I can:

> On the one hand, people of all nations proclaim not only their readiness but their longing for peace and harmony, for an end to the harrowing apprehensions

tormenting their daily lives. On the other, uncritical assent is given to the proposition that human beings are incorrigibly selfish and aggressive and thus incapable of erecting a social system at once progressive and peaceful, dynamic and harmonious, a system giving free play to individual creativity and initiative but based on co-operation and reciprocity.

As the need for peace becomes more urgent, this fundamental contradiction, which hinders its realization, demands a reassessment of the assumptions upon which the commonly held view of mankind's historical predicament is based. Dispassionately examined, the evidence reveals that such conduct, far from expressing man's true self, represents a distortion of the human spirit. Satisfaction on this point will enable all people to set in motion constructive social forces which, because they are consistent with human nature, will encourage harmony and co-operation instead of war and conflict.

A candid acknowledgement that prejudice, war and exploitation have been the expression of immature stages in a vast historical process and that the human race is today experiencing the unavoidable tumult which marks its collective coming of age is not a reason for despair but a prerequisite to undertaking the stupendous enterprise of building a peaceful world. (p. 1)

The Statement goes on to clarify the value and motivating influence of spirituality:

There are spiritual principles, or what some call human values, by which solutions can be found for every social problem. Any well-intentioned group can in a general sense devise practical solutions to its problems, but good intentions and practical knowledge are usually not enough. The essential merit of spiritual principle is that it not only presents a perspective which harmonizes with that which is immanent in human nature, it also induces an attitude, a dynamic, a will, an aspiration, which facilitate the discovery and implementation of practical measures. (p. 4)

Peace in the world starts within one's self and moves to peace in a family, community, city, state and nation. Just as I think peace is possible in the world, I also think racial "peace" is possible if we see ourselves and our circumstances in a new light as described above. In that spirit I hope Blacks and Whites will extend each other an olive branch in peace and continue to grow from that new space at the intersection of our spirit lives.

*Notes:

I was almost finished with this book when Barack Hussein Obama was elected the 44th president of the United States on November 4, 2008. The book was sent to the publisher before he was inaugurated. Though he is mentioned in earlier portions of the book, it is not until the end that his election is acknowledged. Both the election of a President with African American heritage and his inauguration released a tremendous spirit of hope in the US of America and in the world, yet as some would suggest, we are not in a "post-racial" era because of it. There is work to be done to sustain the hope offered by his election and it is my desire that this book be of assistance toward that end.

Seeing Heaven in the
Face of Black Men

Introduction

(Please read the Preface as it outlines the purpose for the book.)

As far as I know I have been Black, in some form, all of my life. Though I once was a Negro, an Afro-American, an African American, a Person of Color and of African descent, I remain Black or Brown depending on your vision or version. I was born in 1953 so I had to have been Colored once as well. The abbreviation would be something like CNBAAPA (Colored, Negro, Black, Afro-American, African American, Person of Color or of African descent.)

Issues of race confronted me at birth. I was born and spent the first ten years of my life in the village of Deephaven in the suburb of Minnetonka, Minnesota. At that time Deephaven had two racial/cultural groups of people: White folks and our family. (I heard Frans Johansson, author of *The Medici Effect* say that in a speech once and realized it fit my situation as well) Our family was the only Black family for literally miles around. So I knew I was "different" and quickly learned, from the time I had cognition, not so desirable. More on that in a minute.

We all have challenges in life and I'm a believer the Creator does not give us more than we can handle, though at times I do wonder. Whether we realize it at the time or not, the tests we face in life are truly gifts. Over time the value of my *birthplace gift* has become increasingly clear, so I have no gripes about the hand I was dealt in Minnetonka, Minnesota. It did, however, give me a particular vantage point and because of those early and subsequent experiences, it is clear to me, the race issue will be with me from "womb to tomb."

The year 1952 set the stage for my entrance into the world in 1953. A big struggle ensued when, in that year, my parents tried to purchase a home in the above-mentioned Minnetonka, Minnesota. Our future neighbors were up in arms, vigorously protesting the sale of a home to a "Negro family" ("Race Prejudice Blooms," 1952). My parents where put through all kinds of changes including personal and physical threats. Though the neighbors could not legally keep my parents out, they told them "there were other ways" to deal with us. The ringleader of the group told my dad if he moved in he "would do all he could to make it so miserable for him that he would move." My dad asked him why he didn't want us in the neighborhood, and he candidly replied "he was prejudiced against Negroes." My dad said, "I am going to do all I can to stay, no matter what happens" ("Protest Against Negro Family," 1952).

Because they were able to secure a lawyer through the NAACP, my parents were able to purchase their new home. According to an article appearing in the largest newspaper in Minnesota, those same angry neighbors agreed they would never again sell a home to a Negro family and even wanted to bribe the seller to break the contract, pledging money to pay for any subsequent lawsuits ("Protest Against Negro Family," 1952). I sometimes wonder what prompted the person to sell her home to my mom and dad in the first place and what flack they might have gotten for doing so. My mom tells me the seller, a single White female, was afraid the neighbors were going to do something to her as well. Regardless, I was born the following year into this emotionally charged environment. For me "womb to tomb" is not too farfetched.

My earliest and most vivid recollections, before kindergarten and elementary school, were of feeling emotionally unsafe, insecure and afraid of the world. For some time I didn't understand why people made fun of me, didn't want me to come to their houses, avoided talking to me but at the same time whispered about me. I couldn't understand why the girls didn't want to sit by me on the school bus or walk with me in the hallways. At a certain point it became clear it was because of my color. One day, during recess, a big White boy called me a nigger. As young as I was, I felt enraged and almost hurt him badly. I'm not even sure why I had such a vehement reaction to that word, because there was no way, at my young age, I could have fully comprehended its meaning. However, I remember it lit and burned my fuse in the space of seconds. I spent much of my time in those early elementary school days wishing I could be like everyone else.

My parents loved us and worked extremely hard to provide for us but weren't fully aware of the emotional confusion and pain we were going through. I was depressed at a very early age. I remember being so insecure in kindergarten that during nap time I wet all over myself because I was too nervous to walk across the room to the bathroom. That happened only once but was indicative of how I felt. From the time I can remember, it just felt like my whole life, including relationships, was perilous, tenuous, uncertain and full of anxiety.

Though my parents may not have been aware of the degree of our confusion, I am eternally grateful to them as it was during these early years they modeled for us and taught us the need to love, have spiritual strength and rely on God. Religion and spirituality have long been the sustaining force for African Americans in the US of America and in that regard our family was no different. (I say US of America instead of just America because there is a Central, North and South America and not just a US of America; and I say US instead of United States to remind you and me that this whole effort to move forward is about all of US.) I now understand more clearly that they were trying to teach us the exact opposite of what we were experiencing in our daily lives. They were setting an expectation for our behavior.

As members of the Bahá'í Faith, my parents were grounded in the belief in the oneness and unity of the human family and the belief that prejudice of any kind opposes the will and purpose of the Creator and of creation, violating the most fundamental principle of justice for all. They believed and still believe the religions come from the one same Source and contain truth that should guide our behavior and attitudes. At a most fundamental level, they taught us to live by the golden rule. Rather than being a mere slogan, they taught us by example that this was the core of living a good life—a spiritual life, if you will. They taught us that religion and spirituality should create unity and justice, not disunity. Most importantly they taught us that human beings are noble and that I needed to behave in that way and choose to maintain my dignity in dealing with life's challenges.

This last point, I later internalized to include how I needed to deal with the challenges of racism and prejudice. My parents modeled that nobility and graciousness. During our childhood, I never heard them talk badly about anyone, including White folks. Given the circumstances, I find that extremely admirable.

I now understand that their concept of religion truly meant a way of living that transcended a particular religious affiliation. Religion of any kind can motivate spirituality. Spirituality encompasses how you treat, meet and greet others and how you handle life's challenges. It has more to do with how you live your faith than it does with what you call yourself.

However, at the time, the spirituality Mom and Dad tried to convey to me only sunk in partially. It was sort of a mixed blessing. At the time it didn't help me very much to know I was created in the image and likeness of God and God's love would sustain me in times of woe. I was simply trying to survive emotionally from day to day and God's love was just too abstract. Interestingly enough, I did respond on some level to the principle of unity and oneness of all people and likewise to the principle of religious unity. Unity of all people sounded good to me because it was what I wanted to feel. Similarly the unity and equality of religions felt like a better bet to me especially when I'd hear so many other kids talk about folk going to hell if they didn't believe this or that. I'm fairly certain the idea of rejecting others because of their religion didn't sit well with me as I was being rejected every day because of my color.

That said I also had to deal with the fact that, in this almost entirely Christian environment, my parents were members of this "strange" religion called Bahá'í. So, far from making me feel more secure and grounded, I felt further outcast as both Black and Bahá'í! I could not lie about my skin color, but I could and did lie about my religion. If asked by other kids what my religion was, I would often tell them I was Christian. I believe my faith of choice was Lutheran; remember this was Minnesota.

My sister, in later conversations, described our time in Minnetonka as *traumatic*. For a long time I didn't accept her description. I would say to her it was just the way life was and simply our cross to bear, consciously or unconsciously dismissing the gravity of the experience. As I reflected on this over time, with the help of counseling to reconcile some of my emotional baggage, I came to accept the word *traumatic* as the only accurate way to describe the overriding emotions of our entire childhood.

You might wonder about the reason for my parents' move to a place like Minnetonka, Minnesota, in 1952, particularly since my dad grew up in a similar environment decades before. His was the only Black family in Boone, Iowa, way back in the day. They would later explain that their primary concern was that we receive a good education, which of course was a noble motivation. A good education has been an enduring issue for CNBAAPA folk from day one. "To make it we couldn't be just as smart, we had to be smarter, not just as good but better," as the saying goes. My brother and sister and I have had many a talk with my parents about the "learning" that took place waking up Black in US of America in Minnetonka, Minnesota. We no doubt received a good school education and a good education about race and racism.

Our family has debated the pros and cons and the "what ifs" regarding that time in our lives. In addition to a good education, we did not live in a poor urban area and were spared some of the challenges of that environment and, yes, to some degree we learned how to relate to White folk and "survive" in that world. No, we didn't develop a sense of identity or a sense of belonging, we didn't have role models or Black playmates outside our immediate family, and we suffered isolation and exclusion—sometimes subtle, sometimes overt. The verdict remains now and forever "out" on whether we would have been better or worse off growing up somewhere else. The thing about life is that some things you will never know for sure. I do know for sure about those times that I made it through them and suffered deep emotional wounds. I also know for sure that I gained spiritual strength, capacity and sagacity, much of that materializing with age. Life tends to bring gifts of fortitude, even in sorrow and pain and often because of it. I am grateful to my parents for doing what they felt was the right thing. I hope I live up to their example with my children and grandchildren.

On another grateful and "up note," I did learn early on that some White folk stand up for justice for justice's sake. A

6

Jewish lawyer remained a dear family friend to the end of his life. Without him we would've never gotten our home. An elderly White woman made sure that the humiliating experience my parents faced appeared in the newspaper, actually writing the story herself. A few Whites in the area welcomed us and some others were willing to struggle with their prejudices and make efforts to accept us. I include this up note not because it changed the overall climate of that time and place, but rather because it represents an important part of my experience, my truth and my hope.

So what did I learn from those early years? I learned consciously and subconsciously that I didn't fit in; my color was a detriment; the world was not an emotionally safe place; and whatever being Black meant, White people were uneasy and even angry about it. They did not trust it; so it was better to try to be like them if I wanted to have any life at all. I also learned that some White people cared and would stand up for me.

I learned very little if anything about other Black people except from the few visits with relatives, a few of our parents' friends and the occasional Black Bahá'í who would come from a distance. I remember being uncomfortable around the few Black kids we had contact with because I didn't feel like them, talk like them or act like them. It took me a long time and a lot of heartache to realize being Black was a noble and beautiful thing.

When I was ten or eleven, we moved from Minnetonka to a demographically similar place closer to the city of Minneapolis. Different place, similar experiences, but now I was approaching the late elementary and early junior high years as they called them then. They're called middle school years now, but by whatever name, it is often a time of turmoil and uncertainty. I still had no clue about who I really was, where or how I fit in or what it meant to be a Negro. I tried real hard to fit in because that's what junior high kids want to do, at least with each other.

White kids ice-skated so I learned to ice-skate. In a short time, my brother and I learned to skate with the best of them. I also tried to fit in by identifying with what these kids thought was cool. I zeroed in on everything from their favorite TV shows to their hobbies. I still felt the color barrier though; the discomfort felt by so many other kids being around me and my discomfort being around them. I might have looked like I was "one of the guys" to some, but I knew I was simply not like them and I had no alternatives to choose from. I hung out with different kids for short periods of time, but what I clearly remember is that rarely did anyone seek my company. I felt like I was always chasing them or I would be left out. I remember starting to develop one friendship with a kid that during high school would evolve into a solid and good friendship. At that early stage I felt like even though we hung out, I was competing to be accepted in his crowd. I found out years later, his mother was asked by one of her neighbors if she was a "nigger lover." She said, "I guess I am." I realize now, though I always felt off balance and out of place, there must have also been subtle and not so subtle pressure on some White folks just having me around. I now wonder how many other White folks got flack for having me in their home or neighborhood.

A vivid memory, indelibly etched in my mind, is of the bully in my junior high school standing up in the middle of the lunchroom, staring straight at me and viciously shouting, "You Black nigger!" He shouted and just looked at me with a menacing stare, daring me to say something back. Everyone watched and no one said anything. Even if someone wanted to they were probably too scared. I shrunk and walked away in humiliation and fear. Unlike my first experience with the "N"-word in elementary school, this guy scared me to death. He just seemed so big and so mean. That experience solidified my sense that somehow in this battle, it was me against the world. True or not, that is what became embedded in my psyche.

The first, but not first ever, big time crush I had on a girl was in the eighth or ninth grade. She was White of course, there being almost no Black girls in the school, and she liked me too. But, she told me she could not take the pressure from her friends if she spent time with me; told me straight up. This story repeated itself in various forms several times with several girls. She cried and I cried. I ended up telling her I understood, so she would not feel bad, but I felt terrible. Junior high was a rough one.

I was angry inside, desperate and rootless and became more rebellious. I started smoking cigarettes, actually in fifth grade, and drinking in seventh grade. (I quit drinking by eleventh grade, but I smoked on and off until my late twenties.) I ran away from home in eighth or ninth grade. At times I got along best with kids who were considered troublemakers. I started stealing, not everything and anything, but it included cars, clothes, women's handbags and most things in between. No weapons were ever used, thank God; however I had some harrowing experiences. My life of crime ended when I got caught after crashing a stolen car in my own neighborhood. My neighbor was a police detective and I ended up in his office at the police station. How embarrassing was that?

When I was fifteen, my parents decided to open a foster home for troubled youth. (Probably sounds like I needed to be the first placement.) They needed a bigger house and the one which suited their needs was in a predominately Black neighborhood. My sister had graduated from high school and was no longer at home; so it was just me and my brother. We had as many as six foster brothers at a time, mostly Black. This was my first real exposure to Black kids in close proximity for any length of time. Most of them were from broken homes.

While some had minor criminal records, they were not what you would call hardened. I have to say I learned something about who I was as a Black person from all of them. I learned about "Black" music, hair products, colognes, clothes, speech patterns and communication styles, hand shakes and greetings. I learned there was a whole "Black" identity separate from White folk.

I was so starved to be accepted and feel normal I overcompensated and tried to become the very essence of "real Blackness." I particularly gravitated to one of the boys, who, for the sake of this narrative, we'll call Jimmy. He was a tall, slick-dressing, smooth-talking young man who was more than willing to show me the road to Blackness via his personal style. I changed my walk, talk and dress. I also "copped" an attitude, as folk used to say.

Now in high school, I remember many of the White kids being astonished at my metamorphosis. I was bitter and didn't really care what they thought, at least on the surface anyway. My "super fly" friend went to the same school with me and we liked to strut our stuff! After several months he got kicked out of our home for continuous violation of house and school rules. I settled back into the rut of wanting to be accepted, but with at least some small sense of who I was as a Black person. Jimmy taught me some good things and some not so good things, but I have to thank him for all of it. Most importantly he modeled pride in being Black. As James Brown said, "say it loud, I'm Black and I'm proud" (Brown, 1968). Such was Jimmy, loud and proud.

Somewhere around that time a really popular, older White boy, whom we'll call Joe, seemed to take to me for some unknown reason. Man, I thought I was cool. I hung out with Joe and he displayed me like a trophy, but I was too starstruck to care. All I knew was this popular White dude kept telling me how cool

I was and I was getting attention. Plus, his Cuban girlfriend—we'll call her Maria—would always confide in me when they were going through rough times. She would drive me around in her red GTO. We would talk on the phone for hours and became friends. She was gorgeous and, needless to say, I had a crush on her. At one point I even think she had a bit of a crush on me, but that could have been wishful thinking. I do remember it was Maria who one day told me she wanted to teach me to kiss. She gave me one kissing lesson, so maybe she did sort of like me. As far as Joe went, after a time the cool feeling I got being around him sort of wore off and I moved on.

Soon after that I got my first real girlfriend, whom we'll call Sue. Sue was White. No surprise there; my school still only had about three Black students maximum, including me and my brother. Sue was sort of an outcast and didn't care what the other kids felt about her going out with someone Black. Her family did their best to accept our relationship but I could tell it wasn't easy. I was just glad her mom and step-dad didn't prohibit her from seeing me. I will forever be grateful to her. Having a girlfriend who really cared about me, my *Blackness* and all, was just what I needed to survive at the time. Our precarious relationship was on and off again throughout my high school years. Sometimes it was great and other times we were like oil and water. However Sue broke the ice. That experience had a profound impact on both of our lives I feel blessed we reconnected after many years and continue to be good friends to this day.

By my late junior and early senior years, I was having a better time of things. I started to excel in athletics and was an all star in football and captain of the baseball team. It seems excelling in sports has frequently been a door to a *level* of acceptance in portions of the White community and it appeared that was the case for me. It increased my popularity in general and with girls as well which is a key issue in high school. The Civil

Rights Movement had taken place around this time and I have come to believe that it also had an impact on my increased acceptance.

My increasing popularity notwithstanding, I was worn out and wanted to drop out during my senior year. My grades were bad and, according to my recollection, I graduated at a pretty low rank in my class. I thank God for baseball season as that is what really kept me in school. We had a motley crew of rich and lower income kids and even a tad of ethnic diversity. Our coach was fun loving, and we all seemed to jell. (By the way, as captain I emphasized, if nothing else, we were going to be unified. I tried to lead by example like my parents.) That whole experience represented the first time in my life I really had a feeling of accomplishment. We were a game short of becoming state champions. Though, at the time I sensed my new-found popularity had more to do with my athletic achievements than it did with changing attitudes, I focused on the fact that my social life was improving. Though somewhat recklessly, I took full advantage of the change.

During my high school years I developed a few close friends, kids who cared about me regardless of race, and several good acquaintances. There was a category of kids who were nervous about getting too close, but who liked me at a safe distance, and then there were those who wanted nothing to do with me. I also had a few older young adult friends who welcomed me to their homes. I remember one woman in particular, ten years my senior and the sister of a boy I could say was really a friend. Her home became a hangout for me for a period of time, and it felt like a safe haven as she welcomed me with open arms. She could chide me or joke with me and still maintain her "elder" status. We became and remain good friends.

During one of my many break up times with Sue, I dated another girl we'll call Shelly. Shelly attended a different school and the boys at our school always said that school had the prettiest cheerleaders. My guess is that they gave little consideration to the cheerleaders at the black schools and embarrassingly enough I probably didn't either. Anyway Shelly, to my recollection, was captain of the team. Didn't I think I was somebody? Not really. I was still surprised when a White girl accepted me and didn't back away later. Equally surprising was my experience with Shelly's parents. They were proud to have me as their daughter's boyfriend. This was a new experience for me—a White family actually embracing my relationship with their daughter; not like a show piece, but as a real person. They told me, in a conversation early on, they'd raised their children to treat everyone equally, and they intended to stand by that. My antenna was always up to see if that would indeed be true. As I watched and observed I realized they really liked having me around. They would introduce me to their friends, without hesitation, as "Shelly's boyfriend." Shelly was the same way. That relationship proved another huge emotional boost. We too remain good friends to this day.

It would appear, life was pretty good, but inside I was still mixed up and insecure. I no longer wanted to be more "White like," but I still didn't know what it meant to be Black. Going out with the prettiest girls helped my self-esteem, however superficial that may seem now. Not surprisingly, it failed to diminish my basic inner turmoil. "Who am I?" remained the question of the day.

By this time in my life I had tried anger, frustration, bitterness, fitting in, not fitting in, rejecting self, and rejecting others, all Blackness, no Blackness and focusing on girls. The results were emptiness and confusion. I needed to try something else. Something told me I needed to focus more on God or religion or spirituality, not even being sure what that all meant. However for most of my life, in the back of my mind, I had a feeling I needed to figure it out. I'm sure it had to do with my parents' influence. I made a commitment to cultivate my "spiritual nature" more fully as, in my mind at least, I had tried everything else. After some investigation and soul searching, I officially became a member of the Bahá'í Faith and started on that journey. I told myself it was worth a try.

This represents an abbreviated history of my middle and high school years. Again the question is what did I learn from this time in my life? The lessons were almost the same as they were in my elementary years, just somewhat more nuanced. I learned I did not fit in, my color was a detriment, the world was not an emotionally safe place and whatever being Black meant, many White people were uneasy and even angry about it and they did not trust it. Though I started to reject this notion, I realized, the more I acted like them the more I was accepted. I also learned there are White people who care and who will stand up for what is right

I did learn more about other Black folk, besides my relatives, and though most of it was from my foster brothers, who had their own problems, they still had good qualities and helped me more than they could know.

I realized well after the fact, most of the kids I knew best in middle and high school had no idea I had such a tough time. I went to a couple of my high school reunions because there were a few people I wanted to see. One thing I learned at one of the reunions shocked me. At least a few of my class-mates actually thought *I had it made* in high school and *had it together*. I remember one woman told me that during high school she felt like I was "the man." I don't know what to make of that, but I have a few thoughts.

One thought is the students had no idea what it was like to be a lone Black in an all-White environment. It could also mean those who were friendly to me felt like everything was okay, assuming I was experiencing what they were experiencing on a day-to-day basis. Many of these folks were not necessarily mean-spirited. In many cases, they conveyed their discomfort with me through unconscious, non-verbal cues and simply did not realize it. Also I know I pretended pretty well and that no doubt created some confusion on their part. And finally it could mean that, over time, I became very sensitive to rejection and negative reactions to me and was blind to overtures that might have been genuine. Probably it was some of all this and more.

It would not be until college that I would have a broader cross section of experiences with Black folk. It was during that time I really began to have a more wholesome and proud racial identity. During college I married, and we had our first child. After college and a brief stint working in juvenile corrections, I worked for several years as a Minority Affairs Director at St. Cloud University in Minnesota. This was my first opportunity to address racism in an institutional setting. In that job, I began to find an outlet for the frustrations of the injustice I had felt all of my life. I was driven and I threw myself into the work. After almost five years I was emotionally spent, but I had developed an even stronger racial/cultural identity. As I look back, I realize this period of passionate devotion to the race work was one of the most defining and affirming times of my life. I remain proud of what I accomplished during those years, by the grace of God.

My years in St. Cloud as a student and professional were however, not with out racial pain. For me part of the pain was that for many Blacks I was not Black enough and therefore ostracized or ignored. Of course that was not across the board but substantial enough to cut deep. For many Whites I was too Black, expected too much change in my role as Minority Affairs director and was not grateful enough for the small gains that the University was making. That dynamic forced

15

me to come to a greater clarity about what being Black meant for me.

It was several years after having our second child that we moved from Minnesota to South Carolina. In that state, where race plays a prominent role in all aspects of life, I started a business with a friend in the field of diversity training. Of course the focus was on race and that has been the primary focus of my work since. After twenty years in South Carolina, my family moved to Washington, DC.

So now you know a bit about from whence I have come and about my frame of reference for writing this book. As I look back on these early years I see how deeply they shaped my current perspectives on moving the US of America to a higher level of racial unity and justice. My journey continues.

Chapter 1

How the Story Began

(Please read Preface and Introduction first. They are part of the story.)

"It sure is a trip, wakin up Black in America. I said, 'It sure is a trip, wakin up Black in America.' Does anyone hear me? Do you hear what I'm saying? I'm telling anyone that will listen it's a TRIP wakin up Black in America, and it was a trip wakin up Colored, Negro, Afro-American, African America, a Person of Color and of African descent as well." So if you put Black in there after Negro, again you have the abbreviation CNBAAPA.

Anyway, some time ago, I was frustrated and angry about the racial experiences I was having and I thought to myself (and may even have said out loud), "It sure is a trip, wakin up Black in America." That was really how this book started. I took all those feelings and memories and ideas that started flowing through me and I just sat down and started writing. It was like a faucet had been turned on by that one little sentence, and if I didn't start writing, I might drown. The editing and goals came much later.

Once I started writing this book, I would read a news story in the middle of the writing process or hear something on the radio, see something about race on TV, or talk to someone about a race-related subject. If I was moved by it or thought it touched on some perspective or angle I had not included or that needed reinforcement, I put it in the book in "real time" as best I could. As soon as it came my way, I tried to add it to the book, regardless if it fit in with the particular subject I was writing about at the time. So right in the middle of some topic, you might see the words "**NEWS FLASH**." That means something happened at that moment or that day that I just added right as it happened or when I started writing again. If you're confused, don't worry: you'll understand once you run into it.

I also decided to write this book as informally and naturally as possible to convey the type of thoughts and experiences I and others like me have daily. I wrote much of it as if I were thinking my thoughts out loud and sharing them with you. Sometimes they take on an almost conversation like form. At times I will lay things out in detail to make my points. Other times I will write in short-clipped sentences when I feel I just need to get to the point or if the words just naturally flow that way.

Since I wrote this book on and off for eight plus years, some of my experiences will be recent and some not as recent, which in many ways is a good thing as it gives perspective over a period of time. The order of chapters, for the most part, is based on my flow of consciousness and, figuratively speaking, these chapters are written as sort of "a day in the life." Also, something may come up at one point in the story and then some variation of the same theme somewhere else. That is how race has worked in my life. I will see, hear and experience one thing and then some permutation of it will come up somewhere else during my day/life. I don't introduce this redundancy for redundancy's sake; it simply represents the redundancy of my experiences.

It is written primarily in the first person and represents my personal experiences, though I include the perspectives of others as well. It is their reality fused with my reality that constitutes my outlook in this book. In either case, whether I write about my experiences or my intersection with others' experiences, they are representative of a *portion* of common Black reality.

That being said, as I wrote my flow-of-consciousness story, I realized that many Colored, Negro, Black, Afro-American, African American, Person of Color and African descent folks in America could write on this same theme—a day in the life of a Black person—and it would come out pretty much like my story. Their stories would simply have different examples of the same challenges—different characters but similar experiences. When I asked some of my CNBAAPA friends to read parts of my story, they did so, and almost matter-of-factly said, "Yeah, that's true," along with a few instances of "Amen" and "Good job." To them, there was nothing revolutionary about the representation of many of my experiences—it was just life, *and often some version of their own.* (What some particularly liked were the approaches suggested for resolution, unity and justice.) On the other hand, when I showed it to some White friends, they told me most White people they know have very little clue Black folk might experience life in this manner in the US of America.

That is the point. As has been stated by many others before me, White and Black folk too often live in parallel experiential and psychological universes. Until we allow these parallel universes to intersect, or at the very least begin to *acknowledge and accept* that Blacks and Whites often have very different experiences, America will continue to be riddled, rattled and plagued with the matter of race.

Here's an important note before I move on. Folk have asked me if I think all White folk are prejudice. The question is asked as if one is either prejudice or not prejudice. I say prejudice exists on a continuum and often only manifests itself when one is in the situation. It isn't about being all prejudice or all not prejudice. Some folk think because they have a friend or two of another race they are not prejudice. Well guess what? I'm married to a woman, have two daughters, three granddaughters, a mother and a sister all of whom I love. Does that mean I am free of sexism and in all situations will treat women equitably?

Anyway, the continuum starts at the bigoted kind of prejudice that we are all familiar with such as the Ku Klux Klan type. Well in between that and being prejudice free there are all kinds of things that require attention. I will name only a few. Would I send my kids to a good school that had a large number or majority of Black students? A similar question can be asked about where I would choose to live. As a White female do I clutch my handbag when I see a Black man coming my way? Because I say hello and am friendly to my African descent co-workers does that automatically mean I'm not prejudice? Does my friendliness to my Black co-workers translate to all other situations? For example, if I'm looking for a used car and I drive by a used car lot where I see a number of Black workers in the lot, would I go there and look for a car? Prejudice comes out situationally so to assume lack of prejudice is to stop paying attention to opportunities for real growth and change. What did I feel like when I saw that car lot full of Black attendants? Did I hesitate to stop or just drive by and not stop at all? What went through my head at the time? What gut level fears or anxieties might have been operating subconsciously? This book is about the need to pay attention and be intentional about removing our prejudices.

Moving right along. In being honest about all this, I didn't want my book to be grim or humorless so I make some attempts at humor or lightness. So some parts of the book are written in a tongue-in-cheek, folksy way. When I get too heavy for too long I just get weary. Other parts are just straightforward everyday language.

Speaking of folksy let me tell you what happened when I first started writing this book. It started coming out in sort of a conversational and folksy way at first. I couldn't really help it; even started leaving g's off some of the words that are sup-posed to end in -ing. I'm not doing that because I don't know any better. I'm doing it because I used to read the works of the late and great Mr. Langston Hughes over and over again. He wrote about race and found a way to state hard truths in a folksy, but straightforward way. Took some of the edge off so his words could really be heard. He was truly a genius in con-veying his meaning through prose and poetry though I think he decided to keep the "g" on the end of most of his words. For me, takin the "g" off some of the words just gave me that folksy Langston Hughes feeling.

Langston Speaks

Let me share a little bit of the genius of Brother Langston: He created a character named Jesse B. Semple (Just B. Simple) and in conversation form had him tell stories about the impact of race in his life. Mr. Hughes, through the character of Jesse, told these stories in such a way that you would feel like you were sittin somewhere on a porch swing right beside him. He would say things like "I have had so many hardships in this life it's a wonder I'll live until I die" (Hughes, 1967, p. 1). Normally, Jesse was conversing with someone who would re-spond to him or ask him questions. The following abbreviated vignette exemplifies the type of divide that I hope to bridge with this book and also gives you a taste of the Langston flavor. It's surely one of my favorite of his stories. It's titled "Coffee Break."

Jesse has an interaction with his boss who is White, like most bosses, as Jesse clarifies. Semple's boss keeps hounding him, asking just what does the Negro want? The inference is, since Colored folk have famous singers, athletes and some politi-cians in high places we have it made; so what more could we expect or want? Semple is annoyed and tells his boss to ask someone else because he is not "The Negro." His boss can't seem to let it go. Semple tells him a sarcastic story from a Moms Mabley comedy routine, about *Little Cindy Ella* and her prom date with the president of the Ku Klux Klan. After wearing magic slippers that turned her into a blonde princess, Little Cindy Ella returns to her Black self at the midnight hour, landing her in jail. The boss doesn't quite get Jesse's effort at explaining the reality of integration through this *Cindy Ella* story. He continues to insist that all is well for Jesse and Negroes and that they are no longer oppressed. He keeps asking Jesse what he (The Negro) wants.

> Semple responds: "To get out of jail" he tells the boss. "What jail?" "The jail you got me in." Me?" yells my boss. "I have not got you in jail. Why, boy, I like you. I am a liberal. I voted for Kennedy. And this time for Johnson. I believe in integration. Now that you got it, though, what more do you want?" "Reintegration," I said. 'Meaning by that, what?" "That you be integrated with me, not me with you." "Do you mean that I come and live here in Harlem?" asked my boss.
>
> "Never!" "I live in Harlem," I said. "You are adjusted to it,' said my boss. "But there is so much crime in Harlem." "There are no two-hundred-thousand-dollar bank robberies, though" I said, "of which there was three lately elsewhere—all done by white folks, and nary one in Harlem. The biggest and best crime is outside of Harlem. We never has no half-million-dollar jewelry robberies, no missing sapphires. You better come uptown with me and reintegrate." "Negroes are the ones who want to be integrated," said my boss. "And white folks are the ones who do not want to be," I said. "Up to a point, we do," said my boss. "That is what THE Negro wants," I said, "to remove that point."

"The coffee break is over," said my boss. (Hughes, 1967, p. 80–82)

Hughes had a folksy, disarming way of getting his point across. I first read some of those stories over twenty-five years ago but they just stuck in my head. I remember the spirit of his stories like I read them yesterday, especially "Coffee Break."

I add some objective data and research in various places to accentuate or make a point or because I was reading it at the time. However the purpose of this book is not to prove things with research, but to express life experiences and reflections and what I think will help the US of America move from its *race base* to another place. Therefore, I have four specific goals:

1. I want the title of this book to help create a new image about Black men in the US of America. I want to help promote this image among black folk in general, and particularly among Black men. The goal of course is to understand the implications of "heaven" as a metaphor for the spirituality (strength, dignity, beauty, capacity) we possess and then vow to manifest that spirituality more fully in service to our families, communities, the nation and world at large.

2. I want White folk to examine their images of Black folk, to adopt the "heaven" image as their basis for viewing black men and then do their part to facilitate the atmosphere and conditions necessary to establish unity and justice, thus helping to make this vision a reality.

3. I want Black folk and White folk to realize we (Blacks) are not crazy or oversensitive and,

notwithstanding racial progress, we still experience what we experience. It is not just in our heads and, though our spirituality can aid us in transcending this persistent and debilitating obstacle, justice demands that it be removed from the playing field. Similarly, I want African Americans to be firmly convinced, from the inside out, that we are *no better or worse* than any other group in this country. Because of the mix and blend of beauty and the beast in our communities some aspects need to be respectively celebrated or rectified. Whites and other communities have their beauties and their beasts as well, their own version of things that need to be celebrated or rectified. Black and White are equal in our capacity for lofty and noble behavior or for destructive and immoral behavior. Like everything else, both beauty and beast come out of a cultural context and, therefore, *may* manifest themselves differently in the Black and White communities.

4. I want Blacks and Whites to realize we are inextricably bound together by history and circumstance. It will take a much deeper consciousness of our oneness and interconnectedness, a *spiritual* transformation of attitudes and behaviors, and a willingness to mutually sacrifice for each other's well-being, if we are to solidify the unifying good will and healing potential generated by the energy surrounding what I call the *Obama(s) phenomenon.*

Because you may not have read the preface and because talk of spirituality and or religion is sensitive, I feel a need to repeat what I mean by spiritual or spirituality. In a broad sense, spirituality is motivated by the core or common purpose of all major religions of the world. It is about the desire and willingness to think and act in a noble, honorable and spiritual, or what some call transpersonal (beyond personality) manner. However, choosing to live life from a spiritual or transpersonal frame of reference does not require that folk claim allegiance to one or the other of these religions. Spirituality is defined as that quality and depth of consciousness that realizes an interconnectedness with all humanity. When drawn upon, it impels us to act and react from our noble and better selves and live in integrity, even in the face of seemingly insurmountable challenges. We each have within us, access to a quality of consciousness that, when chosen, allows us to sense and be guided by our highest and best self and to be conscious of the sacredness of our life's purpose; specifically how we are intended to act toward and react to others. Spirituality has more to do with the quality of principled responses, first in thought and then in action, than it is does with any material, emotional or physical outcome. In short it is about the ability to conquer our lower nature with our higher nature and thus to sacrifice our baser egocentric needs and responses, to a higher and more profound self; a self that believes, as succinctly stated by Dr. Eunice Gifford, co-director for the Institute of Self Transcendence in Atlanta, Georgia, "when deep speaks to deep, deep responds."

It is spirituality that, in the heat of our daily challenges and inner struggles with race, provides us with a transformative way of responding, lifting us through, out and above our emotional and protective impulses. It can lift us through the emotional pain and anger associated with race and transform it into motivation, will and strength to build unity and justice. All too often we admire that demonstration of character in others, yet fail to choose it for ourselves. Spirituality then has more to do with how we live our faith than it does with what we call ourselves.

25

There is another point I want to make clear before getting fully into my story. I conduct race relations/diversity training and consultations for a living and have been doing so a long time. As a Black man leading workshops on race, I find that many White folk automatically think that I say what I say because I'm on the side of Colored folks and sort of against them. After all I'm Black so I must be on *their side*. Some could easily feel that way about this book; that I am only on the side of folks of African descent. Truth be told, I'm only on one side and that's the side of gettin or keepin (dependin how you see it) this race stuff moving forward. Far as I'm concerned there is no other side.

We've been so blessed in this country and unto whomsoever much is given, of him much is required. That's just the way it is. Can't play with God is a lesson I learned. *If we don't make things work here in the US of America, with all we've been blessed with, we'd better find a rock to hide under. The problem is, there's nowhere to hide from the Almighty.* Sooner or later He might take a closer look and decide to "jack us up" a bit. Got a feelin none of us would like that. Not gettin over these sick worn out old prejudices is not gonna fly much longer, the way I see it. To fail to solve our race problem means to steal freedom's hope right out from the rest of the world because, like it or not, folk still pay close attention to what we do here; the good, the bad and the ugly. To fail to overcome race prejudice is to send a message to that same world, that racism will always exist, even in a democracy and even in a country that stands for equality and justice. What kind of hope is that to offer to the world? What kind of gratitude does that show for all we've been blessed with? The God I believe in, to the best of my knowledge, won't stand for that forever. No sir! No ma'am! Truth is, God won't have to do anything to us if we keep breaking these spiritual laws of love, unity and justice. Might sound strange but we will be bringing ourselves down and God will only be watching in sadness. I say, let's not let that happen! So what's my point? Point is I'm not writin this book for Blacks and against Whites or any variation on that theme. I'm writin it for the reasons I just said. We in the US of America gotta get this right.

Finally, I believe other People of Color in the US of America have major issues to address as well, but the intent of this story is to talk about the Black/White issue. It is the one I'm most personally familiar with. Similarly I'm the most familiar with a Black male perspective. However much of what I am sharing applies equally to Black women; no denigration intended against any group I have not explicitly included.

Chapter 2

Seeing Heaven in the Face of Black Men

This is the first big **NEWS FLASH** which will explain better than anything else what I want this book to help create. This flash caused me to change the title of the book (It was titled Wakin Up Black in America.)—it was so powerful. It is some-thing that hit me smack dab, and I mean smack dab, in the middle of my head and heart! I was talking with some Black folk at this annual gathering of African American men and each one was talkin about what the gathering meant to them. One brother said words that shook me to my core! He said "I never thought I'd see heaven in the face of a Black man," meanin he saw heaven in the face of Black *men* at this gath-ering. All kind of feelings and thoughts rushed to my head, heart and soul. Oh man! I thought about prejudice and how Black men have been so marginalized and so "ghettoized." At the same time I thought of all that beauty and brightness and strength in so many brothers that so often gets lost in the focus on the criminal Black man, the drug-riddled Black man, the no good father Black man. My heart was *leapin and limpin* at the same time. This man's words were no joke and their implications were deep, deeper and deepest. I wondered to myself how many U.S. Americans *expect* to see heaven in the face of a Black man! A host of other images no doubt come to mind, from danger to death, from the hood to hip hop, but not heaven in the face of a Black man. This brother's words spoke volumes about race relations, racial perceptions and racial stereotypes—how Black men (and women) are still portrayed, presented and far too often denigrated. (It was clear to me, he was not coming from a denigrating perspective but more one of awe and wonder.)

I thought about his statement for many a day and night and have not stopped thinking about it since. Later I found out, at least according to Eric Butterworth in a book titled *Discover the Power within You*, the word "heaven" comes from Greek roots that mean "expanding" (Butterworth, 1992). This fact made the metaphor even more powerful to me; I had a vision of an expanding dignity, honor and strength. Then it struck me, I should change my friend's statement about not expectin to see heaven in the face of a black man. I started thinkin and repeatin out loud, sayin it in different ways till I settled on many versions, all having the same energy. *Seeing heaven in the face of a Black man, I see heaven in the face of Black men, I saw heaven in the face of a Black man, and seeing heaven in the face of Black men all sounded good to me.*

I started thinking about all the dignified, honorable, creative and committed Black men I know and I thought to myself what a powerful and striking image heaven is when thinking of Black men. Heaven to me, in addition to expanding, means spirituality, soul, strength, true manhood, love, caring, compassion, resilience, sacrifice, perseverance, wisdom, laughter, joy, creativity, sincerity, genuineness and the list goes on. As they used to say, back in my day, "makes you want to holler," but in a good way. Fact is the more I said it the more I realized how much I'd seen it. I'd seen "heaven in the face of a Black man" all over the world. Seen it in young, old and every age in between. But the media, books, educators, too many White folk, some Black folk and others got my mind all twisted up to the point that I sometimes think more about the other stuff than the heaven stuff. NO MORE I said to myself. No more!

There's a lot of heaven in the face of Black men and that's what I'm gonna look for and expect to see. That determination doesn't make me blind to other stuff; it just makes me focus on what can help me and others glow and grow. Heard it said if you look at a person the way they are they only become worse, but look at them the way they could be and they'll become what they should be. Amen!

When Caucasian folk and Black folk have more of that heaven image in their mind, I will know for sure, the US of America has taken a big step in the journey toward racial unity and justice. Indeed it does "make you wanna holler."

NEWS FLASH OVER

I mention the media several times and often in terms of how it sensationalizes and exacerbates stories, situations and circumstances. The media has tremendous sway, for good or bad, and shapes a lot of "group think" sentiments in the US of America. That being said, the media has served in many circumstances, in an honorable fashion. At various times throughout our history, it has exposed racial injustices such as what happened to my parents and other situations that were much worse or that might have remained hidden. These situations, without media exposure, often would have gone unchecked. Surely in many cases it could have exercised more initiative but in fact, did so in other cases. Members of the media, like all institutions and people, sometimes lose the best part of themselves, allowing them to engage in behavior that does not serve us or their profession well. So, I believe in giving credit where credit is due and at the same time I believe the media has played a huge role in embedding stereotypes in the consciousness of US Americans and the world at large.

Chapter 3

Wakin Up Colored, Negro, Black, Afro-American, African American, a Person of Color and a Person of African Descent in the US of America (CNBAAPA)

I woke up this morning Colored as I always am, Negro as I always am, Black as I always am, Afro-American as I always am, African American as I always am, a Person of Color as I always am and a Person of African descent. People who look like me have been all of those things at one time or another and mostly in my lifetime. I didn't sleep real well last night. Thinking I ate too much before bed. Good night's sleep is important because it can sometimes be tiring, going through, working through and living through my day(s) as Negro in the US of America. In short, wakin up Black in the US of America can wear you out. Not complaining, mind you, as I love a lot of things about this country and I've traveled enough to know U.S. Americans of Color of whatever ilk have better possibilities here than in a whole lot of other places. (Truth be told, it makes me and lots of other Black folk both sad and glad, living like we have to in the US of America.) On the other hand, this is a democracy and a place that is all about freedom, liberty and justice for all, so I think it shouldn't make me so tired wakin up Black (CNBAAPA) in the US of America. Tellin you up front, I have higher expectations for my country than I do for some other places; especially since folk of my hue were responsible for building so much of it up.

We got a "No Child Left Behind" campaign and I think we better get a "No Race Left Behind" campaign. We're runnin way late with race, so my plan is, we start this campaign in March when daylight saving time starts. That way we'll *spring forward* and jump start this thing and just plain skip the *fall back* season. There's legislation passed for No Child Left Behind so now we can get No Race Left Behind legislation, and we can identify failing cities and kick folk out who are not springin forward in workin for racial justice. Let those folks go somewhere for a "time out" till they decide they want to spring forward. Give them a chance to pray and meditate awhile till they get right with themselves. Know that won't happen but it should. As I'm slowly wakin up that's what runs through my head about what we need in the US of America.

I'm thinkin and feeling this morning, White folk and Negro folk really don't understand each other in a deep way. We just like to pretend we do but we really don't. So much bad blood's passed between us that we see each other through dirty lenses and keep our distance. It's a natural fact however, the *minority* generally knows the majority better than the other way around. Minority has to study the *majority* or those in power to figure out how to make it in their world. Women study men the same way and employees study the boss. It's really about survival. But even if Colored folk know Caucasian folk better than the other way around, we still don't know them very well. General knowledge is not good enough to solve our problems. We need to take a closer look because it may sometimes feel like nothing has changed and therefore it's not worth lookin. I think some things have. Some things are still pretty messed up between the races and I'll get to that, but one thing I have noticed in my travels is, more White folk are more casually and naturally friendly to me than in years past. Many more folk seem comfortable just kickin things around with me and not just about sports. Not a big thing some may say, but for me it feels better than the way it used to. Feels also like more White folk, especially the young ones, are reachin out and more Black folk, particularly the young ones are wantin to reach back. I think there's a spirit in the air; so we need to take a closer look, acknowledge what we've accomplished, dig in and connect deeper so we can finish the job. Anyway that's all a part of what I feel like as I try to wake up this morning. When I feel such things I know I am plugged into what I call my high road self or as I said in the preface and introduction (which you should really read if you haven't) my spiritual or transpersonal self. The other part of me is feelin other things. The battle begins.

Here's what I mean. There's two parts to me; my high road self that is hopeful and my low road self. On my *low road self* days I don't even want to get to know White folk any better because I've been hurt and disappointed so many times. I'm guessin when White folk have low road days they don't care to work on this thing either. Funny how my thoughts work: one minute I can feel good about all this and the next I can feel hopeless and want to retreat to my Negro corner. Like this morning—part of me is feelin good, and another part of me is feelin like I'm better off just stickin with my own and just bein civil to White folk. Save me the trouble of having to keep goin over the same old ground. I mean we've made some real gains in my adult lifetime, which I consider the post-Civil-Rights/integration years. We lost a whole lot too. Folk say we desegregated but never really fully integrated. I think that's true. We closed up shop in our neighborhoods but weren't allowed to open up shop in other neighborhoods. As Jesse B. Semple said it's time you "come integrate with me not just me with you." Too many Black folk still havin to do the majority of reachin out, stretchin out, and burning out. Sadly, the way I see it is too many White folk are still holdin out, runnin out and waitin us out.

Told you a good night's sleep is important. I can get testy about all this when I'm tired and then you get some of my *woke up on the wrong side of the bed feelings.* Indeed, separation and keepin with my own kind can sound appealing on my low road days. On my high road days I know it is illogical, ill-conceived and it makes me ill. We did that already and there's no going back. Truth be told, plenty of folk on my side of the tracks have given up hope even when they've had a good night's sleep. "Been there, done that" is their mantra. Many of them are getting on in years, lived through the sixties and saw the life and hope literally shot out of this country. They feel like we left our soul back there and never found it again. Some hold out hope Obama can move us on up. Time will tell.

But tired of all this many folks are. And please understand what I mean when I say me and others of my hue get tired wakin up Black in US of America. What I really mean is going through our day/week/month, we get tired. I'm not talkin sleepy tired as that's cured by eight hours plus an extra nap. I'm talking "butt weary" tired that lingers on. Part of going through our "day" often means we are either made aware of, or realize we have to be aware of our color, almost from our very wakin up time. That can make a person more tired than you would think.

Let me give you just one small example for right now. I love goin on vacation in the mountains because to me mountains are beautiful to behold. Mountains are often in isolated rural areas where no or few African Americans live and where some folk don't want Black folk to be. In some places in the South, Confederate flags hang on houses and trucks—not about hate for all people, but for some it is. How do I know who is which? When I get to hikin or walkin in the mountains, I'm lookin over my shoulder as a reflex. Walkin late at night when the stars are so bright is a great thing, but it's pitch black out and when I see White folk in pickup trucks drive by something starts happening in my stomach. I think about not driving on those isolated roads after dark in case I get a flat tire. Runs through my head about all those people who'd been putting out nooses as a joke. Who's just makin a bad joke and who is serious? I think about the stares I got when I walked around town earlier that day. When I'm in a cabin that's real isolated, I'm wondering who might not want me there. Now remember, I'm just tryin to go on vacation to relax, but all these thoughts are a part of it. I control them, but they're never too far from the surface. That's just one small example of what gets tiring. Thinkin White folk aren't going through those changes when they're on vacation in the mountains.

I ask the White folk who hear or read this to put yourself in a frame of mind, asking, why might I feel this way? What would make a reasonable person see and feel things this way, think thoughts like I do when I'm in the mountains. Please don't go pokin holes in it before feelin and hearin what's being said. Instead ask the questions, ponder and reflect. More than likely it'll make more sense to you if you do that. More'n likely you will see some truth in it. Doesn't mean you have to accept everything I'm sayin. Just means you're makin an earnest effort to believe my sincerity and acknowledging, it represents my truth, my experiences, my challenges. That indeed is my hope on this early and tired morning.

On my low road days I don't have a lot of hope White folk are going to take time to sort through this stuff and on my high road days I feel a new spirit of hope. Indeed on this day the battle has begun and there's nothing easy about it.

Wakin up—My Day Begins in Earnest

Like I told you, a good night's sleep is important. Sometimes that bed feels so good specially snugglin with my wife, and I'm talkin just a sweet snuggle, as we nod off. First thing I like to do when I get up, after takin care of the necessities, is to go outside and breathe the morning air; that is if it's not too hot, which it usually isn't so early in the morning. So this particular morning, I went out to do just that, to get my newspaper and stretch out a little. Those first few stretches in the morning feel good too, cuz for me, some parts wake up slower than others. Low and behold, I looked in my neighbor's yard and see his newspaper blowin around on the ground. He's a pretty good fella so I thought I'd pick it up and go knock on his door and give it to him, knowin how he likes to read the paper early in the morning just like I do. Only difference is he wakes up White every day. I often wonder, and I mean truly wonder, what it's like wakin up White in America. I got no clue, and White folk don't have a clue about wakin up Black and that's why we need to listen to each other. I got a very strong feeling wakin up White is a whole lot different than wakin up Black in more ways than two. Anyway, I go knock on his door and because it's early I guess the thought flashes through my head, I want to make sure he sees me real good, because if he just sees a *dark* person at his door, I'm not sure what he might think. Wish I didn't think that way but I do, and that's what went through my mind. I think he might think some Colored man is coming to rob him. So I make sure he can get a good look at me through that peephole of his. I have one of those peepholes too; comes in handy. Anyway, I hope he recognizes me. Well, guess he did because he opened the door and was happy to get his paper.

I wonder why I was worried. Am I just paranoid or would he have really been afraid seeing a *dark* face at his door? I mean if he didn't recognize me right off and just saw my darker hue, would he have thought "robbery time"? Would he have just seen a Negro face first, thought "robbery time" second, and not even taken time to see it was his neighbor? *Maybe so and maybe not*; maybe he would have felt the same about a White person approaching his door so early in the morning. Nah, I don't think so. Guess you have to decide for yourself, but like I said, I don't think so.

Chapter 4

Cops, Killings and Dilemmas

I need to make my point in a very serious way now. I saw on TV the other day a true story about an undercover White cop who accidentally shot an undercover African American cop. As the story was reported, the White cop was in the middle of a drug bust outside of a bar. Inside was an off-duty under-cover CNBAAPA cop having a drink. The Black cop, dressed in his casual, off-duty clothes, heard the noise outside, went out to try and help, and the White cop turned around and saw the Afro-American cop with his gun out and shot and killed him in that split second. Turned out the two had gone to the training academy together. Anyway, this was a sad story for everyone, but the point is, the White cop only had a second to make a decision and looks like he saw a Black man with a gun and did not see his academy buddy. Not sure what he saw, but my guess is, a Colored man with a gun brought up some quick images in his head, and they weren't good. Stereotypes are strong in our society and sometimes folk see what the stereotype taught them to see, whether they want to or not. I am guessin that's what that *White cop couldn't have helped but see*. I'm glad my neighbor had more than a split second to see my face. Not thinking he would have shot me through the door. Maybe so, maybe not, and I sure hope not.

By the way, I wish I could say I don't see how the White cop could have done what he did, sad, tragic and heart-sickening as it is. Though I can't excuse it, I truly doubt he was malicious or trying to kill another cop. He may or may not even have been consciously prejudiced. He, like so many folk in the US of America, had negative images instilled in his mind from the time he was two and a half years old according to early childhood thinkers and researchers. That's what my wife has been tellin me, and I researched it on my own. At two-and-a-half years, children are already starting to act and react based on prejudices. That's a fact. So this man had lots of years to build up strong negative images about Black men with guns, *whether he wanted to or not.* Those images are no joke and especially when you have a split second to make a life-or-death decision: anxiety and fear can bring them out and just like that—reaction, reflex, and bang!—he's dead. Being Black in the US of America can cost you your life, no "maybe" about it.

I know what some of you are thinkin. You're thinkin about me sayin I'm glad my neighbor got more than a second to look at my face, wondering if I think he would've shot me. You're thinkin this fifty-somethin Negro is losin his paranoid mind and my neighbor would not have been concerned about my Blackness. He would have just been concerned about some person being at his door so early in the morning and the color would have made no difference. I say to that, *maybe so,* maybe not, but a stronger maybe so. I say to you that is what I feel from my life experience. I remember feeling a *tightness and anxiety* until he opened the door and saw it was me. Not big-time anxiety, but enough. Over time anxiety wears on a person.

I am barely into sharing my story here, and I bet I got some folks heated up with me already. Stick with me, my brothers and sisters of all hues, stick with me.

Scary-Looking Black Folks and Africa

Anyway, time to get back in the house, read my paper and get that first cup of coffee. Love that first sip of that first cup of coffee in the morning, though I'm tryin to quit. My wife is hooked, so when I smell it brewin in the morning, sometimes

I just give in. I know me and a lot of White folks have that in common, both lovin coffee and tryin to quit at the same time.

I read the local news first to keep up with what's happening in my community. Soon as I open the paper, I see a picture of three Black fellas who just got arrested for some kind a crime. First thing comes to my mind is "they" sure look awful spooky and like some serious thugs. Then I say to myself, "newspaper can sure make Black folk look thuggish." Not sure I ever saw any Negroes in real life that look like those pictures, but that may just be me. I know if they look like that to me, they definitely strike fear in the minds of some White folk; especially for those who don't know many CNBAAPA folk up close and personal. Those pictures could scare a lot of Black folk too, and that's the truth.

Well, let me get to the rest of the paper. Lot of things going on in this world I'd say, and not all good. The way the news and papers show it, those fifty-three countries on the African continent seem like they got nothing but problems. Every time I turn around I read about some famine, AIDS, or some sort of drought or civil war. Even with that portrayal, I always had something tuggin at me to go to Africa and see at least one country for myself. Knew there had to be more to Africa than bad stuff and animals.

A lot of folk talk about goin to Africa to go on a safari. That's all well and good, but I knew Africa had to have much more than animals. You'd think from what you see and hear there'd be no cars, airplanes, trains, hotels and restaurants on that continent. Not sure I have ever seen much of that on the news, but maybe I am just forgetting about it. On the other hand, if I have to think that hard they must not show much "civilization" about Africa on TV. I sometimes think we never get a full picture of lots of things and that's why we believe so many half truths—not just about Africa and not just about

39

race. Sorry to say it, but half-truths raise up half-wits; gets folks all confused; then they start making assumptions. I am here to declare that it is indeed hard to find the whole truth about anything nowadays!

Anyway since my ancestors are from Africa (yours too), I decided to go see for myself; at least visit some kin folk in one country. I'll tell you something. There were some pretty savvy, shrewd and loving people where I went. I saw heaven in the face of a lot of those beautiful, dark brothers and sisters. I had wondered if they run around half dressed like I usually saw them on TV in those documentaries. My guess was in some places they did and in others they would be fully clothed. Really I knew that would be the case before I went. Well on my trip to Uganda, I saw folks in suits, dresses, traditional wear and everything in between. They even sell our magazines on their street corners, and in this case, were promoting some of the uncivilized things the US of America does.

I'll digress for a minute and explain. They were selling some of those "girlie" magazines that show women on the cover half or less dressed. I'm not talking about Playboy either, but just our regular main line magazines. Felt so strange being in the middle of "the continent" and looking down seeing all that mess. Same thing happened when I was in the Tortola in the British Virgin Islands. Saw a bunch of the native folk huddled around a TV in an outdoor bar, and they were watching folk jump in and out of bed on one of the US of America soap operas. Those magazines plus TV shows and movies make people come to this country expecting to find *easy* half-dressed women. That's how we export stereotypes about women, race and all sorts of things.

Getting back to Africa, I wonder if White folk accept they are the kin-folk of African people just like I am. As I understand it, that's where scientists think civilization began, so White folk are related to Africans just like I am. I wonder if knowing that makes them want to go back and find their roots. I think for most folk, travels would end in Europe regardless of what scientists say about their origin. I'm not sure if a lot of White folk want to be related to those African folk. That's speculation on my part. Not trying to offend, but that's what I think. On the other hand I have European ancestry and I am not all that excited about going to Europe to find my kin folk. I guess partly because I know my European ancestry came not necessarily from a consensual union of man and wife. I think you know what I'm saying. So I guess I don't feel real excited about my European roots. If I could get past those feelings, I probably would discover some interesting things about my European ancestors.

In their heart of hearts, I do think if White folk really internalized, in a sincere and genuine way that their ancestors originated in Africa, over time it would help them and their children become more accepting of their African American brothers and sisters. Just a thought I had this morning.

Anyway, think about this. Since we are all from Africa wouldn't it be a great thing for African descendants and Caucasian children to go back as far as they could to find out if they have any common ancestry? They might find some painful information and some exciting stuff too. That might help everyone get over this prejudice thing or at least confront it early on. That's a pipe dream, I know, but I think children could handle it just fine and would work out anything that came up. What an education it would be for everyone! And it might help bring about some healing while they're still young and not so jaded. Chances are they wouldn't be able to find everything about their common ancestry, but just going through it together couldn't help but make them feel more connected!

My trip to Uganda made me feel proud of my ancestors and relatives, so many strong, spiritual, intelligent and creative folk. Africa is a place all of us can be proud to come from, and I believe if more White folk went there to meet their kin folk or just to meet folk in general they'd feel proud too, proud of their relatives that live in that part of the world. There's a special vibrant spirit in the people I've met from so many countries in Africa. We could all use some spirited energy from that side of our ancestry, Caucasians and Negroes alike. So I encourage you all, go visit, not just the animals, but especially the people.

Speaking of common ancestry and commonalities reminds me of a good thing that happened a while back in South Carolina. Some descendants of former slave owners and descendants of former slaves got together for a reunion of sorts. The descendants of former slave owners established a scholarship fund to send some of the descendants of former slaves to college. Now that is something worthwhile. Not just talkin about makin things better but doing something about it. Some good people deciding it's time to heal and then taking some action to make it happen! Sure wish I could have been a fly on the wall as they talked through feelings about their mutual history. God bless both sets of descendants for letting their spirit and experiences meet at the intersection and create new possibilities.

Sports and Us

Well, back to reading my newspaper. I love sports, especially basketball, so I want to see how my favorite teams did last night. I like teams that play the game the way it's supposed to be played, like an interdependent team, passing the ball, gettin everyone involved so they're not just standing around expectin the superstar to do it all. Now don't I just sound like the expert? Though you didn't ask, I want you to know I still take my fifty-somethin self on the b-ball court with the young fellas. I don't embarrass myself either.

Tell you one thing; CNBAAPA folk have truly taken professional basketball by storm. We're doing more in tennis than ever before with Venus and Serena Williams and a few others in the wings and old Tiger Woods is really doin his thing in golf. We even have several Colored folk in hockey and some stars that I only recently found out about. I heard some of them get called names but are accepted by most of the fans and players. I used to skate as a kid and was pretty good at it but I never thought of hockey. Magic Johnson and others are trying to make sure we're represented in NASCAR. We're coming into all the sports and even those that have a long tradition of bein all White. Not many of us in some of them yet, but as they used to say back in the day: "weez a comin." Now I'm proud of our sports legacy but sure don't like it that we still get pigeonholed. As long as we entertain or are playing sports we're accepted, but when it comes to coaches, board room executives, management, we still get passed over far too often. We are absent from head coaching jobs in some of the very sports we have excelled in, particularly in college football. Some sports are better than others, but college football is real bad off.

Sportscasters always talk about the "athleticism" of Black folk when they talk about how we play and very rarely about how we use our heads or think when we play. Not the same way they talk about great White athletes. Always talk about how these White players are thinkin or out-thinkin other players, using their minds to play the game. I noticed that big time with Serena and Venus. Their athleticism, power and speed are extolled, but almost no reference to how smart they play. It was worse when they first started, but even now, after all they have accomplished, very rarely do sportscasters talk about how smart they must be. Let me tell you all somethin: you can't win as much as they have won without havin a whole lot of brain power. That kind of condescension stuff gets real old and is just plain insulting. Plus, too many people have worked too hard and too long to get treated that way and then later get passed over time and again for "thinking positions" in management and the like, because they are seen as simply "athletes." Good old Tony Dungy was a classic case who, finally, after being passed over for head coaching positions time and again for lesser talent, got his shot—and what a job he did with the Indianapolis Colts, and in Tampa Bay, for that matter.

Heard some of my lighter-hued (White) brothers refer to certain Black athletes as thoroughbreds, which was supposed to be a compliment. Respect and dignity is what this is about. You'll hear me say that again and again. Folk really gotta start lookin deeper at what they think and what they say.

Makes me think back to one of my heroes, ole Hank Aaron. Though he was extolled by many, he never did get the respect and dignity he deserved for breaking the home run record that stood for decades. He did however get a whole lot of death threats instead. Here he breaks baseball's greatest record and hits more total home runs than the mighty Babe Ruth. Then he gets a bunch of hate mail sent to him, some even threatening his life. He got up to 3000 letters a day, and a lot of them were race-related hate mail. A couple of samples follow:

> "Dear Nigger Henry,
>
> You are (not) going to break this record established by the great Babe Ruth if I can help it. . . . Whites are far more superior than jungle bunnies. . . . My gun is watching your every Black move."
>
> "Dear Henry Aaron,

How about some sickle cell anemia, Hank?"

The letters came from all over, but most were postmarked in northern cities. They were filled with hate. More hate than Aaron had ever imagined. "This," Aaron said about the letters, "changed me" (Schwartz, 2008).

Aaron had support too, from White and Colored folk, including Babe Ruth's wife who suggested the Babe would have been thrilled about Hank breaking the record. But Aaron still got all that hate mail; doubtful that any of it was from Negroes. Ask yourself how he must have felt at this pinnacle in his career, reaching this milestone and then getting rocked by all this hate mail. *But, let me try to be fair here.* I wonder, if Hank had been White, would he have gotten racist hate mail because he was about to break the record? Well, the truth of the matter is, I really don't wonder about this one because had he been White, of course he wouldn't have gotten racist hate mail—from Negroes or Caucasians. He may have gotten ugly mail in general, which I know Roger Maris did when he was attempting to break the mighty Babe's single season home run record. I feel for him and his family, but his color was sure not the reason he got that mail. Hate is hate, but I tell you hating because the person who is going to break the record has too much melanin is over the top. So when I say Black people have to deal with all of the challenges White people deal with, in addition to the color factor, this is what I'm talking about; that four letter addition called race. And let me say this; it's about time Hank becomes the icon that the mighty Babe has been for so many years. Hank broke the record but it is as if he is still a footnote to Babe Ruth whose record he broke.

Some of you are probably thinkin what the man who was rifling questions at Jesse B. Semple was thinkin. African Americans have folk like Oprah Winfrey, Tiger Woods, Michael Jordan, Colin Powell, Maya Angelou and Condoleezza Rice, who have apparently made it so to speak and even have been revered by a lot of White folk. What more could we want? I say, yes, we have all those folks and more that have made it and been *accepted* to some degree or the other, no doubt. And I say, there is a history in this country of Whites more readily accepting certain kinds of Black people. The two that come to mind the most are those who are such superstars in their fields, they dazzle everyone and those who are very humble and/or don't talk about race too much, if ever. Again, not by their own definition, or by their own wishes, but more by the definition of many White folks, they represent the good Blacks. In large part because they *don't complain/talk* about race or make it a *crutch*, as some of my lighter-hued brothers and sisters put it. I'm not criticizing anyone who doesn't talk publically about race; I'm observing. Those who do talk about it have a much harder way to go to be *accepted.* And those who are superstars often are accepted with limitations.

Let me illustrate my point with a story about Arthur Ashe, a former African American tennis player, who was accepted much more fully before he started talking about things considered political and racial. "The mild-mannered" man who was often described as "Mr. Cool" almost lost that label when a reporter, seeking to express her empathy for his terminal AIDS-related illness, allowed that AIDS must be the heaviest burden he has ever had to bear.

"No, it isn't," he writes. "It's a burden, all right ... but being Black is the greatest burden I've had to bear." Ashe adds: "No question about it. Race has always been my biggest burden, having to live as a minority in America. Even now it continues to feel like an extra weight tied around me. Race is for me a more onerous burden than AIDS" (Johnson, 1993). The story continues thus:

When one of his close associates, who is White, read the quote in the reporter's story, he promptly called Ashe, suggesting that it must have been a misquote; surely he has nothing to complain about. He is rich and famous. He has it made, the friend stated. Moreover, since AIDS is finally fatal, what can be worse than death Ashe was asked? Ashe's response is worth the price of the book. It invigorates the mind, expands the soul. It educates the head and softens the heart. Like his athletic hero Jackie Robinson, who broke racial barriers in baseball when he was hired to play with the Brooklyn Dodgers, the tan tennis titan had crossed another color line when he discovered that what started as a triumph turned into a tragedy. Thus he had another heavy burden to bear.

Ashe recounts the exhilaration he felt when he was exalted to the captaincy of America's coveted Davis Cup team. He was the first Black to attain the position and only the second captain in over 30 years to lead the U.S. Davis Cup team to consecutive victories in 1981–82.

But this shining honor began to tarnish, and he resigned from the Davis Cup captaincy. Since the surprise resignation came at a time when he was raising his level of political participation, JET wanted to know if his interest in human rights and his ongoing opposition to the practice of apartheid in South Africa had something to do with the USTA decision not to ask him to continue as Davis Cup captain.

Ashe remembers the call from JET'S sports editor and recounts the question and answer interview in his book. He notes the story appeared, headlined: "Ashe Says Activist Role May Be Part Of His Ouster As

Davis Cup Team Captain." He writes, "Happily, it was accurate and fair." (Johnson, 1993)

Arthur Ashe was a great U.S American and a credit to the *human race,* but once he started talking about race and racism his status plummeted.

Now let me digress and tell you this: trying to be fair all the time gets ***tiring*** too; always having to try and make sure you're looking at both sides of things, even when you know something is "real" racially wrong. If you don't try real hard to be fair, someone will accuse you of "playin the race card" or dwelling on the negative too much or being oversensitive. Truth be told, my experience is, even if you try to see all sides of things, and you mention race as a factor in something, someone will still accuse you of playin the race card. That is, if you bring race up as a factor in ANYTHING. Unless you can absolutely five-hundred percent prove race was a factor, which is often hard to do, probably some White person is going to accuse you of playing that card!

Well, anyway, back to Hank. As you know, he broke the Babe's homerun record, but spent some serious time in anger and sadness because of those racist reactions and threats on his life. Truly this was a dark stain on the legacy of the world of baseball and on the US of America. Hank's story, like so many others, is the story of dignity and honor; who's afforded it and who's not.

I'm tryin to see the upside of things and not just the downside so let me tell you, I've been noticing, some of the major league baseball teams like Pittsburgh, Philadelphia and others are takin more time to pay tribute to the old Negro baseball leagues. These were leagues Black folks had to play in because they were not allowed to play in the major leagues, which was a Whites-only league till Jackie Robinson broke the color

48

barrier in 1948. Now, some major league baseball teams are really singing their praises. These Negro league ball players are another group of "never say die" heroes who simply did not give up because of their love of the game. Their stories can inspire all U.S. Americans and I encourage you to read them yourself and to your children. I know there's heaven in the face of those Black men because I had the good fortune to meet some of them. Fact is, there were three women who played in the Negro leagues and I met one of them. Indeed there was heaven in her face too!

Chapter 5

A Common Dilemma

Now here's the dilemma for me and many other CNBAAPA folks in America. We're told to work hard so that we can live the American dream too. In the next breath we are told to be patient and not expect too much too fast, that things are getting better and we just have to hang in there and "be positive." Worse yet, we get told the playing field is level, and we should just stop talkin about race. Then we get passed up for promotions, or other kinds of advancement over and over, get paid less for similar work, don't get hired even when qualified, get put in prison quicker and longer than White folk, get kicked out of school more frequently even for similar stuff; yet we're told we shouldn't talk about race or racism. We should only talk about how things have gotten so much better and be grateful we live in the US of America. Most Negro folk got a boatload of stories about the kind of discrimination they see or experience, but we're supposed to hush up about all that.

Give you an example of one I've heard in many forms over the years and one I experienced first-hand. An Afro-American fella worked at a company for many years and trained several people, all White, who eventually got promoted over him. He was told this had nothing to do with race, to be patient and keep working hard, not to play the race card or get bitter and his time would come.

Something like that happened to me once and the folks who perpetrated the offense actually admitted to me, I mean face-to-face: they had not promoted me because of race. They had not been conscious of it till I broke it all down for them. Here's what happened. A White female younger than me, who had worked in the organization for only nine months, got promoted over me, and I had been workin there three years and had top-notch evaluations. I talked to the guy who made the final decision to hire her, and we hashed it out. To his credit, he said he was wrong—said it had to have been race as the deciding factor, but he had not seen it before we talked. He felt real bad and teared up right in front of me. She still got the promotion and I went back to my old job with a heartfelt apology. My case is not unique. It's unique that the guy had the dignity to admit he was wrong. Didn't get me the job, but restored some of my faith in humanity. The job would have been nice though. I earned it.

And when we do succeed, *a lot* of times we're resented by enough folk to make it uncomfortable, like old Hank. Or we feel like our competence is suspect and often times like we're under a microscope with folk looking for the first sign of ineptness. The unspoken is whether we can perform as well as Caucasians. Or folk are in some wonderment about how we got *ahead*. Some folk act as if we just got promoted because of affirmative action. God forbid we make a mistake, because then it becomes "see, I told you so."

Or even worse, if we get in a position to hire folk, if we hire a person the same color as us, the whispers start that we are giving Negroes preferential treatment. I think that is still part of the fear of many White Americans, that if we get ahead we will shut them out and just take care of *our own*—in this case hire our own. If White folk only knew what confusion and dilemmas we face. Some of us have to overcome our own stereotypes about other Black folk. That's right, we get brainwashed by the same society that brainwashes White folk. In other words, we might think Caucasians are more competent than CNBAAPA folk, so we might lean toward Whites first. Or we might hire Caucasians instead of Colored folk so we can feel like we're fittin in or so we can stay in the good graces of folks who may be in a position to promote, demote or remote us later. Or, like I said, we may want to hire a Colored person but would worry about how that might be seen. God forbid we hire two Negroes in a row!! You see, even if we had the nerve to think about hiring two *qualified* Black folk in a row many of us would think twice. I don't care how qualified the Colored folk are, the whispers would rise up big time! It is complicated and *tiring* but these are things many people go through simply *wakin up Black in the US of America.* God knows, we often have to rack our brains tryin to fit in and not to lose ourselves at the same time.

Give me a minute before going on, and let me tell you something I heard once. It was one of those blunt statements that if you get past the bluntness of it, you can really see the point. It was something said to a person talkin about whether race issues were *getting better.* Man was describing why you can be glad and hurt at the same time when bad things start to get better. He said if a man stabs you in the back and the blade goes in eight inches and then someone pulls it out four or five inches, things are a lot better, but that last three or four inches still hurts like you know what! Well, I guess eight inches represents the knife of slavery, segregation, inequity, etc., and the four or five inches the knife has been pulled out is up till now. The three or four inches that is left still hurts a whole lot; plus, the knife gets twisted fairly often and that hurts too. It's been in there so long, it's creatin all kinds of related problems, and it's hard to heal until it comes out all the way. Reflect on the implications of that a minute. I don't suggest stickin a knife in someone to see what it feels like when it only comes out part way. Let's all just use our imagination but that's how race things are in my view and why it's so complicated addressing them and for sure why it is not a simple answer as to how much progress has been made.

Does all this dilemma stuff and me feeling like Black folk are constantly under a microscope sound a bit paranoid? Maybe so. Am I a bit paranoid? Probably so, but the *bit* is based on real experiences. It comes straight from my and many other black folks' lives. And as for the bit of paranoia, my brother jokingly, and sometimes not jokingly, tells me, "because you're paranoid doesn't mean they aren't out to get you." I may be imagining some of it, but I'm sure not imaginin all of it. It's real. And figuring out how to sort through all of it makes a brother weary.

I'm thinking, White folk don't have to worry about all of that stuff. If they hire other Caucasians, do they worry about what their colleagues and employees think? Do they worry those Whites are going to be under a microscope because CNBAAPA folk will wonder if they're really qualified? They may think about it but I don't really think it's a big-time worry like it is for CNBAAPA folk. Do they conclude that they better not hire two European Americans in a row, or else no other Whites might get promoted in the company for fear those folks might hire other Whites? All things being equal, if Whites hire other Whites they don't have to worry about a whole lot, unless there is an affirmative action plan, and even then it usually isn't a big-time worry. Most affirmative action programs, contrary to popular opinion are simply goals for hiring protected class folks (women, minorities and others), not legally enforceable mandates. If the goals are not met, often there are few if any consequences.

Speaking of Double Standards

Speaking of what's right and what's not, you may have figured out by now, double standards and what looks and feels like hypocrisy are among my hot button issues. Here's one of example from the sports pages and basketball which like I said I love to read about. There have been some problems with fights and carryin on in pro-basketball which makes me

53

real sad because I love the game. Anyway, I keep hearing code words, like "too many thugs" in basketball. I know they're talking about Afro-American folk when they say "thugs." Everyone is up in arms about the increasing violence. Makes me mad even though I agree some things have gotten out of hand. My take is, violence in sports really started in hockey and has been *sanctioned* for years. Those boys take off their gloves game after game and the referees stand there and watch them fight till they get bloody. Sometimes folks in the stands go buck wild and I hear nary a word about "thugs" taking over the game, even though such fights happen all the time. Now and then someone will mention it, but you don't hear too many folk makin a big thing of it. Give you an example how bad it is. Twenty seconds into a hockey game one player knocked out the other. Here was the explanation:

> But to Fedoruk and NHL insiders, there was a method to the madness. Fedoruk knew he was a marked man since roughing up Rangers captain Jaromir Jagr on Feb. 17. That violated the unspoken code of fighting, intimidation and revenge.
>
> As the Rangers' "enforcer" or "policeman," Orr had to send a message, says Fedoruk. Since hockey's code of honor says premeditated fights should occur at the start of a game, period or shift, the punches flew almost as soon as the puck dropped. Despite suffering a concussion, Fedoruk says Orr did the right thing.
>
> He had to let his teammates know they would be protected and safe, that they wouldn't get run by us," he says." (McCarthy, 2007)

Way I see it, fighting in hockey is sanctioned violence. Where's the uproar about all this? I say if hockey players were mostly Black and fightin all the time, we'd be hearin all kinds of noise about it and you all know it. Some of you all will say race is not the main factor in this. I'm here to tell you, I see RACE as the primary reason one sport gets a free pass and another doesn't. Looks and feels like a double standard. Different lenses, different realities, different perspectives.

NEWS FLASH

I was reading an altogether different newspaper today and there was actually a feature story on violence in hockey. It portrayed an individual who is called *an enforcer*. Apparently most teams have at least one or two enforcers who specialize in intimidation and fighting. Article was not on the front page of the sports section but on the front page of the entire newspaper with a picture smack dab in the middle of the page. Now this was a big time major newspaper that I will not name. Well guess what? The feature story was on a black hockey player. One of the few stories about a black hockey player and fighting in the National Hockey League and it's about *an enforcer*.

Well it was an extremely well-written and touching story about this man's life of abuse, abandonment and neglect and how he was trying to pull his life together, how he didn't want to fight but was cast in this role and couldn't shake it, so he embraced it.

You wondering what I felt about this article? My initial reaction was frustration—I can't believe this is front page news—and anger. I mean why have this on the front page, why a black player, why not include other players who are enforcers? I know this was a home town fella, but it definitely could have been done to show the range of enforcers more clearly or other hockey players of Color doing other things besides fighting.

On the other hand the content of the article was very well constructed with clear attempts to avoid judgments of the family or the "enforcer." On the other hand, I am tired reading stories about African Americans and their broken homes and their less than stellar child rearing-practices. I'm especially tired of reading about violent Black men, particularly in this case where, based on sheer numbers, the majority of the violence is carried out by White men. On the other hand....

Reminds me of the movie *Fiddler on the Roof*. The main character, a Jewish man, was in a quandary as to whether he should accept his daughter's relationship with a non-Jew. He went back and forth looking at the pros and cons. Pondering out loud he would say things like "on the one hand it could be good" and would pause briefly and then say, "but on the other hand it could be bad," and he would give reasons for each. After several "on the one hand but on the other hand" scenarios he stopped and emphatically said, "there is no other hand!" That is how I feel so often in my attempts to weigh both sides of things; "there is no other hand!" Stop focusing on the violent Black man!

NEWS FLASH OVER

Well then, back to my day. It's almost time to go down to the civic club to give my talk on race relations in America and how that impacts business.

Trying to put this newspaper down, but race seems to be peeking out at me again. I am reading another article on this sports thing about Black coaches. Only this time it breaks it down. There are only three Black coaches in Division One football in the NCAA men's ranks out of 119. Basketball is better with twenty-two percent of coaches being Black, though that is less than half the percentage of Black players. Let me lay out the football situation in raw numbers:

- Fifty percent of all NCAA football athletes are Black, translating into twenty-five percent Black assistant coaches; equals three percent Black head football coaches.

- Fifty percent of all NCAA football athletes are White; translating into seventy-five percent White assistant coaches; equals ninety-seven percent White head football coaches.

The source of these statistics, Terry Bowden, who happens to be White, goes on to state the following:

> A profession that so desperately seeks a level playing field offers nothing close to one for the Black athlete who aspires to rise to the pinnacle of the college coaching profession.

> Plainly and simply, folks, this is discrimination. More precisely this is one of the last and greatest bastions of discrimination within all of American sports. In college football, we are winning games, building programs and making millions of dollars with the sweat and blood of African-American athletes. I should know. In the last dozen years, my family alone has made more than thirty million as Division I-A head football coaches." (Bowden, 2005)

I'm not suggesting that the percentage of coaches should exactly mirror the percentage of players, but come on, folk, something is *real* wrong with this picture.

There are some Afro-Americans raising a big fuss about all this and some White folk are saying things like, "why do Black folk bring race into everything?" "The person most qualified should get the job." Well, I will tell you, it is simply dumbfounding and defying common sense that the only qualified coaches seem to always be White. Seems to me, White folk get the benefit of the doubt and get hired, and Black folk get the doubt and are not hired. Then when special programs get set up to affirmatively seek ways to get African American folk in the pipeline, you hear cries of reverse discrimination, even in a situation where you have almost no Negro representation. As the young folk used to say, "What's up with that?"

Pro-football has made some strides primarily, if not exclusively, thanks to the *Rooney rule*. It requires teams to interview at least one minority candidate for each head coaching position. This was instituted in 2002 and at that time there were only two head coaches of darker hue. In 2007 there were seven before two were fired (Brown, 2007).

Pro-basketball has done much better in hiring Black head coaches, but their tenure lasts significantly less time than their white counterparts regardless of the win/loss record (Leonhardt & Fessenden, 2005). Can this all be based on race? Maybe so, maybe not, but I say in part race is a factor and that part can make the difference between being hired or fired. Put it this way, folk can argue all they want about how big a part race plays in these livelihood type hiring decisions. I say size doesn't matter, impact does. The impact is that it plays a big enough part to prevent qualified folk from getting hired and I'd say that makes it a big enough size.

Still wondering: if race is such a non-issue in some folk's minds, and the playing field is so level, why do we still have such glaring issues blinding and binding us? Maybe we should just all admit we have made progress in some areas, and in other areas we have a long way to go. Let's quit actin like African Americans and concerned Whites need to stop bringing race into things. If folk had not done so, all those other sports would still be all White in the coaching and player ranks. Do you think folk would have just woken up one day without outside pressure and said, "Sure would be nice if we had more Black coaches and players," and then headed out to find them? Only time that happens is when folk see a dollar in it and even then....

Yes, Colored folk are grateful progress has been made! Does that mean we should be satisfied as if the job were done when we know better? I am a strong believer in being grateful, no matter what the circumstances. It promotes and evokes a certain humility that I believe we can all use more of. Humility is an important quality of being human. However, being grateful and being satisfied are two different things. People who look like me have been in this country for several centuries now, so I expect we should be a lot further down the road toward equity and justice. So, yes, I'm grateful to have what I have and, no, I'm not satisfied to be part way home. I ask my White brothers and sisters: would you be satisfied?

Reverse Discrimination Revisited

Let's revisit affirmative action and the concept of reverse discrimination for a minute. I think White folks have the best affirmative action program goin. Lots of them get jobs because of *who they know* and not because they are most qualified, so I'm told. When I do my race workshops, White and Black folks come up to me all the time and tell me that. Sometimes they'll tell it right in the workshop and usually neither Colored folk nor Caucasian folk deny it's true. They tell me about folks who got jobs because of their daddy or mommy or someone they knew that knew someone that knew someone. "This is the best affirmative action program going," I say to myself, and sometimes I say it out loud. Not only does that program work automatically, but it is virtually unchallenged, was not set up to right a past wrong, does not depend on the applicant's qualifications, and is capricious based on who knows whom, who lives by whom, who plays golf with whom, or who goes to church with whom. If you know the right people, qualified or not, someone can talk someone else into giving you a break with no affirmative action stigma attached. People say if Black folk get hired due to affirmative action it carries a stigma, that we couldn't make it on our own. Well, I say, a whole lot of people in the US of America don't just "make it on their own." Lots of preferential treatment in this society with no stigma attached; no public outcry. What I hear uproars about is "X" Negro got hired to meet a quota and not because of their qualifications. If US of Americans are concerned about merit and quality, I say it's time to put a stop to what some call the "good ole boys" system of hiring. Truth be told, this kind of double standard doesn't sit well with a lot of my dark-skinned brothers and sisters, or me for that matter. It is a fact, in the US of America, Caucasian folk are more commonly than People of Color in a position to know people in high places or to be well-connected. And it's a fact, those folk got in those places when Colored folk couldn't. I don't mean wouldn't, I mean couldn't. And it's a fact, most people like to hire folk and be around folk that look and act like them. Some call it comfort zone. Whites still do most of the hiring and still feel more comfortable with folk like themselves. And some are just downright prejudiced, consciously or not. Surely not everyone is like that, but enough are to make some kind of affirmative action program important—even if I would prefer we could do away with them. I ask you to think about it before getting upset about reverse discrimination. Have we really come so far that you think race doesn't matter when folk hire people? Not sure what some White folk, who affirmative action programs upset, are worried about when they still have the highest-paying jobs, get hired first and fired last. Check it out for yourself. We are still not at equal pay for equal work either; so it's not about reverse discrimination it's about *reverse fairness*. That's what we need to be looking at. It's about putting the car in reverse; drivin back and takin a look to make sure I didn't get driven by, just to get to you!

Civil Rights Act of 1964 legally forbade discrimination in the workplace, and that was only forty-five plus years ago. I don't believe, after legally discriminating in the workplace and all other places for over three hundred and fifty plus years of US history that it all just sort of disappeared in the last forty years. So I'm all for some kind of "reverse fairness" in my life. The playing field is only level if you are standin on top of the wall Negro folk are still running into.

And while we're on this topic I got something else to say. Affirmative action programs never were about hiring just anyone because they were a certain color or gender, regardless of qualification. It was always about goals, never about hiring the unqualified. Folk talk like Negroes as a group think we should get hired just because we're Black. Some Black folk might think that, but MOST surely don't.

And while we're still on this, something sticks in my craw about all this. It's not just Blacks that benefit from affirmative action; but when people get upset about it, seems like Black folk take the heat. I know a bunch of White women benefited from affirmative action, but for some reason it doesn't seem like so much public flack comes their way. Personally I'm very glad they benefited and others who have been unjustly treated as well. A lot of women, of all colors, have been on the firing line working for justice. But you gotta agree, the primary flack seems to be against those of us of darker hues. Folks suing all the time, feeling they got cheated out of some college spot, contract or job because of "preferential treatment" for Blacks. Don't hear much suing because White women took a spot and if it happens it sure doesn't make the news like it does for Colored folk. Why is that?

Okay, so here's the bottom line with affirmative action: the argument goes something like this—"Race should not be a factor or matter when hiring, the best person should get the job." I agree that race *should not* matter but too many studies and experience say it does and not in a way that benefits folk of Color. So for example's sake, let's say twenty percent of the folk in hiring positions are impacted negatively by the race or gender of an interviewee. Those who say no to affirmative action programs are basically saying, "too bad for those folks who are interviewed by that twenty percent. That twenty percentage should be left free to discriminate if they want to because we can't have any kind of programs in place to stop that for fear some of us might not get a job. Those Colored folk unlucky enough to be discriminated against just have to grin and bear not getting the job. Leave things the way they are, wait for time alone to heal everything and bye and bye that twenty percent will disappear. Affirmative action is not the answer. We need to be colorblind." The message to folk like me is "since things have gotten better, though not nearly equal, we can dump affirmative action programs." Many folk realize things are not equal but the message is since they're *better* that should be good enough for "you all." ("Just what does the Negro want.") Whether spoken or not, that's the take away. Someone tell me what to make of that.

So if affirmative actions programs aren't perfect I say help make them better but get rid of them **only** when they have accomplished their goal not when they have barely approached it.

Chapter 6

Remembering Columbine Differently, Then There Was Rwanda and Darfur

I'm back to my newspaper. I know I have to get ready to go, but this grabbed me. I'm reading about one of the anniversaries of the tragedy in Columbine where a couple of White boys shot and killed several classmates at random. I remember looking up from my newspaper several years ago and seeing the aftermath of the school shootings in that predominately White neighborhood. They had it all over the TV. Oh, here we go again, I remember thinking to myself. I feel real bad about my feelings on this, but every time I hear them talk about those shooting incidents, at the schools where those White boys killed a bunch of folk, I really get upset. Now, at Columbine they're recounted, because at least one of the shooters got *bullied*, he got a gun and started takin his schoolmates out at random. Call me oversensitive, but the way I see it, when CNBAAPA boys do things like killin folk in their neighborhoods, nobody tries to figure out the social causes or interviews folk on TV to find out how bad the boys felt when they got picked on or "bullied." All I hear is "time to crack down on crime, three strikes and you're out, tougher drug laws," etc. I don't hear the same cry for "understanding" what is going on in Black communities all over America as when something bad happens in White neighborhoods. It feels like prejudice to me. Maybe it's not conscious prejudice but it feels like it nonetheless. When a White child dies, or kills, or acts up in a really awful way, we need to examine our whole country and see what's gone wrong "with America's kids" (heard that on TV). Victims' and the killers' friends are interviewed on TV to try to understand why. When a CNBAAPA person kills or robs, you better lock him up quick to discourage others. When something bad happens in a White neighborhood like I read in the editorial page the other day, folk say things like, "this just isn't supposed to happen here." I wonder where things like that "should happen" and if folks really care when they do happen other places…. I have to ask a hard, painful, and sensitive question that many CNBAAPA folk ask themselves all the time. *Is the life of a CNBAAPA child in America viewed as important as the life of a Caucasian child? Is it as important to understand the cause of why CNBAAPA children commit violent crimes against other CNBAAPA children as it is to understand why White children commit such crimes?* Some folk say "well these school shootings and similar mass killings are different because it all happened at one time." I say to that, CNBAAPA killings may not happen at one time but they happen *all the time*, the victims are often young and the cumulative numbers are more staggering, as any Columbine, Santee, Finland, Virginia Tech, Binghamton, rural Alabama, Omaha, Pinelake Health Center or postal shootings combined. Does the fact the killings don't all happen on the same day really matter? And what about all those young black men going to prison? Is that something that should concern the US of America?

I read an editorial by an angry White fella shortly after the Columbine and Santee tragedy. He was adamant in his views. He was real upset because he felt folk are deluding themselves about these school shootings and where and why they are happening. He wrote it several years ago, but it still seems to have relevance. Might need to say a prayer for calm and composure before you read this. Let me share some of what he said and please know I took out the cuss words.

> Two more White children are dead and thirteen are injured, and another "nice" community is scratching its blonde head, utterly perplexed at how a school shooting the likes of the one yesterday in Santee, California could happen. After all, as the Mayor of the town said in an interview with CNN: "We're a solid town,

a good town, with good kids, a good church-going town, an All-American town." Yeah, well maybe that's the problem. I said this after Columbine and no one listened so I'll say it again: White people live in an utter state of self-delusion. We think danger is Black, brown and poor, and if we can just move far enough away from "those people" in the cities we'll be safe. If we can just find an "all-American" town, life will be better, because "things like this just don't happen here."

Well [...] on that. In case you hadn't noticed, "here" is about the only place these kinds of things do happen. Oh sure, there is plenty of violence in urban communities and schools. But mass murder; wholesale slaughter; take-a-gun-and-see-how-many-you can-kill kinda craziness seems made for those safe places: the White suburbs or rural communities. And yet once again, we hear the FBI insist there is no 'profile' of a school shooter. Come again? White boy after White boy after White boy, with very few exceptions to that rule (and none in the mass shooting category), decides to use their classmates for target practice, and yet there is no profile? Imagine if all these killers had been Black: would we still hesitate to put a racial face on the perpetrators? Doubtful. Indeed, if any Black child in America— especially in the mostly White suburbs of Littleton, or Santee—were to openly discuss their plans to murder fellow students, as happened both at Columbine and now Santana High, you can bet your [...] that somebody would have turned them in, and the cops would have beat a path to their doorstep. But when Whites discuss their murderous intentions, our stereotypes of what danger looks like cause us to ignore it—they're just 'talking' and won't really do anything. How many kids have to die before we rethink that nonsense?

How many dazed and confused parents, Mayors and Sheriffs do we have to listen to, describing how "normal" and safe their community is, and how they just can't understand what went wrong? I'll tell you what went wrong and it's not TV, rap music, video games or a lack of prayer in school. What went wrong is that White Americans decided to ignore dysfunction and violence when it only affected other communities, and thereby blinded themselves to the inevitable creeping of chaos which never remains isolated too long. What affects the urban "ghetto" today will be coming to a Wal-Mart near you tomorrow, and unless you address the emptiness, pain, isolation and lack of hope felt by children of color and the poor, then don't be shocked when the support systems aren't there for your kids either. What went wrong is that we allowed ourselves to be lulled into a false sense of security by media representations of crime and violence that portray both as the province of those who are anything but White like us. We ignore the warning signs, because in our minds the warning signs don't live in our neighborhood, but across town, in that place where we lock our car doors on the rare occasion we have to drive there. That false sense of security—the result of racist and classist stereotypes—then gets people killed. And still we act amazed. But listen up my fellow White Americans: your children are no better, no nicer, no more moral, no more decent than anyone else. Dysfunction is all around you, whether you choose to recognize it or not. According to the Centers for Disease Control, and Department of Health and Human Services, it is your children, and not those of the urban ghetto, who are most likely to use drugs. That's right: White high school students are seven times more likely than Blacks to have used cocaine; eight times more likely to have smoked crack; ten times more likely to have used LSD and seven times more likely to have used heroin. In fact, there are more White high school students who have used crystal methamphetamine (the most addictive drug on the streets) than there are Black students who smoke cigarettes. What's more, White youth ages 12–17 are more likely to sell drugs: 34% more likely, in fact than their Black counterparts. And it is White youth who are twice as likely to binge drink, and nearly twice as likely as Blacks to drive drunk. And White males are twice as likely to bring a weapon to school as are Black males.

And yet I would bet a valued body part that there aren't 100 White people in Santee, California, or most any other "nice" community who have ever heard a single one of the statistics above. Even though they were collected by government agencies using these folks' tax money for the purpose. Because the media *doesn't report on White dysfunction.* A few years ago, U.S. News ran a story entitled: "A Shocking Look at Blacks and Crime." Yet never have they or any other news outlet discussed the 'shocking' Whiteness of these shoot-em-ups. Indeed, every time media commentators discuss the similarities in these crimes they mention the shooters were boys, they were loners, they got picked on, but never do they seem to notice a certain highly visible melanin deficiency. Color-blind, I guess. White-blind is more like it, as I figure these folks would spot color mighty... quick were some of it to stroll into their community. Santee's Whiteness is so taken for granted by its residents that the Mayor, in that CNN interview, thought nothing of saying on the one hand that the town was 82 percent White, but on the other hand that "this is America." Well that isn't America, and it especially isn't California, where Whites are only half of the population. This is a town that is removed from America, and yet its Mayor thinks they are the normal ones—so much so that when asked about racial diversity, he replied that there weren't many of different "ethni-tis-tities." Not a word. Not even close. I'd like to think that after this one, people would wake up. Take note. Rethink their stereotypes of who the dangerous ones are. But deep down, I know better. The folks hitting the snooze button on this none-too-subtle alarm are my own people, after all, and I know their blindness like the back of my hand. (Wise, 2001)

This guy is talking pretty straight and he sounds mad, the kind of anger born of frustrated caring and perhaps having to make the argument over and over to deaf ears. His tone is harsh perhaps, but meaning of his words ring true. Well he said what many CNBAAPA folk are feeling, but know, if they said anything like it in any tone, they would be ostracized, labeled oversensitive, insensitive and militant. The US of America cannot value one group over another like this and then wonder why folk like me get hurt, then angry. Worse yet, I feel bad because of how I feel. I want to grieve like everyone else about these kinds of tragedies, but I have to fight these feelings of humiliation, and God knows it is not just my imagination. Sometimes I wish I could put my head in the sand and act like I don't see what I see. It would be a lot easier in some ways. I bet I wouldn't get so *tired*. I'm also betting I'd lose my self respect.

I care about all children but I am not sure the US of America does. I and other CNBAAPA folk get *real weary* watching this double standard and acting like it doesn't bother us, because it does and especially when it comes to Black children.

A most painful example for me is that of missing or kidnapped Children of Color. It is clear that those missing children rarely, if ever, get the kind of national media coverage White children get. What is the message in that? And it happens *in your face* over and over again. So while I watch White children get day-in and day-out coverage and feel sad for their plight, I am torn by other feelings of humiliation. Where are the missing Black children's faces? Where are they and why aren't they?

Since we're on the subject of tragedies, let me say that one of the most challenging and painful things I had to deal with in recent years was the genocide in Rwanda. Over a million—yes, you heard that right—over a million of our/yourAfrican brothers and sisters where slaughtered. Yet again an agonizing question is raised in the minds of folks like me. How many dark-skinned folks have to die before a nation cares enough to really do something about it? Apparently a million was not enough? When is an atrocity so appalling that some sort of action is the only moral response possible? Later we said about Rwanda, "never again." Then there was Darfur.

As a proud person of color, I want you to hear me and "feel" me because I'm telling you, your African American family hurts over this kinda stuff. How could so many dark-skinned people be allowed to perish? Do we care? Did we see these men, women and children as valued members of the human race with dreams and cares like everyone else? Could we not imagine there was heaven in these faces and not just mere flesh and bone? Do I see race as a factor in all this? My head, heart and life experience can not see it otherwise.

I know some folk feel we neglected the ethnic cleansing in the mid nineties in Bosnia for too long as well. (Estimates I read stated there were over 100,000 deaths.) We may or may not have but my point here is not to make some political statement about our government. I'm trying to convey the emotional challenges that have an impact on the everyday life of Black folk. White folk weren't feeling their race was devalued, for example, because of the response to Bosnia. Most Black folk I know feel their race was brutally devalued by the response to Rwanda and Darfur and that if it was a million White folk slaughtered anywhere, the response would have been different. I like many African Americans believe our nation's response, consciously or unconsciously, was at least in part based on race.

How do I come to that conclusion and how can I *support* that belief you might ask? I come to that conclusion the way we all come to conclusions; through research, observation, feelings, and experiences. I'm bringing these tragedies up because I'm human and stuff like this is gut wrenching and because these are pain and anger-producing factors that drive wedges between CNBAAPA folk and Caucasians. These are the kinds of things that cause deep hard feelings and widen the chasm.

Chapter 7

Pride and Passion

Well, I don't want to dwell on all that; I just get too mad. Actually, it hurts me. I use the word "hurt" several times because some folk have a hard time saying that out loud. No one wants to sound like a wimp and a whiner, especially a "brotha." But the truth is, whether old or young, this kind of thing, happenin over and over, hurts my sense of self, my pride and dignity. I can hide that shadow under a veneer of okayness, but it will creep out sure enough. Like I said some folk just throw in the towel and say, I'm done tryin to get along with Caucasians in the US of A, done expecting a fair shake. On my good days I tell them, "hey man, see the glass half full, we can do this, don't give up now." But some still feel, deep inside, the meaning of the words attributed to Malclom X and spoken by Denzel Washington in the movie *Malcolm X*: "I say and I say it again, you've been had. You've been took. You've been hoodwinked, bamboozled, led astray, run amok" (Washington, 1992).

I almost hesitate to bring up Malcolm X because some folk will cut me off right there thinkin he was so "militant" and "hostile" and "anti-U.S American." Therein is another dilemma. Negroes feel like we have to filter our words in terms of who we talk about and what we say in front of White folk because if we are connecting with the wrong folk or saying things in the "wrong" way they're going to think we are "too Black." It's irritating in general, but if Caucasian folk have any kind of authority over you, you don't want to mention certain Black people nor do you want to act to bothered about race stuff. Brother Malcolm stood adamantly for freedom for Black people, believed in self-help, straightened out a lot of wayward brothers in the neighborhood, and had a dignified and honorable family life, did not drink or smoke after he became a Muslim, and yet he gets maligned. He got hot under the collar about seeing Black people maimed, crippled and abused in the US of America, so yeah, he got angry and said some things he probably shouldn't have. Look at what was going on at the time and you can understand why he was so angry and incensed.

Check this out: past presidents and other White leaders who held slaves and/or who disliked or even hated Black folk after slavery have bridges named after them, monuments on street corners and parks and streets named in their honor. It's okay for White folk to talk about them in front of us, but us talking about someone like Malcolm is not cool and like a major taboo. I speak from experience. It is as if White folk can ignore the negative and often reprehensible attitudes some of their heroes had about Black folks and bring them up as if we should honor them too and as if those attitudes are irrelevant. I want to say to them, "don't you know these heroes of yours hated people like me or held us in slavery? And in too many cases they acted in such a way that led to our deaths. So please don't talk about them as if I should revere them the same way you do." Sometimes I do say that and other times I don't say anything. The past is the past, I'm told by many of my White brothers and sisters and some Black ones too. Sometimes I'm cool with that but other times it's a trip for me. I'm not saying we should tear down all those monuments or change the names of all those streets. I'm saying, many White heroes weren't perfect; neither should the Black ones have to be. As Langston Hughes said in one of his famous poems, "I too am America."

Well, Malcolm did his best to set things right and even had hope for race reconciliation at the end of his life. He went on his pilgrimage to Mecca and saw dark and light-skinned Muslims together in belief and spirit. He came back to the US of America with hope that could happen here. He changed from feeling like there was no hope of reconciling White and Black folk to holding out hope. This was a dramatic shift for him and an example of true leadership. He was a seeker of truth and showed the willingness to change based on new information and experiences. Throughout his entire life he let go of many previous beliefs or positions, no matter how difficult and however unpopular it made him. He was courageous so I won't apologize for him, nor feel like I need to explain away some of his angry statements. No indeed. He's one of my heroes and I'm proud of him!

Wish all folk, Black and White would read about his life and, just as an exercise, do a gut check. Would you have the courage to risk your life for your beliefs knowing people were out to kill you and perhaps your family as well? I know Martin Luther King and Patrick Henry made statements about finding something worth dying for so you'd be fit to live and demanding liberty or death. I believe all that and I also believe it's easier said than done. Malcolm did it. There are lessons in his life for everyone if we're willing to meet at the intersection in the spirit of sharing different experiences and different realities.

Chapter 8

Costing Money to Be CNBAAPA

Anyway, I better get dressed to go give my diversity talk for this local civic group. I'm pretty much prepared for it as it is a short talk, thank God. I applaud them for meeting for a strict amount of time so early in the morning. Anyway, I better look sharp. *I don't want those people to "look" at me and think I am not qualified, cuz I know I'll be scrutinized when I walk through that door, and not just by Caucasians but by Colored folk too.* Last time I went to a place like that driving my "nice car," a fellow looked at me, then at my car and kinda shook his head and sayin something about how I could afford all that? I didn't hear all of what he said but I heard that part. Anyway, I think I'll drive my Corolla, which I am trying real hard to sell. It is difficult to sell a car, so I have a "for sale" sign in the car window. To make sure folk don't miss it, I put one on each side. My wife said that may help. "Who knows," she said, "you might drive right by someone who wants a car just like ours." That's what she said but here I go again thinking there are White and Black folk who will look at me, and look at the "for sale" sign in the car and not even consider calling me, even if they need a car like mine. I know it sounds paranoid and over the edge, but I bet some folk would look at me and see a Black person ***and never even think about why they would not consider calling me. They, in many cases unconsciously, would not call, even if they needed or wanted a car like mine.*** They would not necessarily ever think the words "don't call because he's Black"; it would simply never come to their conscious mind to think to call. Ponder it before you dismiss it. I think this is how deep the whole race thing in America goes. I don't think my car example applies to everyone, but it's true of plenty of folk and definitely enough folk to narrow the possibilities of me makin a sale. It costs money in the US of America to be Colored, Negro, Black, Afro-American, African American, or a Person of Color. Black and White folk can be skittish about seeking services and goods from Negroes. Brainwashing goes deep and that can cost you cold hard cash!

Fact is, I saw a show on TV, which said CNBAAPA US of Americans pay more for cars than their White U.S American counterparts. We Negroes, so the show says, are not seen as sophisticated buyers in comparison to Whites, so car salesmen get over on us. It amounts to Afro-Americans paying millions of dollars a year more than White folk. They had the hard facts and numbers to back it up. Now Colored folk gotta own part of that deal as well and try to get hip to what's goin on, but it's wrong to take advantage of folk just because you can, isn't it? This kind of thing can make you *mad* even if you don't want it to. But see, I don't want to play the race card, so I try to do what a lot of folk tell me to do about things like this. They say, "Just don't let it bother you." "Don't let it bother me," I ponder to myself. That takes a lot of energy but it takes more of my energy to let it bother me! Straight up though, it trips my trigger (manner of speakin, nothing to do with guns I assure you) that folk lookin like me are being systematically taken advantage of. Not cool. So inevitably and after a battle with myself to regain myself, I take some deep breaths and try not to let it bother me. Let me tell you something: don't ever underestimate the power of deep, slow breaths to center and calm yourself.

NEWS FLASH

News stories just came on discussing sub-prime mortgages and who gained and who lost the most. Bottom line: a lot of folk got messed over, but the numbers of Colored folk was way up. Some got duped and some just got big eyes over what looked like a shortcut to easy money.

As we have found out the sub-prime fiasco was nothing but greed; folk with big money trying to get bigger and preying on the dreams and hopes of common folk. When too much *green* is in the mix, *mean* is not far behind. That's why spirituality is important in this whole thing. Something has to check the greed and materialistic bent. Temptation is a real thing and "money is honey" to some. Folk need something to check that sweet tooth when it kicks in gear. Sweet tooth for money can pull folk down a steep dark decline. Think about it. Slavery and Jim Crow, drug selling, sex trafficking, most wars, robbery, burglary, fraud, sub-primes, killing for life insurance, arson for house insurance, slum lording and a whole lot more slime, grime and crime come from that sweet tooth. Well I could go on and so could you. The manifestations are many, but the cause is the same. Point being however when greed kicks in it often kicks folks of Color the first and the worst, and sub primes were no exception.

NEWS FLASH OVER

Giving a Simple Talk

Well, I am getting close to arriving at the place I will be giving my speech, so I better get ready. *I wonder how many Negroes will be members of this civic club.* I know it shouldn't matter but it does, and that is what comes to my mind as I drive into the parking lot. I will find out soon enough. Walkin in the room everyone seems to look up at the same time. I catch a few eyes and hear a few comments. One White guy says, just loud enough for me to hear it, "I guess we're going to get diversified today." I hear a few chuckles around him. I catch the eye of a *brother* as he nods at me lookin sort of nervous, probably hopin I don't say anything too rough or get too carried away about race during my talk. I see a *sister* who genuinely has that look that says, "Oh I am so glad you're here." About forty people in the room and about five People of Color: Four CNBAAPA and one, I believe, is Latino. I'm thinking that this group might be like so many others I have spoken to. The Caucasian folk think, as a CNBAAPA man, I'm probably going to blame them for all of the problems of Colored folk and likely indicate they're all prejudiced one way or another. The *nervous* Afro-American guy is worried I might be too militant or harsh and mess things up for him and other CNBAAPA folk who are trying to make it in this group. The sister, who looked glad to see me, hopes I will really tell it like it is, because she feels and fears that if she ever speaks her mind fully, folk in the club may not be very welcoming to her thereafter. Or she feels *tired* of being the lone voice speaking up about race issues. Chances are the Latino is feeling like all I will do is talk about the CNBAAPA folk and White folk and leave his culture out of the diversity picture altogether.

So this little thirty minute talk is not quite so simple after all. The question I always ask myself is: How do I talk about this issue in an honest, but fair way and not offend someone? The answer I always give myself is the same. *I can't!* Someone is going to be offended by my Colored, Negro, Black, Afro-American, African American, Person of Color, Person of African descent self, one way or the other. All Black folk do not do diversity training or speeches on race relations, so I am not suggesting they face the exact same dilemma I do here, preparing to give this speech—the "damned if you do and damned if you don't" dilemma I mean. Anyway, in my talk, if I am honest about things, I will offend someone and be accused of whining or playing the race card, and if I sugarcoat it, everyone will think that things are really not so bad. Or else, particularly the Colored folk will think I am out of touch with reality and dismiss me. So I'm gonna tell the truth, hopefully in the right spirit, and let the chips fall where they may.

On second thought, many Colored folk do face a similar dilemma even if they are not diversity training folk. I mean the "dammed if you do or dammed if you don't dilemma." When my brother read this, he said this isn't a "second thought" at all. He said he thought of it right away. His thought was "every Black person he knows deals with the dilemma when race comes up." I think he's right, and I'll give you an example. I have a Black friend who works in corporate America. He tells me he faces racial prejudice all the time, but is afraid to say anything because he'll be accused of being too race conscious. He's decided to keep to himself, not making waves and just doing his job. Then people suggested he had a chip on his shoulder and wondered why he was so standoffish. Finally, he spoke up and talked to his team about how he was feeling. He told them how other employees whom he helped train were promoted over him, how he seems to still have to prove himself after all these years, and how he feels like he's under a microscope all the time. He told them he doesn't want to use race as an excuse but he feels he has proved himself time and again and still gets passed over. He told them being seen as a *nice hard workin guy* was not enough anymore, and since he didn't want to get labeled as an angry Black man he didn't say anything, 'til now.

He told me the folk understood "up to a point." They saw his perspective, but felt he was being a little too sensitive, and maybe race was not the reason he didn't get promoted. Even if race was part of it, his time would come. They told him, in essence, to try not to dwell on it or let it bother him so much and try to stay positive. At least one person, sort of defensively reminded him, not all White people have it easy either. Conversation didn't really help ease his frustration and pain because he could tell they just didn't get it.

He tells me now things have gotten "chilly" again. He's back to just keepin to himself, but now it doesn't seem to bother anyone. He's going to try to bide his time till retirement or hopefully something better might come along somewhere else. He feels like he blew any chance he might've had in being moved up because the word is out. "Damned if you do and damned if you don't!" Anyway, that's his story, and I don't want to judge all of corporate America by his experience. Maybe he was just not qualified? But maybe he was qualified and just got shafted. I don't really know the situation because I wasn't there, but when you've heard as many stories like this as I have… well, let me just say it again; different lenses, difference experiences, different realities.

When will we as US of Americans, Black and White, humble ourselves enough, call on our best selves, our spiritual selves if you will, *so we can really hear and feel each other?* When will the conversations Blacks have with Blacks about race and Whites have with Whites, be shared across race? When will Blacks feel free to share how they really feel with Whites and vice versa with an assurance that there will be no retaliation? Won't happen without the kind of courage my friend showed and it won't continue to happen if folk don't dig deeper and try to understand more. "Do you hear me calling"? I'm not callin for me; I'm callin for the future of the US of America.

Because I love sports I will use another sports example to make my point. This example can be extrapolated to dynamics that take place in the broader US of America community. It has to do with a retired boxing champion who, only after he retired, was able to share his true feelings about the racial experiences he had during his boxing career. They had to do with his feelings about the way sports announcers exhibited racial bias on HBO.

"They talk about Kelly Pavlik, a White fighter, like he's the second coming. Or they go crazy over Manny Pacquiao. But I'm a Black fighter," Mayweather said. "Is it racial? Absolutely. They praise White fighters, they praise Hispanic fighters, whatever. But Black fighters, they never praise."

"I've noticed it for a long time but I couldn't say anything because I had to do business with them. I'll still do business with them, but I'm done holding my tongue." His response, after finally sharing his true feelings is also telling. "I'm happy. I feel clear. I feel free as a bird," he told the newspaper. "I feel good that I can finally speak out, and say the things I want to say."

What was the response from HBO? HBO Sports president Ross Greenburg said in a statement that the network, which has carried many of Mayweather's fights, "was disappointed to hear of the boxer's remarks and denied his claims." He went on to say "His (referring to Mayweather) remarks regarding HBO broadcasters and executives are unfortunate and we could not disagree more." (Smith, 2008)

Mayweather felt dissed and HBO says, "no way." What would have happened had there been an open enough environment to talk about these issues privately? What would have happened if HBO had opened themselves up to really hearing Mayweather's perspective? Or if he had decided to talk to them privately because he had enough faith in the relationship and believed they would be able to engage in a genuine dialogue? Chances are, when you listen openly to people they will listen to your side too. Who knows, but the result couldn't be worse than the current one. Distrust no doubt has deepened and the issue has been made public. Where does that leave us? I'd say it leaves us more divided. Perhaps HBO and Mayweather will sit down and talk things through now. That would be the best outcome at this point and then perhaps everyone could learn something. If not, another notch in the race coffin. Whites see another "whiner" and Blacks see another example of "institutional racism." Point is that this example typifies where we are with dialogue about race in the US of America. Anger, finger pointing, blamin and no resolution seems, too often, to be the norm. We can do better!

Do you see where spirituality has to kick in, the concept of sacrificing for each other, transforming pain into strength, humbling ourselves so we can create a new energy around all this and move forward? If not, it's just my emotional pain meeting with your emotional denial and the beat goes on.

Chapter 9

It's More Than the Big Stuff and the Little Stuff

Let me say this right now because I'm feeling it for some reason: the accusation that I'm oversensitive or just plain wrong about what I feel or see does get old. I get real tired constantly analyzing what I am feeling, seeing, witnessing and hearing to make sure I'm not being overly sensitive. But I keep tellin myself I have to try to be fair and open-minded if I want White folk to do the same. (I imagine they get tired of always hearing they are racist or prejudiced.) On the other hand, it seems many folk don't see racial prejudice unless it's the most blatant kind, like a Black church getting burned down by someone White, or a Black man getting dragged to death behind a car just because of his race, or a Black woman getting raped and tortured by six White folk who tell her that's how niggers get treated. (I believe that tragic story only made the national news for just a few short days. I can't help but wonder if six Black men imprisoned, tortured and repeatedly raped a White woman, would it have been in the news longer?) These types of events are clearly acknowledged and abhorred by Black and White alike but are often viewed by Whites as aberrations and not symptomatic of endemic racial prejudice.

And before I go on let me share with you the details of the woman referred to above who was raped and held captive for at least six days, and some think much longer. Here is what happened to her. Ms. Williams, a twenty-year-old Black woman, was kidnapped by six White career criminals in August of 2007, held captive in a desolate mobile home trailer for several days and perhaps up to a month. During that time, in addition to being taunted with the word "nigger," she was beaten, raped, fed animal feces, stabbed, strangled, forced to lick blood and threatened with death if she tried to escape. One of the perpetrators will be eligible for parole in just six and a half years and I'm not sure about the others. The perpetrators, both male and female, have had a total of 108 criminal charges against them since 1991 including first degree murder. By the way, Ms. Williams apparently also has learning disabilities (Michaels, 2007).

So my questions are: If this were a White woman and six Black folk who were the perpetrators of this heinous crime, what would the outcome have been? What would the jail sentences have been? How long would it have stayed in the newspaper? How much public outrage would there be? Whose lives really matter in the US of America? I had to share this story with you all, not to be sensational, but this crime was outrageously horrendous and extremely hurtful especially as it was dismissed so quickly; in part, reports stated, to avoid excessive bad publicity for the city in which it happened.

Black folk sharing racial experiences, other than ones that are universally abhorred, are most frequently met with incredulity or denial. Let me tell you something that is a blood boiler for me. Pardon me, but I find it the essence of arrogance to deny other people's experience just because you may not experience the same kinds of things. I find it even more arrogant to suggest that Colored folk, as a group, try to bring race into everything. I wonder if those who make such accusations realize how thoroughly *draining* it is to bring race up as an issue? Drudging up things that are painful, anger-producing and anxiety-laden is not most people's idea of a good time. I know I have better things to do, and most Negroes I know do too. I like to read, play basketball, play scrabble, pray, meditate, help folk out, work out, write short stories and long stories, go to the country, memorize famous lines and whole parts of movies, go for walks, tell jokes, eat out, eat in, cook out, hang out with my wife and grandkids and family and just plain be. Most folk I know, Black or White, like to do some of that stuff too. (Well maybe not memorize famous parts of movies. If you do, let me know and we can have a contest.) Most of us would rather do that kind of stuff instead of getting into verbal race wars. So to suggest that folk of African descent bring race issues up lightly and all the time is not only arrogant, but ignorant. I'm bein harsh, I know, but come on! Think about it. Soon as you bring up race you get labeled, often for life! I am not saying that no Colored folk ever bring race into things where it doesn't belong, but in my experience, it is more the *exception* than the rule and certainly does not represent the majority of Black folk.

Let me explain a little something here. There are a lot of different kinds of Black folk, color-wise, temperament-wise and otherwise. **Some**, (emphasis on the word some), folk do simply want to complain and constantly talk about the "White man" and prejudice as the reason they aren't makin it. They perhaps have given up psychologically and physically and, yes, some of them just sit on their butts. Others may not be on their butts, however they got something stuck in their craw regarding White folk and can't seem to let it go or have just given up trying to reconcile with them. Then there are a lot of folk who talk about the "White man" and prejudice, and they're working hard to be just and fair, to be open, doing their best to raise a family, workin hard, but are still frustrated with racism. Some just don't want to talk about it at all, nor do they admit it's still an issue in the US of America. These groups aren't the same. The first has given up for a whole lot of reasons that include but may not be limited to racism. The second one is probably workin hard, paying taxes, yet just doesn't want to even deal with White folk anymore. The third is where I and a whole lot of other folks are: wantin to let go of all this race stuff, but realizin it's not ready to let go of us. We're gonna make sure it's addressed so long as it's an issue in our lives and the lives of our children and families. How could anyone expect otherwise?

84

Think about it and while you're thinkin about it, think about how Caucasians bring race into a whole bunch of stuff where it doesn't belong. A lot of White folk have, over many years, blamed Black folk for so many of the problems in their life or in the life of the US of America. African Americans have been or are constantly blamed for the reason why their kids don't have jobs (affirmative action), why their kids can't get into schools (affirmative action), why the economy (before the sub-prime fiasco) is bad (entitlements), why there is such immorality, why there is so much crime. Some were even blamin Barack Obama ahead of time sayin he would bring down the country by steering his policies toward the twelve percent of the population he "represents."

In general there are many Whites that don't want to live in neighborhoods with Black folk, don't want to use Black professionals for services, hire Blacks for jobs, etc. This is my take about race being brought into things where it doesn't belong and no doubt some folks would dispute it.

When some White folk bring race into this kind of stuff, it is often either an oversimplification of the issues and sometimes it simply is ignorance and or prejudice. For example there is absolutely no way an African American President, would have the capability, even if he or she wanted to, to steer policies only toward those in his race. How can anyone think that Blacks will automatically bring property values down and then use that as excuse not to move in a mixed neighborhood? On the other hand some move out when Blacks move in. Is it possible some just don't want to live around too many Black folk? And why would you not use a professional because of the color of their skin? It happens my friends, it happens. I have an idea based on that last point. African Americans use the services of White folks all the time. To level the playing field, White folks could affirmatively attempt to use services provided by Blacks for *some* of their needs. Some would ask, "why should I go out of my way to do that?" I would respond to that, "Because you care enough to reach past what is comfortable so you can build unity and trust." I would also say, "It is this kind of behavior that will not only address financial disparities but will also offer ways to build bonds of fellowship across racial and social boundaries." And finally I would say it is a way for some Caucasians to have contact with folk of Color on equal footing. There are many Caucasians, because of work situations and neighborhood choice that do not have contact with People of Color other than in service roles in restaurants, hotels etc. It is this kind of going out your way outreach that can help change that and make a difference. What do you think about that idea? Maybe try to think about it spiritually instead of emotionally.

So back to my main point, I still say that the vast majority of Black folk prefer not bringing race into things where it doesn't belong. The reason many folk see it the other way—the *rule rather than the exception*—is that they simply refuse to hear and feel what folk are saying or believe what is being said. If a person refuses to believe it, then they don't have to do anything about it. They can write me and others off as whining Negroes playin the race card and therefore avoid seeing the need to change their lives at all.

The System of Advantage

Some folk even try to tell me that what is happening to me really isn't. They really do tell me that. Don't let me get too carried away or be judgmental, but I have to say that it is incomprehensible that some of my Caucasian brothers and sisters will tell me my experiences aren't real and that what I'm experiencing I'm really not and then proceed to explain to me what is really going on, or that my experiences aren't any different from theirs. That's like a man claiming that a woman

86

isn't really going through the experiences she is having, then explaining to her what she is really experiencing, and that it's the same as a man's experience. Lord, help me!

You also got some Negro folk, high and low alike, tellin all who will listen we gotta stop makin race an excuse. They're saying we gotta quit blamin the White man and start disciplining our children more and make sure they get off the street, stay in school and stop gettin into gangs.

Generally, these folk are just blastin away at mostly poor Colored folks. Have to say, I agree with some of the blastin AND have to say I don't think it's that simple. Don't believe it makes sense to simply "blame the victim" as they used to say back in the day. Gotta say the answer lies in both the "victim" and the "victimizer" taking responsibility for what was created over so many years. One group can't do it alone, so the way I see it, focusin on one at the exclusion of the other is getting us nowhere. And the victimizer is not just White folk as individuals, nor is it just those Colored folk who are brainwashed into thinkin they're nothin, so they act like nothing, and treat everyone else like they're nothing. It's also "the system" that still favors the majority US of America population. Let me give you a very fundamental and age old example: folk write textbooks for schools and colleges that don't tell the whole truth and don't include contributions of Afro-Americans. Teachers doesn't have to be prejudiced in their hearts, all they have to do is teach from the book, and because it's not including contributions of Black folk or their perspectives, a *system of advantage* lives on. (Students tell me they only learn about the same African Americans year after year.) The victimizer becomes the *educational system* not just or necessarily the person teaching. The students being taught from these textbooks simply learn the "facts" and perpetuate the myths. More often than not, these textbooks contain a tad more truth than they used to, but much of it is watered down so students will say things like I heard again recently: "Blacks haven't done that much to contribute so why should we try to add more things to the textbooks or teach about them?" Another comment was that, "Blacks were not allowed to participate freely in the US of America for so long so they weren't able to contribute much." The latter statement was intended to be understanding, but it was still very misinformed.

And of course, teacher training programs, for the most part, don't teach from a oneness or multicultural perspective; so the teachers are not in a position to supplement the textbook. And if they somehow have educated themselves to a broader understanding, they are often not reinforced for sharing this knowledge in the classroom. On the contrary, they can be blocked or shut down.

Another example is the war on drugs. Laws got written that said a person can get locked up for using five grams of crack cocaine or five hundred grams of cocaine. Since law enforcement believed Black folk used more crack cocaine, the less expensive version of cocaine, and said that made them more violent, they were targeted and then filled up the jails; minimum time: five years. Turns out it was debatable who was using how much of what and if one drug actually made one more violent than the other. Either way, Blacks were "systematically" targeted and sent to the slammer in record numbers.

If you don't target folk using cocaine they stay out of jail and even if you do, chances are they won't have five hundred grams, so you are not going to put them away anyway. So all you have to do is follow the criminal justice "system" of laws and you're promoting a "system of advantage based on race" (Tatum, 2003, p.7), or disadvantage, depending on your vantage point

I use this cocaine/crack cocaine example because it stripped the African American community of so many men that it has contributed to the breakdown of some Black communities all over the United Sates. How much is five grams of crack cocaine, you might ask. I was listening to a talk one day and the speaker explained it this way. If you took two packages, the size of the sweetener *Equal* and filled them to the top, that would be about five grams. Now there is talk of making the laws more equitable and I believe some steps have been taken in that direction. I say, "go ahead, please do and thank you," and with a heavy, heavy heart I also say, "damage done!"

And let me throw this in there. With the privatization of prisons there is a whole industry rising up that is quite profitable. In other words folks invest in the prison industry for profit. Does that sound a bit strange and might I say immoral? Who are the folks who are going to prison in massive numbers? What a nice set up? Black men continue to be excessively demonized, therefore devalued, therefore their excessive incarcerations are normalized, folk make money and no one blinks. Would I be paranoid to wonder if the profiteers want and try to continue to find ways to keep folk in prison longer who look like me?

Already mentioned police profiling, but a friend recently told me their friend, who is Black, had been pulled over by the police twenty-six times. And no they weren't doing anything wrong. Some in the White community and perhaps others in communities will question this and say, "No, that can't be true. They must have been doing something wrong." I can tell you that I think that reaction is based on the fact that you can't imagine Afro-American folk could have such a vastly different experience than you.

So when I say "victimizer" I am not just talking about individuals being victimizers, I am talking about the system that creates advantage based on race. It really is that simple and that elaborate and that fool-proof.

Any individual, *group or culture* that creates any system is going to bring to it whatever biases they have as individuals and as a group. So during all those years Blacks were slaves, living under Jim Crow and the "Black codes" and segregation, and Native American folks were shoved aside to make room for the Europeans, European folk created the educational, political, economic, criminal justice and all other systems. Those systems reflect the good points of Europeans and the bad points and biases. Well, prejudice and racism have been part of America from the beginning; so it has been and is manifest in our systems. How could anyone assume otherwise? If folk still have prejudices, consciously or not, it's going to be reflected in the policies and practices of the systems, both formally and informally. Some folk say, well, if Black folk created the system, they would have put their biases in too. I say, maybe so and maybe not, but since they didn't, there's no use talkin about it. What we need to talk about is how to make the current system good for everyone and reflect the biases of none.

Mindsets are gonna have to do some serious changin to fix this; like I've been sayin a whole new consciousness if you will. Here is an apt analogy I'm borrowing from the Bahá'í teachings about that new consciousness. I think you'll like it. All humanity can be referred to as "the body" of humanity and can be likened to a human body where every limb and member is critical to the whole and needs to work in harmony for the body to fully function. For example you might think your thumb nail is not that important till you slam it in a door. Not only does your thumb hurt, so does a lot of the rest of your body. Your eyes water, your stomach gets queasy, you feel drained, etc. When part of the human body is hurt, the whole body suffers. If I pull a hamstring muscle in one leg my other leg suffers because it has to compensate. It is not important why I have a pulled muscle; what is important is that my other leg and the rest of my body compensate to help the healing. It will do no good to point fingers at the hurt leg and blame it and then refuse to help it. The whole body will eventually suffer. So it is with the body of humanity. If part of the body is sick or hurting or not fully developed for whatever reason, the rest of the body of humanity better kick in and help or ultimately it will suffer as well.

In this new consciousness, does it make sense to allow Black folk to continue to suffer from past and current discrimination? Does it make sense to point fingers and blame Black folk and at the same time not create an environment for them to heal and develop? Who suffers if we don't heal? And does it make sense for Colored folk to turn our backs on those Caucasian folk who suffer from conscious or unconscious prejudicial or racist attitudes and do nothing to reach out and help? Who suffers if they don't heal? In both cases the whole body suffers, the whole body of humanity. In both cases "they" are "we." This is simply truth, in plain terms. So whaddya say—we try out a new consciousness?

This ailment of prejudice and racism has a particular need for healing, as it is related to so many of the other symptoms of disease in the body of humanity; so again I ask my White brothers and sisters who have remained on the periphery of this issue to check in and play your part for all of our sakes.

Black folk need to look deep within also and say, "yeah, I been victimized, but I can't act like a victim." With God's help, and the God power within, I got to take charge of my life, my children's education, my family and community and heal and continue to move, taking advantage of opportunities that are available. Don't give up reaching out to White folk either.

We need to reach out to White folk because they can offer us something and because they got problems in their communities too, and we have experiences that can help them. In addition to being creatively smart, know how to make a way out of no way, know how to bounce back without allowing setbacks to destroy us, we still know the value of extended family. We know about rolling with the punches, being spontaneous and flexible, how to connect and show emotions, how to exhibit common sense, how to bring spirituality to life and integrate it into our daily lives. We are a loyal people, and we know how to get along with all sorts of folk, how to make folk feel welcome; and we sure know music, dance, dress, good food and good humor. Not saying that all folk of African descent have these qualities nor am I sayin that's all we have. Neither am I sayin no White folk have these qualities. My experience is every culture has gifts and these and others exist at a high rate of frequency among Colored folk. Point is White folk have gifts that can help Black folk and Black folk have crucial contributions to make to the well bein of White folk. I believe the Almighty made it so we'd all have gifts to share with each other and that things would work out if we shared and would not if we didn't.

Like I always say, "we're two halves of a (w)hole we gotta climb out of together." Back to my human body analogy, if part of the body is sick and neglected, eventually the sickness will spread to the whole body. But if each part helps the other part, the whole body will prosper. Otherwise, as brother Tim Wise said, troubles will soon come to a Wal-Mart near you.

I remember when I started lifting weights and doing arm curls. My right arm was real strong in certain areas and my left one was weak in certain areas and so I felt out of balance. So what I thought was, I would just do maintenance work on my right arm and not try to make it stronger for the time being. I would work like crazy on my left arm till it got as strong as my right

92

arm and once they were equal I would kick in big time on both arms. Some would say I was giving my left arm "preferential treatment." I would say my body is better off when both arms are strong. I think I'm making a pretty good case here so early in the morning.

Sorry, I got a little off track. Where was I? Oh yeah, my talk to the civic group. (Bet you forgot all about that but I didn't) It went pretty well. The requisite percentage of people weren't interested. A number of Caucasian folk came up after and said it really made them think and sincerely thanked me. The Black woman and the Afro-American man both thanked me and said that they hoped it would help. The person who I thought was Latino was actually from Greece. He told me a lot of people think he is Latino and often start a conversation with him in Spanish or try to talk to him about "Latino issues." He said they often say something like "Buenos Dias" (good morning) or "Que pasa?" (What's up?); just trying to connect in a humorous way, though at times it feels a tad condescending. He said he mostly just plays it off, but other times it gets on his nerves a bit. No big deal. When he tells them he is from Greece, they just say somethin like "oh—sorry about that—I was just kidding" followed by an awkward moment or a hasty exit. (I was glad I did not say "Como estas?" or something like that because the thought crossed my mind.)

Anyway I have to get home. As I leave, the guy from Greece thanks me and says he can relate to a lot of what I said because he is darker hued. He finds that is a turn off to some folk. Generally, he said, once people find out he is from Greece he has no problem, but when they think he is Latino sometimes, according to him, people are a little less friendly. As I leave he says "Adios" and smiles.

Chapter 10

Cops Again and Who Are "the Good Ones"

If I get home quick, I might be able to drop my kids off at school and finish reading the paper before I really have to get into my work day. Like I said I love it that these civic groups are in out before 8:00 am. Who knows, someone may see my car on the way home and, as my wife says, "It might just be the one they're looking for." I look out my car window and think to myself, "Oh no, here comes a cop, I better slow down." I think to myself, police folk see speeders a mile away, as my driving record will attest, so I'd better chill.

I'm thinkin and knowin Black folk have had a whole lot of run-ins with the police and relations aren't always the best. Back to this profilin thing again. There's been a lot of talk and supporting research for some years about racial profiling and that Blacks in a whole lot of places get profiled more than others. In fact, in some states it sounds like race has definitely been a factor in who gets stopped and who doesn't, who is suspected of drug use and who isn't. A whole lot of Black men I've met have been stopped randomly, and I'm not talking for speeding. I remember a friend of mine's father got stopped and beat up and was scared to death he wouldn't get out of jail alive. So definitely some of them see color as well as speeders, and color can make a huge difference.

The profiling horror stories and statistics make the news and the news influences me too, so when I see a cop I'm not sure which ones will see my color as a negative and which ones won't. That's why I get a little edgy anytime I see a policeman comin my way unless, for some reason, I called them myself. How does the saying go? "Everyone dislikes a cop till they need one." Well I don't dislike them; I just get anxious around them in certain circumstances. Interesting thing I just realized while I was writing this: I don't get real nervous when I see a police woman. Not sure what that means, maybe it's because I don't fear as much bodily harm from a woman or maybe I've had more bad experiences with men cops. As a male, maybe part of me feels like I still got the power. I hope I don't offend any women by saying that, but I guess it could be offensive. Should I worry about women cops thinkin I'm sexist because I don't fear them like I do the men cops? Maybe it is partly sexism. Need to think about that some more, because I'm definitely not an equal opportunity worrier.

I just hope this cop drivin by me is a "good one." Let me confess here, because I know I'm being a tad cynical. I'm thinkin it might help to explain what I mean using the phrase "a good one." Some of you probably already know. Sarcasm and cynicism comes from the fact that much of my life, Caucasian folk have suggested I am a "good one" (a good Black) and "why can't more Colored folk act more like "you" (me). They say things like "you sound/act just like anyone else," meaning anyone else White. Then the line comes that makes every CNBAAPA person bristle: "You're so articulate." Might be meant to be a compliment but it often feels like they're sayin (consciously or not), "unlike the other, Blacks I know," or they sort of seem pleased and surprised to find me "so articulate." They state, almost incredulously, they can't imagine me having racial problems in society because I am just like them. Feels as if I passed some unspoken test and now I'm being awarded the *gold standard of approval* as "a good one." Seems, because they know a little about me on the outside they think they know me on the inside and what I face wakin up Black in the US of America. I find that gold standard approval thinking hard to swallow and hard to understand. Like I said this may be done unconsciously and if so I encourage folk to bring it to consciousness and toss it. Anyway, being singled out as one of the "good ones" feels patronizing so I guess that comment I just made slipped out as a sort of unconscious, made conscious "get back." Some days, especially bad night sleep days, my cup runneth over and stuff just comes out.

To tell the truth, "get backs" bother me when I engage in them, because I truly want to just love my White brothers and sisters and get past all this. May sound hokey but life is about love, and I stand on that. Many other Negroes want to keep reaching out too. But when things happen over and over that are aggravating, Negroes will go off and start talking much stuff about White folks, like with this articulate thing or some other aggravation. It isn't always pretty either because, like I said, it's usually when folk are sick of dealing with something over and over again that the rage and anger strike. Even with that, there are usually Colored folk in the group that remind everyone "not all white folk are like that." Most times, many of the Black folk will agree, but still be honest about what gets on their last nerve. "You're right brother, it's not all of them, just like it's not all of us messin up, but man I'm sick of... (whatever the issue is). I know some White folk that are cool, but some of them are just trippin." My point is that even in rage many of us are not ready to throw in the towel. The anger is real and the desire to get past it, to settle it, to work it out is also real. Not for everyone but for many. By the way, are you all gettin yet why it is we need to call on that deep spiritual/ transpersonal power to deal with all this? It's no joke folks, no joke at all. I'm guessin, some White folk are probably trippin right now about what I am saying, but I'm asking you, brother to brother or brother to sister, to stay with me!

Let me add this with pride. Black folk have a whole lot of resilience that truly deserves admiration. Many of us have had more experiences with prejudice than we can count and most of us are *still* willing to reach across the table to White folk, and meet them more than halfway. Many of us still try real hard not to judge all Whites by the many discriminatory experiences we've had. Now if you really stop and think about how hard that is, you will marvel at it too. The ability to forgive or at least put things behind us is something all Afro-Americans can be proud of and something that deserves more attention than the whole "playin the race card" thing.

Now on the other hand, my White brothers and sisters, I must tell you straight up again, some Colored folks are mad for life, because they've had it up to here with tryin and cryin and havin to, the way they see it, deal with too much lyin. So you see we all got to get movin on this thing before more folk decide to fold up and hold up for life. I'm guessing some White folk have thrown in the towel as well. Resignation and apathy, White or Black, will do us all in.

If the Shoe Were on the Other Foot

Colored folk like my own curious self can't help but wonder if the shoe were on the other foot would White folk be so forgiving. I hear statements like, "well I was not prejudiced until I had this experience in the army or at work, or with a neighbor where a Black person was so hostile or negative and after that I was not the same." I hear folk tellin me they're prejudiced because of affirmative action, or having a neighbor of darker hue who didn't keep up their yard, or carry their load at work, or cussed them out. I even hear things like, "I was less prejudiced once, but when people like Louis Farrakhan, Jesse Jackson and Al Sharpton (or whoever) keep pushin race and racism in *our* face I can't help but feelin what I feel."

So it sounds like some Caucasian folk are prejudiced not based on personal interactions, but based on disagreeing with what a couple Black folk say who are in the news. When I hear the reasons some White folk give for being prejudiced, I wonder if they would put up with as many bad experiences with African Americans as so many of us have had with them and still try to give us the benefit of the doubt and not give up. (That's a mouth full and I don't like all the "them and us" talk but that is a real tough one for me to think about.) I don't know the answer but I must say and say out loud, if things are gonna change, White folk have to tough it out just like so many of us do. No free lunch for any of us on this deal. I have to pray hard so I don't stay hard hearted against you and you have to do the same. And if you don't pray, then do whatever else softens you up enough to come back to your senses and keep on keepin on. You can hardly be prejudiced because of a few bad experiences and then expect us to be patient and forbearing and open after hundreds of experiences. If one or two experiences "made" you prejudiced then some of that prejudice poison must have been there in the first place, consciously or not and those one or two experiences just brought it all out. So I ask you to check it out with yourself; preferably after some prayers.

So my White brothers and sisters, know that I and many folk like me can't help but wonder; if the shoe were on the other foot, if you had a lot of bad experiences with folk of my hue, would you be forgiving and still be willing to reach out to us? We wonder because we so often get *dogged* for being angry and impatient with our racial experiences. In our moments of frustration we say out loud or to ourselves, "White folk would never put up with that from us and still be willing to reach out and forgive." Right or wrong, when we feel your antagonism toward us or your impatience with our impatience, those kinds of thoughts rush to the surface and spill over.

But since the shoe is not on the other foot, I guess I might as well let that go, at least till I wonder about it again.

Chapter 11

Going Along to Get Along, Threatening Blacks and the "N"-Word

Before I finish telling you about the policeman drivin by me and me gettin nervous, let me mention what I heard on the radio: it's a **NEWS FLASH.** You're now aware that many Colored folk spend a lot of energy trying to fit in and be acceptable? I already told you, many Afro-American folk in the workplace feel like their behavior receives greater scrutiny than their White counterparts; so a lot of them feel like they gotta be careful. This **NEWS FLASH** is a clarifying example of what I mean and the challenge of trying to address it.

Donovan McNabb, the great African American quarterback up in Philly, said publically he felt like Negro quarterbacks were scrutinized more than White ones especially when they made mistakes. He said that was "his experience." Well, in his many years of being quarterback, he had not been one to focus on race. You should have heard the sports announcers and media coming out against him in such an indignant manner, saying he was playing the race card and why after all this time did he play that card. Sportscasters were sayin things like he used to always be such a *classy* guy but now he'd gone over the edge. For the most part they went ballistic on McNabb, decrying his nerve and craziness for thinking such things. Didn't appear many of them went to McNabb to try to get a better understanding of why he said what he said—they just went off on him.

All Donovan McNabb was saying, in my reading of it, is that although Caucasian quarterbacks are scrutinized for their ability or lack thereof, it is not based on the color of their skin. For

Negroes, skin color is a key factor, again according his own "experience."

The other part of this **NEWSFLASH** has to do with a sports radio talk show I heard about the same issue. A self-identified Caucasian man called in. Radio talk show host asked the caller why he thought McNabb played the "race card." Caller was real calm and in a very matter-of-fact, unemotional manner, stated that he would "not call it playing the race card." Then he said some things that even shook me. He said that in his travels he watches a lot of football games in sports bars and said it is usually with a bunch of other Caucasian folk. He said coast to coast, in almost every case, once these football game watchers get a few drinks in them, they start using the "N"-word over and over. White man emphasized this happens all the time! Point I think he was makin is that if this is the feeling of folk once they loosen up, perhaps Donovan McNabb is not necessarily "paranoid." Couldn't believe what happened next. Talk radio host acted like he never heard the caller make the statement about the "N"-word being used over and over. Didn't ask the man to clarify, didn't say he found it disgusting, and didn't say a thing about it! No acknowledgement of the reality the caller was trying to make him see, just kept on talking about the race card being played by McNabb. (I assure you that I don't think every sports bar with White folk in the US of America is like this, so don't miss the point.)

So I asked myself why this radio talk show host just moved past this caller's point. Not sure, but I have experienced that sort of ignoring behavior more than twice or thrice in discussions about race. Darker-hued brother/sister will bring up a point about race that pretty much nails it and a lighter-hued brother/sister will get silent, minimize it or simply ask another question. "Yeah I know a bunch of Black people get stopped by the police but some of them probably deserve it or are guilty anyway. Plus you can't expect the cops to be perfect."

That, I guess, justifies profiling in his/her mind because some of them are guilty and cops aren't perfect Then they will move on and add another question or problem in the Black community. "There's no excuse for so many of them girls getting pregnant. That's gotta stop. They can't keep doing that and then blame it on racism." The first point gets minimized and now there's a new problem Colored folk need to fix, and, of course, none of the problems, in their minds are related to legacy of racism. "After all racism didn't cause those girls to get pregnant. They simply made a choice." And so much for any in-depth discussion of how race may be related to a number of these problems. The outcome of this approach: The Problem is effectively minimized, the fault lies in the deviant behavior of Black folk and ramifications of racism live on.

More to the point of McNabb's story and the radio talk show host. Folk say things like, "well Black people use the 'N–word' too." Again the point is minimized; the blame is passed because Blacks have dirty hands too. They use the "N." Because Black people use the word, then somehow it justifies the use of the word by our lighter-hued brothers and sisters or makes it understandable anyway.

Now truly, would it have been so hard for this talk show host to take in what the caller said and acknowledge what a significant statement he was making and ask his callers to reflect on that a bit? "Acknowledge the point and call for reflection and thoughtfulness," I say. We all might learn something. So the issue in this case is one of deflection versus reflection.

NEWS FLASH OVER

Now about McNabb speaking his mind about race, if Black folk were talking to each other about that situation someone would say something like: "As long as the brother 'stays in his place' he's okay, but let him step out of his place, speak up for himself, challenge what he sees as wrong and he's seen as *ungrateful* and/or *uppity*." Some folk get downright raw and will say they would be seen as an *uppity nigger*. That would be the type of conversation among many Black folk I know; because that's how many of us feel.

Some Black folk (particularly men) say they are perceived as a threat or uppity even if they just dress too nice. Get sarcastic comments that feel like resentment toward them when they're decked out. Comments about how they can afford to dress like that all the time, just like the nice car problem I told you about with me. In past years I can't say I ever had the "decked out" problem, as my wardrobe was pretty basic. Some, over the years, have suggested it is less than basic. Definitely never been resented for it, made fun of maybe, but no one ever used to ask me how I could afford my clothes!

Seriously, Black folk are perceived as threats and or uppity in so many ways. For example now a days I mostly dress in African garb which actually is pretty classy. Folk make that out to have all kinds of meaning. I remember one person told me when observing my garb "You must be real Black." She meant I must be an Afro-centric brother. Some folk indeed think I'm trying to make some kind of statement by wearing my African garb. It is indeed stylish wear in my view but I have to think before I wear it some places as it is perceived in so many unusual ways. Mostly I wear it everywhere now and am willing to deal with whatever comes but I often have to think about whether it will put folk off. I remember for one diversity workshop something told me not to wear it. I told the person who hired me I'd made that decision. She told me, had I decided otherwise I would not have been well received. Now this was a diversity workshop I'm talking about. I almost always wear my African clothing to diversity workshops because I figure if folk can't accept diversity in clothes then we surely aren't going to make any head way on the deeper issues. Even wore it to a black tie affair once. If I had a 9–5 job I'm not sure if my employer would agree with my African wear.

Point is that so much of who we are and what we do is unacceptable to too much of the US of America. So who sets the standard for acceptability? Using the subject of what is appropriate workplace clothing as an example, folk tell me we gotta have standards for the workplace and for everything for that matter. I tell them I agree but disagree on who is allowed to set them. Then I get the comment that suggests we can't lower "our" standards for anyone or that we have to maintain high standards, the assumption being that if I, as a Black man, am involved or Black people are involved in setting a standard, I/we must want to, somehow, lower it. Is it possible I could have high standards that are simply different from conventional standards and that if we put our sense of standards together it could work for everyone? I've had this conversation about everything from standards for school behavior to the kind of celebrations that should be allowed in football games after a touchdown. Back in the day I had those conversations about acceptable ways to sing *The Star Spangled Banner* and how one should behave while it was being sung. Many folk felt like it deserved almost a church-like reverence and that equated to silence in their minds. Then Marvin Gaye came along and sang it at the NBA All-Star game in 1983; the fans seemed compelled to engage in a lively call and response. For the most part that ended that discussion. Subsequently there has been more creativity in singing the National Anthem. All versions surely are not equal in quality but neither were they when one style was the norm.

I got off track a little, but not much. So if CNBAAPA folk are too outspoken or assertive, they get perceived as bein aggressive or militant. If they seem too smart or walk and talk with too much confidence, drive too nice a car, ask too many questions, are into their heritage and culture and show pride, oftentimes White folk act put off. Many Black folk say they have to "cool their jets" and act a bit deferential if they want to fit in, when they're workin around a bunch of folk of lighter hue. Yes, I'm still talkin in the 21st century. Reminds me a lot of my time way back in the day in Minnesota. The issue is still about fitting in. Point being, they are saying if I am my "Black, Colored, African American self," things won't go too well for me. They say "I have to wait till I go home to be my full Black self." As one man put it, in a video about race called *Color of Fear,* "We have to shuffle in corporate America, it's a 1990's shuffle, but a shuffle nonetheless. I can't wait to go home so I can be Black again" (Wah, 1994).

I sincerely hope the question White folk will ask themselves is why CNBAAPA folk, or at least a good number of us, might feel this way? Could there be something to why we feel this way? Bottom line; I'm asking White folk who aren't, to please pay attention. I'm not accusin you, blamin you or chastising you; I'm simply sharing with you some things you may not know, knowledge about experiences you may not have. I'm not gonna beg you to try to understand. As best I can, I'm tryin to be respectful and human, as an equal partner in all this, tryin to meet you half-way and walk and talk this through.

I still believe talkin works sometimes, depending on the spirit in the room. I remember, in one workshop I conducted on race issues, an African American woman expressed her sense that, if too many Blacks gathered or congregated in the workplace, it made White folk nervous. Let me give some background on this sort of thing before finishing her story. This is another one of those tough issues for me. Black folks often get accused of self-segregating. Here is how the argument usually goes. "If Blacks want to be integrated or accepted why do they self-segregate? Why can't they just join in? They seem to always hang out together during lunch or on breaks. Why can't they just mix in?" Here is what I and many black folks say or at least think: "Why is it when we are together or sit together it's called self-segregation but when you do it it's just normal? At the same time we're sittin together at lunch you are too. So who is self-segregating? Why can't you come and join us? Besides we have to try to fit in so often; sometimes it's just nice to be with folk who are like us so we can be ourselves. You feel the same and that's why you don't come and sit with us at lunch, because you think you'd be uncomfortable."

Another version goes something like this. What would happen if White folks got together for a gathering of White people? Usually I will say that White folk usually don't have to plan to get together because it often just happens. And some exclusive clubs that are not declared as "Whites Only" still virtually are. Usually when People of Color get together, it is not to separate or exclude, but to strengthen our capacity and identity so we can be more effective participants in society or for just general support. Historically White-only gatherings have been used not for the purpose that they could become more effective members of society but rather to strengthen their hold on society by clearly and purposely excluding others. So I ask for what purpose would they get together? Would it be so they could more effectively be represented in society or for strengthening their ability to participate? Mostly the question about what would happen if Whites got together for gatherings of White people, is a theoretical question rather than a question grounded in reality, as Whites folks rarely have to set a time up for them to just be with each other for comfort and identity support. Many workplaces now have affinity groups (Blacks, Women, and Latinos, etc.) made up of various identity groups. Their purpose is to provide support, reinforcement and to create a sense of belonging. The groups are initiated, not for the purpose of cutting themselves off from other workers but rather to address their unique workplace challenges.

A friend of mine, we'll call Jim, who is a White male, had a powerful response when talking with me about why folk had such a big issue with Black folk getting together with each other. It is like the human body analogy in many ways. Jim said the diversity of humanity is like an orchestra made up of many sections that come together to play the music. Some times the various sections of the orchestra need to practice by themselves so they can contribute more effectively to the whole. The goal of practicing apart is to have time to deal with the unique roles and challenges of that section and to refine their particular part and then go back to the whole better prepared. Although each section has a common goal, which is to play the music, they may be at different levels of capacity at any given time to fulfill that goal. Thus time apart is not only appropriate; it is critical! This holds true for human beings of diverse backgrounds as well.

The orchestra analogy is as plain as I can make it.

Why do Blacks need the NAACP Image awards or even Black Beauty Pageants or a Black History month? Again, the reason is to include, not to exclude. Since so few African Americans receive awards from the traditional entertainment industry or are crowned Ms. Whoever, it is important to have something that celebrates the achievements within the Black community for the purpose of acknowledgement and encouragement. Without such programs our contributions would simply not show up in full bloom on the US American screen. Then where would the role models be for Children of Color?

Now then, that simply cannot be that hard to understand. However I have spent many an hour talking with White folk and some Black folks about these kinds of things. Some even call such gatherings racist, comparing them to the exclusionary segregated practices that Blacks have fought so hard against.

You have to decide for yourself if you think it is the same. I say, motive and intent mean everything, so it's not the same.

Here is why this is a sore spot with me: Blacks getting together to support and encourage each other is a way to help us stay strong in our image as honorable and noble human beings. It is a way to give natural reinforcement for just being who we are. Here are a couple of versions of what folk say and think who don't want us getting together: "Things really are just fine for Black folk and there should be no need for such gatherings." A second version goes like this (it's not always spoken like this, but in essence this is what is being said): "I know there are still racial insensitivities and you are not fully accepted in society and have never been, but it's not that bad now and we all have struggles. You can just suck it up like the rest us have to. Definitely don't get together with members of your own group to give support to each other. Same goes for Black History month and all those separate pageants and similar activities. Things are improving so again just grin and bear. It won't be long till racism is a thing of the past." Translation: "Your experience is very much like mine, so you handle it like I do and I will define what the appropriate way is for you to address your feelings of exclusion." I am not being the least bit sarcastic. That fundamentally is the unspoken and sometimes spoken message.

Again I say, "Help me Lord!!" I got some raw spots.

Before I go on let me tell you that this kind of thing is just one example of why I get tired. I hear this stuff all the time, and wonder how many times I am going to have to confront it, talk it through, "justify" why we want to be together sometimes, explain why it is no different than what White folk do, explain why it's not racism, explain that once in a while we just feel like being together because we share common experiences, explain we aren't sitting around during those times just talkin bad about White folk; that it's more about enriching each other than anything else. When White folk challenge me on this, I have choices. I either address or try to clarify it, which I often do and then have to put up with a lot of flack and a lack of willingness to really hear what I'm trying to say. Sometimes folk will at least admit I have a point but truthfully, that has not been the majority in my experience. I can ignore it and leave people to think we are just whiners, that all we do is self-segregate anyway and then complain about how bad we got it. Or if I refuse to answer or talk about it I'll probably be seen as bitter.

All that said, and by the way, thanks for letting me get some of that out of my system, I do believe some folks, who are not just hacking away at Black folks, really do try to understand and still struggle with the idea of separate gatherings, activities, etc. The concept is genuinely difficult to understand for some from all races. Here are few reasons why: (1) Historically, separate gatherings have only meant one thing—exclusion. (2) Unity is often viewed as uniformity or sameness, and therefore any kind of separation and focus on differences is seen as divisive. The concept of unity in diversity, in my view, is not explored or thought of in depth. (3) We trust each other too little not to assume the worst. If we are separating for any reason or having separate activities, it is an affront one way or another. Some less than honorable purpose must be the intent.

The only answer, as far as I can tell, is a new vision going forward, again using the human body and the orchestra as apt analogies to convey that vision. Its actualization requires first accepting it as *the vision*, working to build trust and then maintaining a unity of purpose.

Now there is some context for the issue the lady I mentioned above brought up in the workshop. Remember the one about Colored folk gathering together at work and how she thought it created tension among White folk. She said some of them would even ask the Black folk what they were up too in a sort of half joking half serious way but she could tell they really wanted to know. At first, the White folk in the session were a bit surprised she perceived tension. The group hashed it out. Some of the White folk admitted they thought the Black folk must be talking about them; at least some of the time. Black folk mentioned some of the time they were talking about some of the race challenges they face in the workplace, but it was because they did not feel they could address the issues openly. Most times they said they were just "kickin it around," and their conversation had nothing to do with White folks.

The whole group had a real good and open discussion about it without blaming, accusing or pointin fingers. I think everyone learned something about perception and reality and how important it is to put things on the table to see what is what. It was clear it made everyone think a little, which is what we often don't do when race hits the table. For a minute during that workshop, the *parallel universes* came closer together. Folk met at the intersection.

I for one am willing to sort through what's perception and what's real if folk meet me halfway. But if folk clam up or try to jam me up, I tend to sit up, get up, and get out! Don't underestimate sincere desire to search for truth, and a willingness to consult about it.

Oh my, I almost forgot! Remember, a while back I started telling you about the cop I had to slow down for so I wouldn't get a ticket? He seemed to be looking back and forth between me and my *for sale* sign as he drove by. Maybe he wants to buy my car, I thought nervously. I remember hearing as a kid that the policeman is my friend. Many of them are hard workers and doing the best they can, so I can't judge them all. They have a dangerous job that I could never do. I just hope they realize

109

I'm not dangerous. Anyway, I thought as he got closer, maybe he will buy my car. I mean policemen and policewomen have kids too and one of those kids just may need a 1996 Corolla at a good price. Maybe I don't have to worry about this one.

Damn, he pulled me over, gave me a ticket and bought my car. Just kidding, he drove by *a good buy*.

Chapter 12

Do the Right Thing

Just made it home in time to see my kids off to school, eat some more breakfast, have some more coffee and finish reading an article in the newspaper. Overall, I sure like their school. The teachers seem like they really care. I only wish they had a few more African American teachers. My kids have been exposed to so few African American teachers since they have been in school. The teachers here care, but some of them really don't understand my children's experiences. My brother tells me where he lives the teachers expect so little of Black kids, and in my work I hear that over and over. My teachers tell me my kids are so good, and I believe them; and I also believe they don't realize the challenges my kids and other kids like them face each day, especially but not exclusively, the students of color that don't have much money.

Sometimes my kids, and others I have spoken with over the years, have told me their teachers seems to discipline some of the Black kids, boys in particular, more harshly than the White boys, for some of the same stuff. (Research supports this.) I always tell them to be careful not to look for race to be the reason for this. They assure me they aren't. I remind them to be open-minded and not put all White folk (teachers in this case) in the same category. "Some of those boys," I tell them, "probably really deserve to be disciplined." They all say pretty much the same thing, "yeah but you should see what some of the White kids get away with." I tell them, "Don't dwell on it or let it bother you too much and try to focus on your educa- tion." In the next breath I tell them, "No, let it bother you if you think it's not fair." I tell them, "You can share your feel- ings with your teachers or the principal if you really think it's that bad. I'll come with you or find another adult to go with you if you want me to." They say, "If we do that, we'll get in trouble too." According to their take on things, it seems like teachers get real uncomfortable and sometimes upset when you start talking about race or suggesting race might have anything to do with life in school. "It's a touchy subject," they say. I tell them, "It might be hard but it's right to bring it up, if you think something is not right. First think about it and pray over it," I tell them. "Just be respectful and I will support you if you get in trouble."

I remember in one school I worked with, some boys of African descent had issues with an administrator. They thought he was prejudiced. Again these boys felt they were treated more harshly than the White students. I helped arrange a meeting with the administrator and the principal so this could be shared in a dialogue. It was a tough meeting and the subsequent behavior of this administrator was uneven; however, I truly believe the students felt better inside for addressing it. Some of the students said things improved, but others were not sure it did any good. Wish I could remember more detail, but I do remember I was very proud of them for taking such a risk. Think about what a position those kids were in, though. They had to continue walking the halls of that school after fundamentally sharing with an administrator that they thought he was prejudice.

On the uptake though, I also recall that a few years later this same administrator became a strong supporter of the race unity work we were trying to do in the school and later as a principal in another school. Good for him and good for those students for having heart. Not sure how and why he changed but he did.

At a suburban school where I also conducted diversity training, the percentage of Black students was very small. These kids, by and large, came from middle-income families. I met with them various times, and they generally seemed demoralized. They said no one would listen to them, they felt isolated and definitely felt like outcasts. There was one Black teacher we'll call Aisha who really tried to support them. She was a real go-getter. Aisha and I were determined and tried several approaches to break down barriers across racial boundaries and to engage more of the White faculty, staff and student population. For every step we took forward, there were two backward. Eventually the stress of swimming upstream wore her down. With her already taxing teacher responsibilities, it just got to be too much. This was not an atypical experience for me in many of the schools I worked in—I mean the swimming upstream all the time. I still see that handful of Black students in my mind and their look of resignation. Not bad kids, not lazy kids—just tired kids.

In another situation a White teacher, we'll call her Rachel, was trying to make improvements in relationships between Whites and Blacks in her high school. The setting was a small Southern town that had recently merged a White and a Black school. In her efforts to help the students build greater levels of unity, she supported their decision to attend each other's churches. That kind of thing was a big deal at the time, because the churches were almost completely segregated. She supported purposeful mixing during lunch hour and other times of the day and a lot of racial awareness activities. Several teachers came out against her and ridiculed what she was doing. One day, in the teachers' lounge, a coworker confronted her and said something to the effect of "do you really believe in this oneness shit?" Got so bad for Rachel she ended up moving to another town and switching schools. Rachel got tired waking up White in the US of America trying to do something about race. I don't begrudge her for switching schools, but she was able to get away from it all just by moving.

113

For all practical purposes, she was run out of town. Her transgression was trying to break down barriers between White and Black students. I talked to Rachel several years later and she was doing fine in her new school but said she could not work with students in that way again. I have a lot of respect for her and what she tried to do at her previous school, because she knew goin in she was in for trouble; probably just didn't know how much. Mostly I regret the students losing out on a golden opportunity to learn more about each other. In the back of my mind I am thinking of my friend in corporate America, "dammed if you do and damned if you don't." I tell myself, if these kids and adults stand up for what they believe, it will build character, and put positive energy in the universe no matter how it turns out on the surface. I believe that. However, deep down I'm deflated and have some heartache. I thought we were past some of this. I tell myself to let it go. For the moment I do.

And by the way, in reference to the teacher I just mentioned, lest someone say or think, "well that was in the South and of course they have race problems": I lived in the South for twenty years, in the Midwest for longer than that, and now I live in DC—race prejudice is not unique to anyone of those places. It just plays out differently, sometimes more overt and sometimes more covert. Martin Luther King identified a city in the Midwest as the place where he experienced the most racial hostility. Just don't want anyone to write off prejudice as a Southern problem.

The Mis-education of Education

This all makes me think of the diversity training work I've done with so many schools, trying to encourage educators to develop a more multicultural approach to education. I would suggest that all kids needed to learn about all people's contributions in a natural way and learn about issues of social justice so that they can be good citizens. I'd share activities and lessons with them while simultaneously sharing how they could integrate these within their existing curriculum. The teachers, for the most part, would laugh in agreement when I shared the research that indicates every human being is related to every other human being on the planet by at least fiftieth cousins (Murchie, 1999, p. 345). At the same time it brought quizzical expressions to others' faces. I'd tell them Black folk have known that all along, and that's why we use the term "couz" when we greet someone: "What's up, couz?" I enjoyed presenting that information because it's a fun way to make a serious point; we're all literally one family. Religion and science both agree on that! I'd tell the teachers that the exercises, activities, and reading materials I was leaving with them could help children really internalize that point, so society would eventually not have all the problems with race it has now.

I'd also clarify, from a factual standpoint, that the demographics of our society are changing and that *all* kids will live and work in a much more diverse world than we as adults have been used to. Therefore, a multicultural approach to education is not just a "do gooder" path to take, but is essential in helping our children function in a changing world. I like to emphasize that our children need to spend as much time learning about "human" technology as they do about computer technology, meaning that learning to get along with, relate to and understand diverse human beings has got to be as important as learning how to get along with, relate to and understand technology.

I asked my kids if, in their classes, the teachers were talking about these things or if they ever had assignments to research contributions of people of African descent, Native, Latino, or Asian folk. They told that me during Black history month they do things and during some of the other special months

(Women's, Hispanic, Native American), but that the rest of the year it almost never comes up. They point out that there are a few teachers that are on the case 24/7. "That's better than what it used to be," I try to tell myself.

My kids, as well as many others, tell me White kids resent Black History Month or treat it like it's just for Colored students. Even some Negro students wish they would not have a month dedicated to Blacks as it makes them feel singled out. I try to help them understand that most history lessons share very few contributions from Colored folk and others that are not White and male, so in effect, without giving it a label, the major part of the year is White history year. I explain, since the early 1900s, Carter G. Woodson and other folks have been trying to get Black contributions in the textbooks, but have only made small gains. So we need to keep having Black History Month, Hispanic Heritage Month and Women's History Month, etc., until we can straighten out those textbooks. Besides, I tell them it makes perfect sense, in such a diverse country, to celebrate and highlight the contributions and cultures that comprise it. Many of the Black students I've had this conversation with get the point but are still uncomfortable. They tell me they see a need for it, but because so many of the Caucasian kids get so tense and some of the Black kids get self-conscious, it's just an uncomfortable and even an unpleasant twenty-eight days.

I often try to reflect on things like Black History Month. Is it still necessary? Do we still need it? Is it divisive like so many say? It's good to check out your own thinking once in awhile. What struck me the last time I did my reflecting was how few African American historical figures are regarded by most U.S. Americans as national heroes. The main one generally recognized for his contributions on a national level, is Dr. Martin Luther King Jr. Of course many Black historical figures are revered by African Americans and some Whites as well, but

116

on a national level, who else is there? If I missed one or two I'm open to that. My take is that many people like Frederick Douglas and others had a very significant impact on the over-all moral character of this country. So many heroes, but let me mention one who surely should be a national hero. It might seem arbitrary but his contributions are so awesome and his intellect so keen I have to mention him. His name is George Washington Carver. You've heard of him but his stature needs elevation in my humble opinion. Aside from his scientific ge-nius he was a great humanitarian who turned down large sums of money so he could better serve the masses. That's character. In addition to his contributions to the life-sustaining concept of crop rotation, he developed hundreds of uses for the peanut, sweet potato and soy bean. He is credited with finding three hundred ways to use the peanut and though some uses over-lapped, his discoveries were nothing short of amazing. They included cosmetics, dyes, paints, plastics, gasoline, nitroglyc-erin, lotion, shaving cream, wood stain, leather and cloth dye, rubbing alcohol, hair tonic and even a good old laxative. He also made food products from peanuts including vinegar, in-stant coffee, cocoa, mayonnaise, salad oil and peanut punch. He developed over one hundred uses of the sweet potato in-cluding flour, sugar, instant coffee, yeast, wood stains, paint, medicine and meal for livestock. There is so much more. This information is readily available. The historical time period and context that he was operating in is what elevates this to another level adding luster to his achievements. He was born in 1864, just before slavery "ended." Maybe all this does not make him a national hero but he should be some kind of hero in the US of America.

NEWS FLASH

John Hope Franklin died during the writing of this book and, if anyone deserves to be a national hero, he does. He was something special and unfortunately not well known outside of African American circles. I suggest if you don't know who he was you take a minute to look him up.

NEWS FLASH OVER

Why only one recognized national hero I ask myself? Those who broke the color barriers in sports and other places are often viewed, not as national heroes, but as heroes who helped Blacks advance. Well, every time these color barrier breakers went through hell to break those barriers, they made the entirety of America a nobler and more honorable place. I'd say that deserves national recognition on a broader scale and should be presented in that way. Students and non-students alike could use that perspective. Isn't it character we say we are most concerned with? What greater character can be shown than to put your life on the line for the growth and development of an entire nation? So yes, I conclude we still need Black History Month. Indeed we do!

As for teachers taking a more multicultural approach to education, I've been working with schools for years, and for all those years, I have heard the same thing over and over. "We have too much to do to integrate all these things into our curriculum. We have to worry about test scores and more recently, 'No Child Left Behind.' It's all about accountability and the bottom line," they say. Understanding the truth about each other and how to get along is not in the accountability mix. I understand their dilemma. I have to understand! Teachers truly are overworked and underpaid and have a boatload of responsibilities and too many unnecessary ones in my opinion. My wife is a teacher, so I have second-hand experience with this. At the same time, I see the impact of not doing these things on all our children who drop out, feel devalued, adopt stereotypes, treat their friends in stereotypical ways, separate along racial, cultural and class lines and often dehumanize each other. I see African American children not knowing who they are, confused, alienated, anxious, angry and often without a clue why; without a clue as to their significant role in the development of the US of America, unable to connect with the whole educational process. Some even think that trying to be smart is actin White. (In fairness to the Black kids who think this, some White kids act like trying to be smart is acting like a nerd, so they have their version of all this as well. Only problem is that Black kids are fallin down, over and out and not makin it back.)

A multicultural approach to education will not change all of that, but it sure is a piece in the puzzle. A whole lot has to be done in the school system in our country to improve the overall quality of education and that is indisputable. But at its core, school has to educate young folk to be "more human" with everyone and it must tell the truth. Shouldn't those critical elements be at the core of education? Stand up and say yes!

I'll start the "stand up and say yes" thing. Yes indeed, I do understand the teachers and their challenges. On the other hand, I hear Martin Luther King's words ringin in my ear: "We must use time creatively, and forever realize that the time is always ripe to do right" (King, 1963). I say for multicultural education and social justice, "Yes, time is ripe"—particularly when I see how relatively quickly things like *character education* got integrated into the schools. Not in all schools, but I have been to many schools, and I see "virtues" and "character qualities" written all over the schools. I hear it talked about all the time. I'm quite sure some schools are doing this in a token way and others more seriously, but it did not take long to get it going, relatively speaking. So I ask myself why the same can't be done with multicultural or "oneness" education as I sometimes call it? Isn't treating people right and learning how to get along with all different kinds of folks important to building character? I understand teachers are swamped, but character education made it through that swamp in many schools and quite quickly.

I remember reading the story of a second-grade class whose teacher had been discussing the history of Native peoples. These children became sensitive and understanding about Native Americans concerns and issues. One day they saw a sign of some kind that depicted Native people in a negative light. They told their teacher about it, and they all decided to write letters to their legislators. Eventually that sign got taken down (Tatum, 2003, p. 50). This was a bunch of second graders!!! When I read that story I thought to myself, "Now that's character education; teaching children to stand up for what is right, at the same time, teaching respect for the diversity in America!" My guess is, those children felt real good about their character because of their humanity toward others. Bet they felt good for many days after that, too.

I also think children will develop good character if they know the truth, the whole truth and nothing but the truth. Without truth we end up living a lie, and that is not healthy for anyone. It's like eatin bad food and telling yourself its good for you. You can get away with it for awhile, but sooner or later your whole body pays the price. As Martin Luther King was fond of saying, "Truth crushed to earth will rise again" and, "No lie can last forever!" This one is my favorite, "Truth forever on the scaffold, wrong forever on the throne, yet that scaffold holds the future and behind the dim unknown, standeth God within the shadow, keeping watch above his own" (King, 1957). I can get carried away with Dr. King quotes.

So I am hoping more and more teachers will get trained in their education programs to develop a multicultural/social justice/oneness approach to education. Even if they can't go full bore with training, they can do a lot on their own as there's so much material available to help them. Greatest mistake you can make I'm told, is doing nothing, because you can only do a little. Let me give you an example: I gave a talk once about the beauty of Black men and boys and how much they have to offer and how their depth, insight and creativity were so much needed in the US of America. Told them the Bahá'í Faith Scriptures use the analogy of Black people being as important to sight and insight in the world, as the *pupil is to the eye*. It was a short speech, but a mother of one of the boys in the audience later told me her son really had needed to hear that message at that time and it may have prevented him from committing suicide! Well, that taught me the value of trying to say and do what's in your heart and doing something even if you can only do a little. I say to you wonderful teachers, give it a try, even a little. A good first step would be to simply tell your faculty, principals, etc., that you think this is a good idea. Second step: find an ally, another or several teacher(s) or someone else in the school to work with. Third, work with the ally to do what you can do individually and within the school. How do you eat an elephant? One bite at a time. So go for it!

Bein patient about things like this is getting harder and harder for this Negro. So spirituality is the real deal for me. Relying on God or spirituality isn't a cliché, its survival and revival. Somehow the Almighty straightens me out when I get to thinkin I'm too tired to address this "mell of a hess" as my mom used to say. (If you don't get that phrase just take switch out the beginning letters of "mell" and "hess.") Gives me what I need when I need it, shows me the progress we've made and reminds me of times past. Spirituality helps me pull together long enough to appreciate the good in all this and keep a perspective on the bad. It helps me keep pushin but with the right energy and spirit. Continually have to remind myself if I want the right outcome I have to have the right spirit. That's the challenge in all this folks, maintaining the right spirit.

I know this race thing is gonna keep comin at us till we get it right in this US of America. If the Almighty stooped to gettin mad, He'd be mad as hell at us. I can see it now—God up there just fumin and sayin, "What's wrong with these folk? I made em different colors so they wouldn't get bored and so they'd have some variety in their lives and here they found a way to make it into something bad! Of all things, they're dividing because of color; animals don't even do that! I love em but they sure need work. Hope they learn before they mess everything up." I think the Almighty would say something like that except it would be much more eloquent.

And I have to say right now and out loud, this race thing is a serious matter. I haven't even finished the newspaper yet and look at all we've talked about. May seem like little things to some, but not to me. Besides, even if you think they're little things, I say "absorb this." I read results of a study that said *everyday acts* of discrimination actually can impact the health and life expectancy of CNBAAPA folk in America. This shocked and shook me. The article was based on clear research and said that African Americans suffer higher rates of disease and death due to the cumulative effects of stress, "especially discrimination." This article said that everyday acts of discrimination cause these problems for CNBAAPA folk, such as discourteous treatment, poorer service offered, being made to feel inferior, and being insulted, threatened, or harassed. This research was consistent with research about mistreatment in general that didn't involve race, and similar outcomes occurred. That means that race adds a whole other layer to already stressful situations that all people suffer. Study stated twenty other studies had concluded the same thing (Amersbach, 2002). Being a Negro in America costs money and not only has a negative impact on the quality of my life, but actually costs me some years. Point being is all those "little things" aren't so little.

So it can be real aggravating to me to constantly hear people say, "just don't let things bother you" or "get over it." Does anyone care about any of this? Do facts like I just shared change anyone's views and thoughts? Does it matter? Will someone acknowledge that dark-skinned brothers and sisters suffering health problems and maybe dying younger are not just a "little thing" invented by race card players; that it matters and that we all, together, need to get serious about all this? Well let me tell you, that's a whole lot of stuff to deal with on this day and all of it *before I can finish my breakfast.* Can I get a witness?

Makes You Wanna Holler or at Least Wonder

So then, I really do have to start work now, but before I do, I have to tell you something. Sometimes things happen in my day that I don't want to see as discrimination, but I can't help but wonder. I was in the drugstore and a nice White lady clerk waited on me. I was in line with a Colored woman in front of me, and a White woman behind me. The Colored lady in front of me was returning something and she wasn't happy and made that quite clear to the clerk. The clerk was real nice to her anyway and after she waited on the lady, she told her to have a nice day which made the Colored lady crack a bit of a smile. I came up and the clerk was friendly to me too. And then just as I was about to leave, this White lady clerk waited on the White lady behind me and said to her, "Would you like to fill out an application to receive discounts on certain products in this store?" Now you all know what I was thinkin when I heard that. Well, I stopped in my tracks and asked the clerk at the register what that application was all about. She told me it was for discounts on certain products, but she still did not offer me one, so I asked her if I could have one. She seemed slow to respond, but gave me one. I filled out the application and she gave me the discount card and smiled and very nicely, told me goodbye or to have a nice day or some such thing. Now, I wondered about all this. I tried to figure out all kinds of reasons she may have not offered either of us Colored folk a discount application, because I didn't want to think it was because of our color. I thought to myself, maybe she didn't offer it to the Black lady because she was returnin versus purchasing something and she was so angry. "Okay that could be true," I said to myself. Maybe she didn't offer it to me because I didn't buy enough stuff, although I use that store all the time, and she had waited on me many of those times. The White lady behind me bought several things and maybe that's what triggered the offer to her. Well, that could be why. I say maybe so and maybe not.

Some of you are thinkin big deal; just let it go! Life happens. Well, of course, I let it go. I didn't lose sleep over it. Fact is, if I lost sleep over stuff like that, I'd be up many a night. Hey, maybe then I could find my way into the "Guinness Book of World Records." That'd be something wouldn't it? It would read: *Black man sets record for staying up nights worryin about race issues.* I make light of this stuff sometimes to get through, but like I said, in my heart I know little things add up.

No joke though, this stuff is part of the parallel universe Whites and Blacks live in. Lots of CNBAAPA folk have daily experiences like the one just described and believe me, for the most part we do just "let it go," just like I let it go. I slept like a baby that night. Has an affect over time though, so on my low road days I can be cautious, leery and suspicious of White folks and their behavior, even when they seem friendly like this White store clerk.

Then there's the story I read in *Jet* magazine about a White boy who thought his friends of African descent were exaggerating their claims about discrimination. He was around twenty

124

years old and in college. He decided to have his face chemically changed so he actually looked Black, like he had read in a book that was written in the fifties called *Black Like Me*. Book told the story of a White man doing basically the same thing. Point is this young fella wanted to find out what it was really like to be a Negro in the 1990s.

Story goes he had so many traumatic negative racial experiences, he only lasted four days. He had planned to go a whole semester but said "racism was considerably worse than I thought it would be" and "I couldn't take being constantly pounded with hate" (Solomon, 1994). Imagine that, he was "tapped out" from being a *Black White man* after only four days. He said even the doorman in his building, who usually greeted him daily, didn't recognize him and treated him very coldly. Don't know what came of him after that but that's what the magazine story reported. Four days was all he could take waking up Black in the US of America!!

Reminds me of another story, which I don't seem to be runnin out of at the moment. Several years ago some news people got together and came up with the bright idea of sending an Afro-American man and a European American man around doing normal things to see if they got treated the same; actually followed them with a hidden camera (Amenta, 1987). They had these young men shop, search for used cars, apply for jobs, rent an apartment, etc., the normal things folks do in life. News folk were trying to do the same thing as the White boy who wanted to find out if Colored folk were exaggerating their discrimination claims. They found out the same thing: CNBAAPA folk get treated real different and not in a good way either. Again, even when it appeared folks were being nice to the young Black fella, once he was out of sight they made snide and racist comments about him and/or his race. Tried to rent an apartment and was told it was taken or already rented; then the White fella went, and he was offered

125

the apartment. Black fella was quoted a higher price for a car than his White counterpart, and the salesperson rambled on incoherently about why that happened. All this surprised and shocked the young White fella and disturbed the Colored fella. Neither wanted to believe it, but they either experienced it or saw it right there on camera.

This was just one news show, and I know news folk can sometimes get carried away to make a good story, but real-life things definitely happened that you just couldn't deny. Stories like this are good to see because folks don't believe you when you tell them what happens to you. Sometimes even when you show them in "Black and White," folk will still say, "yeah, but this" and "yeah, but that," tryin to explain it away. All I can say is, we aren't just making all this up, and it might help everyone heal if this were more fully acknowledged. No tryin to explain it away, no minimizing it or tryin to talk us out of it, but simply acknowledging it. Yeah, I know, I said this before, but I'm getting older, so I repeat myself. *Healing* comes from acknowledgement. If more White folk would simply say, "I hear you" and then sit and just feel it for a minute, I think, that would help them and us.

NEWS FLASH

Man, oh man; the media is working this Reverend Jeremiah Wright speech to death. Keep repeating some phrase he said at a sermon about God damning America and then using words like Obama needs to "disown" his minister for what he said. You all no doubt heard it or about it. Acting like this minister is up there with Satan because he's mad at the US of America. The way this sort of thing gets handled is almost diabolical. Sounds bites become truth and the US of America can't seem to get enough of the taste. All the talk show folks get on their high horse condemning Barack for not disowning Reverend

Wright, and now he's shooting down in the polls. You'd have thought these two had plotted to assassinate the President. Seems the Rev was saying that the US of America has done some things for which God will damn it or should damn it; he's suspicious about the government or someone introducing AIDS into the Black community.

Well, how is this so different from the televangelist, on a weekly basis, teaching that the wrath of God is coming for the sins of the US of America and detailing why we are bringing that wrath upon ourselves? This stuff is on TV daily, weekly, monthly.

A couple of White and real prominent conservative type religious folk, (who I won't name) were talking on the TV two days after 9/11 and basically said we probably got what we deserved. Yeah, that's right. Can you imagine what would've happened if a prominent African American said something like that two days after 9/11? Just think about it. Here are the exact words: "And with biological warfare available to these monsters—the Husseins, the Bin Ladens, the Arafats—what we saw on Tuesday, as terrible as it is, could be miniscule if, in fact—God continues to lift the curtain and allow the enemies of America to give us probably what we deserve" (Harris, 2001). I'm not casting aspersions or claiming to know exactly what they meant but who was condemning them, questioning their patriotism and disowning them? I mean two days after 9/11!

What about the founding fathers? They're at the core of U.S. democracy. Would any of them ever say anything that suggests the US of America is capable of doing something real wrong that God might be real mad about? Thomas Jefferson, in his own way, feared that America would get its just due, and he was relating it to our involvement in slavery: "The whole commerce between master and slave is a perpetual exercise of the most boisterous passions, the most unremitting despotism on the one part, and degrading submissions on the other," wrote Jefferson in 1781's *Notes on the State of Virginia.* He asked,

> (Can) the liberties of a nation be thought secure when we have removed their only firm basis, a conviction in the minds of the people that these liberties are the gift of God? That they are not to be violated but with his wrath? Indeed I tremble for my country when I reflect that God is just: that his justice cannot sleep forever. (Nichols, 2008)

Maybe it's time to take down all the monuments in his name and rename all the streets that have been named after him because he said we would receive the wrath of God for our involvement in slavery. How dare he suggest the US of America could do wrong? He didn't use the word "damned," but he used the word "wrath." Translate that anyway you want, but in my translation it's the same thing. Don't get me wrong, I have real mixed feelings about Thomas Jefferson just like he had about people like me, but I'm makin a point, and he seems like a good one to make it with.

My intent is not to stand in defense or condemnation of Reverend Wright, those two religious folk, Thomas Jefferson, Barack Obama or the US of America. I am saying that folk need to step back, take a deep breath, and let go of that double standard. Black folk have had things happen to us in the US of America that make us suspicious and downright angry, done by individuals, communities and the government. So sometimes we say stuff about our country and/or our communities because we've been maimed, defamed and at times left lame. So yeah, we get mad at our country sometimes, not because we hate it or want to leave it, but because it messes with us.

NEWS FLASH OVER

In 1921, some 15,000 Blacks lived in the Greenwood district, a 35-square block area in Tulsa, Oklahoma, that was so prosperous, it was called the Black Wall Street. After trumped up charges were made against a nineteen-year-old Black boy for assaulting a seventeen-year-old White girl, a mob of at least 2,000 White folk burned it to the ground; burned businesses, burned 3,000 homes, killed up to 300 folk and dumped their bodies in mass graves or in the Arkansas river (Cobb, 2001). Many Black folks are aware of that. How do you get away with burning an entire town, destroying an entire economy and killing at least three hundred Black folk with almost no legal consequences? That was 1921. (On the healing side, in the year 2000, efforts were made by White and Black to create educational scholarships for descendants of some of the victims.)

Now, please pay close attention to this next one because it remains in the collective memory of the Black community:

> For forty years, between 1932 and 1972, the U.S. Public Health Service (PHS) conducted an experiment on 399 Black men in the late stages of syphilis. These men, for the most part illiterate sharecroppers from one of the poorest counties in Alabama, were never told what disease they were suffering from or of its seriousness. Informed that they were being treated for 'bad blood,' their doctors had no intention of curing them of syphilis at all. (Brunner, 2003)

The data for the experiment was to be collected from autopsies of the men, and they were thus deliberately left to degenerate under the ravages of tertiary syphilis—which can include tumors, heart disease, paralysis, blindness, insanity, and death.

"As I see it," one of the doctors involved explained, "we have no further interest in these patients until they die."

"By the end of the experiment, 28 of the men had died directly of syphilis, 100 were dead of related complications, 40 of their wives had been infected, and 19 of their children had been born with congenital syphilis." When confronted with this story the public health officials attempted to justify what they were doing as legitimate science and never apologized (Brunner, 2003). The "Tuskegee experiment" did not end until 1972. In 1997, then President Bill Clinton made a formal apology to the eight remaining survivors of this atrocity.

In cities across the US of America, information has been uncovered that Blacks and Latinos have had evidence planted on them by police and subsequently convicted of crimes. This is not a rumor but a proven fact. In Los Angeles, 120 convictions were overturned because of planted evidence, and the city paid out forty-two million dollars in civil settlements. This was in 1999. Similar travesties have happened in New Orleans, Philadelphia, Dallas and Chicago (Duster, 2006). The only upside of all this is that the justice system prevailed for African Americans at least in LA. Not many years ago that would not have happened.

NEWs FLASH

Speakin of which, I was just talkin to an African American friend of mine, who we'll call Neil. He just came from LA, and he said he is routinely stopped by the police out there, and the same was true in DC before he moved. He and his wife were driving to the store in LA just before he came to DC on a trip. They saw a patrol car. He said he knew he was going to get pulled over, so before they could pull him over he turned off into a fast food restaurant parking lot. The police followed

130

him to the parking lot and started randomly yelling questions at him and his wife, asking such things as, "Do you have a record?" His wife was not used to this sort of thing, so it sort of tripped her out. This was April 2008.

NEWS FLASH OVER

I could go on but it shouldn't be necessary. I and many other African Americans know about the kinds of issues cited above and if not those particular ones, many others. So, yes, indeed many of us look deeply into issues that may appear to be one thing on the surface but in "our experience" have often turned out to be another. It's not about dwelling on slavery and the past. I say, and say so often, 'the past and the present often look alike to me."

Negroes like me see a double standard, day in and day out, and now it's croppin up tryin to derail a presidential candidate and unfortunately, some folk are trying to divide Colored and White U.S. Americans over it. To some degree they have already succeeded, and that's the worst of it. I hope that the dialogue around this will bring out some truth and reconciliation. I believe things happen for a reason, and each time race rears its head in an apparently ugly way, an opportunity to use it for good arises. As Martin Luther King said in another context, "America which will you choose?" (Lischer, 1997, p. 160).

After Rev Wright's sermon was played on TV over and over and over, everyone was talking about it including myself. I got worked up some too. It's interesting the things that can help you chill out when you're struggling with emotional stuff. I heard a radio talk show and was paying close attention to some comments he made to his listeners. The host presented some sanity on the whole thing, and for me it was cool that it was

131

a White fella. Now, remember this was shortly after the hue and cry went up for Obama to quit his church because of the Rev's remarks. Host said you don't leave your church because you get mad at the pastor or because you disagree with him. Pastor is one part of the church, and the members are another part, and all are like family. You stay and work with the pastor, and you don't abandon the members of your family. You don't shop ministers and churches, like grocery shopping, just picking them up and putting them down because you don't like something. A bunch of his callers, mostly White, far as I could tell, concurred.

Things like that radio program help me heal a bit and stay hopeful because it shows me there are White folk out there who look at things from all sides and not just the race side. It's one thing to know that theoretically and another to see, feel and experience it. In general, the media is continuing to hack away at this thing like there's no tomorrow, so we'll see what happens.

Oh yeah, forgot to tell you about my car. Remember the Corolla I was trying to sell? The one I pulled your leg about, telling you a cop pulled me over and asked to buy it. My wife, who, by the way, is White, (I bet that surprises some of you) came home yesterday and told me that she has had several people ask her about buyin our car; like when she stopped for groceries, or at the drugstore and other places. I told her no one has asked me about it anywhere. Not gonna make anything of that. We decided it'd be wiser if she drives the car with the "for sale" signs in the window, because she might have better luck being a woman and me being a man. Maybe that's what it was about.

Chapter 13

Black Men, White Women

Since I just told you my wife is White, let's stay with that a minute. That's another race complication in the US of America and in my life. Some White folk may be thinkin at this point that I must have a big time grudge against them and probably find it hard to believe I am married to a White person; and some Colored folk are probably wonderin what I'm doing married to a White person. Some don't care either way, but I'll tell you, in my life I have taken flack from both races for my being married to Caucasian woman. This race thing is really somethin … and the idea of interracial marriage can still bring out the *best or the beast* in both Colored and White folk. Many White folks are afraid of it, thinkin it's going to pollute or dilute their race and some Black folk fear that too. Some CNBAAPA folk still feel like I'm sellin out our culture. African American women have reminded me there are so few Black men around and that African American women have been denigrated for so long, that when another good (or seemingly good) Black man marries a White woman, it can feel like another rejection of their dignity and beauty or another man taken from the possibilities. I don't apologize for who I married, and at the same time I can't and don't blame Black women at all for feeling what they feel, given how America *has treated, viewed and reviewed them*. The pain that many Black women have endured is real and profound. It gets even more complicated because everything has economic ramifications too but we will leave that for now. Bottom line is this race thing is what causes it all—our inabilities to address it honestly, resolve it and move forward.

One thing is certain and that is that the US of America has never ever given Black women their just deserts. They have never gotten recognized for their soulful intelligence, perseverance, creativity, tenderness, toughness and genuine beauty. And despite not being fully appreciated, they're still here. If you look closely, you'll see they have been the backbone of the US of America in so many ways. They've raised our kids (White and Black) and raised our spirits. They've had to be nurturers, disciplinarians, homemakers, bread winners, defenders of the family and community and sometimes all at the same time. They've schooled us and schooled themselves and now are showing up in all facets of the US of America's educational, economic, social, public and private life, while still maintaining home life. They've been beaten down, gotten down and back up and they've showed us true grit in spite of all. You want an example of courage your children can look up to? You need look no further than Black women.

Some folk may be thinking, "But what about all those Black women on welfare?" Well, they grew up gettin up too, and in spite of all, they're still here. Not all model citizens and some are real cons—I'm not blind, but many, many, many are doing the best they can just like those on welfare in the White community. Many are literally geniuses in makin a way out 'a no way. Truth be told, all communities includin the White community got folk *not showin up for life.* So then I ask my White brothers and sisters, do the White women on welfare who may be con artists, represent all White women on welfare and somehow diminish the value of White women overall?

I say it's time to own up and look up to Black women in the US of America. If some come with what might feel like an edge, consider the thought that they might have to be tough. Partly might be because they don't always feel someone's *got their back.* They can tell their story better than I can, but I hope you'll listen when they do. White men, White women, Colored men and all folk; know that Afro-American women have a story to tell that can help us all.

My hat is off to African American women because I know so many have clung to faith and spirituality to thrive and survive and have done it well. So if some African American women have issues with interracial marriage, I say to them, I understand. I understand! My wife says the same thing: how could she/we not?

By the way, I read an article not long ago that said more folk than ever, from both races, approve of interracial marriage and would not mind if their child or grandchild married interracially. Wonder about that even though I do see more folk lookin and checkin for mates and dates across culture and race. Black men and White women have been lookin at each other for awhile. White men been lookin at Black women for awhile, but now some Black women are lookin back. Other ethnic groups and cultures are marrying across color and culture lines too. Somehow the Black male/White female union still seems to loom large in the psyche of the US of America. So I still wonder if folk are really that opened-minded and wouldn't mind if their child married outside their "race," and honestly, especially when the partner would be Colored. It's sorta like folk who, when polled, say they would vote for a particular Black candidate running for office, but when they get in that booth, amnesia or some other kind of –nesia (if there is another kind) kicks in *for some* and they forget what they said. Or they remember but just can't bring themselves to do it! Barack might be changing some of that, but the phenomenon is very real with voting and mating.

Race and interracial stuff can surprise me though as well. Things I think are goin better I find out aren't, and things I think aren't going so well I find out are doing better than I thought. I found out several years ago that South Carolina, with its checkered racial history, had one of the highest per capita percentages of interracial marriages in the country; between Blacks and Whites that is. TV news did a story and interviewed me and my wife. News lady said several interracial couples turned them down because they didn't want flack from co-workers and some family members who, get this, didn't even know they were married interracially! News lady said some fifteen or so couples turned down bein interviewed for those kinds of reasons, and this was not all that long ago. Well, my wife and I ended up on TV, and we didn't get any flack. I'm grateful for that, as I prefer not to receive flack for anything these days, deserved or not. Anyway, the news lady is the one who told us about the high percentage of Black/White marriages.

Bet "dollars to donuts," as one of my friends used to say, folk marrying outside their race/culture will change things for the best in the long run. Sam Cooke said "a change is gonna come" and as interracial/cultural couples start having children and old/young prejudiced relatives see them, my take is it's gonna be hard to hate or dislike those children. Seen that happen over and over. Before you know it, they'll be makin sure no one is makin fun of "our" grandchild, cousin or whatever, because of their mixed heritage. Put folk through some changes while it's changin them, but change many of them it will!! Maybe we're gonna have to marry ourselves out of race prejudice. In part, I believe that to be so true; in part we gotta keep workin at it, and in part some folk are just gonna have to die off, harsh as that may sound.

A thought that often goes through my head that is very touchy to say is that it's important for people marrying interracially to check themselves out and make sure they're marrying for love and good character. They need to make sure the reason is not some kind of social experiment or rebellion *or wannabe stuff.* Telling you all, this race thing has still got us twisted up in the head and some think, subconsciously or consciously that *light* is right. Others lookin to over-identify with the *other color* for reasons more complicated than love and character. I'm talking

136

White to Black and Black to White. Shouldn't say that maybe, but I guess I just did. That might not happen anymore but I'm afraid it did *back in the day* and I'm just not sure *the day* is over. In fact, I'm pretty darn sure it's not. *Some* White women in my day used to marry or at least date Black men as sort of a rebellion against their family or because of a kind of mystique these women saw in Black men. Some Black men had a thing for lightness and Whiteness, sorta like getting the "top prize." Well that ingrained thinkin dies hard and can be up in our subconscious, and I say we all need to check ourselves out. I'm all for folk datin and marrying who they want to, but I'm saying, reflect on some things first. If we're gonna make race relations better, then I humbly suggest we reflect on why we want to relate to the people we care to relate to in the way we want to relate to them. Gonna take some heat for that suggestion, so I wrote it in sort of a convoluted way. That way I have time to get outta here before you all figure out what I'm sayin.

And let me tell you how crazy this race thing is for me. You'll really think I'm whacked out now. Sometimes, "not always," I say in my own defense, when I see another interracial couple walking down the street, it can flash through my mind, "I wonder if they're together for the right reasons?" I mean, some quick thoughts can pop in and out of my head. Is it really about caring for each other or is it some kind of fantasy for the Black person or for the White person? I wonder if some of those sexual stereotypes are part of their attraction to each other. Is it stereotypes about how "hard" Black women are that are kickin in so he's choosing someone of lighter hue? If one seems attractive and the other not so attractive, one or another of those thoughts can roll through my mind quick. When those thoughts start rolling I hang my head in shame for a minute and then ask myself where that's all coming from. I use it as an opportunity to check myself out and grow if I can. Feeling bad won't help but sometimes I can't help it, like

I said, at least for a hot minute. During that minute I say to myself, "Tod you got a lot of nerve thinkin that stuff, what's up with you man?" Thoughts come and go, and those kinds come before they go and then come back again. Gotta feeling I'm not by myself in things like that poppin in and out of my head. We all have some examining to do.

Not sure what that says about me, but that's the way it is. Doesn't make sense in some ways, does it? I mean me having an interracial marriage but questioning others. Maybe I feel like I'm bein judged like that too, so maybe I am sensitive about the thing. Maybe I feel like a sell-out in some ways so I project that onto others. Maybe I have mixed feelings about the challenges involved. Maybe I have some mixed feelings about the whole thing. I realize you can believe in something and because of life experiences still have mixed feelings about it. Spiritually and intellectually, I believe people should choose whatever color person they want as a mate and that interracial and intercultural marriages have a lot to offer. Emotionally though, I can and do have mixed feelings at times. That's just how I experience certain things in my life.

(I don't know how all this plays out with gay and lesbian partners, nor do I know enough to speculate. Again, I am sharing experiences with which I am the most familiar.)

One thing I don't have mixed feelings about is how much I love my wife, my children, grand-children and my in-laws. I could not be any more blessed.

The race factor has definitely added a tricky and sticky dimension to things. My wife and I have talked about all this a whole lot so I'm not sayin anything we haven't pondered together. In thirty-five plus years of marriage there's not a whole lot we haven't talked about.

Since I mentioned my children, let me tell you a story about my daughter and how confusing this interracial stuff is for kids when we don't help them understand it. For some of them it does not compute. I remember one time my wife was walking our youngest daughter, Talia, to the bus. After Talia got on the bus, a Black child asked her who the woman was walkin her to the bus. Talia said it was her mother, and the child's eyes got big and she looked back out the window at my wife and told Talia, "No it can't be." Talia insisted it was her mom, and the girl wouldn't give any ground and kept tellin Talia it wasn't her mom. The child simply could not fathom that a White woman could be Talia's mother even though Talia was not all that dark. It simply did not compute.

Another time I was in a conversation with a White neighbor, and we were talking about race. A side note: my wife has sort of "full lips," and when she is in the sun she could pass for something else besides White. Anyway, I was telling this neighbor woman that it was funny that sometimes when my wife and I would walk in a restaurant people would glance up, look at me and look back at her a few times and look confused, like they didn't know what to make of us as a couple; like they couldn't tell if we were interracial or not. I told her people often are not sure what Alison is. Lady had lived next to us three years and confided she didn't know either.

I was telling a good friend of ours who is Black and has known us for years about my neighbor's response. She smiled and said, "I didn't know what Alison was either till you just told me." Interracial race stuff brings some light moments and some strange moments all at the same time. For example, what my wife experienced taking our daughter to the doctor: our youngest daughter had several health problems, so we took her to the doctor a lot. My wife did a lot of that for a time. We had some great caring doctors, but my wife told me that on more than one visit, particularly when new care providers

139

asked her questions, it was clear they assumed we lived in a housing project or were on welfare.

So that's how race and inter-race stuff is. Much of what happens with it makes no sense, at least on the surface, or it just seems crazy. Most times you can figure it out if you dig deep enough, but many times, even after you figure it out, you find yourself sayin, "this is crazy." It's crazy, cuz folks have made more out of race than was intended and now we gotta work our way back to what it's supposed to mean and not mean.

Talkin about Race, Serena and Venus and the Hope of Young Folk

I'm really gonna finish my newspaper and start my "work day" in a minute, but what I have to say now is work–related; so I'm getting closer to my goal of actually starting my work day. I told you I do race/diversity work for a living and have conducted a lot of workshops on the subject. Try to get people to talk about race honestly with each other, work stuff out and commit to doing something about what they learn. Lately though, a lot of folks been letting me know they don't want to deal with this race thing, don't want to talk about it, don't want to think about it. They come to workshops with a chip on their shoulder. You gotta know, I'm *fair* in those workshops and don't blame Caucasians for the problems or act like Negro folk are always in the right. Mostly I try to get folk to open up to each other. I tell them we need to hear each other's life experience so we know first-hand what every one is goin through and so we can then decide what we can do to move forward together. I say, everyone has a story to tell and that includes Whites as well. I pray hard on this stuff, but I must say there's a boatload of people in those workshops that send a lot of negative energy my way regardless. Worst part is they don't seem to be willing to see the other side and just honestly talk the thing out. Too many of them act like who they are and what they are is "the thing" and that Black folks just need to get on board. Seems to me, it's been happening more lately, and it makes me nervous for the future. Sometimes after the sessions, I have to pray to get that negative energy out of my system. It can get so thick I feel like I have to take a shower when I get home.

Some folks are even downright rude on purpose, like reading a newspaper while I'm talking or pounding on the table or holding conversations the whole time I am presenting. Now these are adults doing this kind of thing! One guy yelled at me, emphatically saying," My boss said I had to come but he didn't say I had to participate!" And he proceeded to sit in the back during the whole session, arms folded, reading the newspaper and just giving me that hard stare any time he looked up. By the way near the end of the workshop I conducted an exercise that required that everyone stand in the back of the room. It just so happened it meant they had to surround him while they did the exercise. Not sure why I did that, I just did it. Was that wrong? Probably at least a tad vindictive, I guess.

In another workshop, one guy was so mad he had to attend a workshop on diversity; his veins were popping out of his neck. I finally asked him to honestly share what he was feel-ing. He blurted out: "I hate this shit." These are the extremes, of course, and everyone isn't like that. Let me tell you, enough are in that range to scare me.

Talking about the behavior in my workshops makes me think about when the Williams sisters first started playing tennis. Not sure what made me think of that but sometimes that's how my mind works. One thing can make you jump to another, and you look back and wonder how you got to this place from that one. Those sisters got that same kind of energy coming their way that I got in those workshops. Way I saw it is many of the sports announcers continually railed on their flaws and how their close friendship as sisters could be a detriment to them and some even suggested it would be better if they weren't so close. Other criticisms flowed; they had too many other interests besides tennis, they didn't respect the game enough, their father controlled them excessively and needed to step aside as their coach, they were too uncomfortable playing each other to name a few. I was amazed at how sports announcers nitpicked them in those early years. In my view they got only begrudging respect when in fact their phenomenal rags to riches story should have elicited nothing but respect. Here were two sisters, fifteen months a part, coming from a rugged area of LA, and taught by their father who was never a tennis player himself and who learned the game from books. These were two African American young women breaking into a predominately White sport; both having equal and breathtaking potential. They have now risen to the top of their sport, brushing off all the criticism, for the most part with a lot of grace, and have almost universal respect. There may not be two siblings in the history of sports that rival their combined success. Call me protective but I really felt they received undue scrutiny and pressure.

Okay let me say the rest of what I'm really thinkin. As I watched these two amazing Black sisters develop in their tennis career I realized they had to be oh so careful. I realized they, unlike so many of their White counterparts, did not have the luxury of yelling at or makin snotty comments to line judges, losing their tempers or slamming their rackets down when they got frustrated like some of the other star players did on a regular basis and in many case were almost revered for. They needed to be well mannered at all times. And certainly they could not talk about the impact race may have been having on their experiences on the tennis circuit, though their father definitely did at times. Had these two Black sisters engaged in any of that, the criticism would have been even more blistering and you know it. "It's not true cuz I said it, but I said it cuz it's true."

I remember Serena Williams was booed in a tennis match because her sister Venus had dropped out of a match between the two sisters the day earlier. Venus had apparently injured herself. In other words, she dropped out of a match in which she would have been playing her sister. By way of background, apparently, the father used to get real nervous or something when the sisters played each other, so he often encouraged them not to enter the same tournaments unless they were what is called "the majors." So a bunch of folk were saying Venus was not really hurt and that she quit so she would not have to play her sister Serena. Well, I don't know if that's true or not because again, I wasn't there. What I do know is that a bunch of fans, mostly not Colored folk, actually booed this young nineteen-year-old girl. And it was some harsh booing. They booed the father and Venus as well when they came to watch Serena play. If you watch tennis at all, you'll know that booing doesn't happen all that often and for sure not like this. I couldn't believe it! After Serena won, she told the audience they were real hard on her, but she loved them anyway and she thanked "Jehovah" for helping her get through it. Later on, she said she could not believe that people jeered her. The way she put it was this: "How many people do you know who would go out and jeer a 19-year-old? I'm just a kid" (Jones, 2001).

Well, I have had some of that same kind of "booing" type behavior in my workshops and I know how it feels at my ripe old age, so I can imagine how this young woman, who pulled herself out of poverty to become one of the best tennis players in the world, must have felt. Not to mention that those fans should have been ashamed of themselves. They must have missed that character education class in school. By the way, I'm not saying, *for sure*, Serena and her family got booed by

143

Caucasian folk because they were Negroes; might've happened if Serena and Venus and their family were White. Maybe so, maybe not, but that's what occurred to me when I was thinkin about rude behavior in my workshops. Wondering how adults can be so childlike.

For me the scenario with Serena is one of those "quacking duck" situations as it relates to whether certain behaviors or attitudes represent racial prejudice or something else. If it looks like a duck, walks like a duck, feels like a duck, quacks like a duck, it's usually a duck. However race stuff is so complicated that sometimes it looks like a duck, walks like a duck, quacks like a duck, and in my experience it can turn out to be a look-a-like and/or just partly a duck. Most times it's definitely at least part duck in my experience, but sometimes it's not a duck at all. I'm glad when that is the case. So was booing the Williams family a product of racial prejudice or just people being rude? Looked like a duck to me, but those types of situations I try to let go of quick, even though I know they're probably at least part duck. They still tend to find a small place in my psyche somewhere. Dr. Eunice, my spiritual psychology teacher, tells me that when things like that happen I need to just say out loud several times, "delete, delete, delete" before they can take hold. I'm tryin that out.

By the way, tell me if this strikes you as strange (it does strike me that way). When I do workshops on diversity, usually the person hiring me meets with me for at least an informal needs assessment. They usually ask me some details about my approach to the topic; they share what the needs of the organization are, etc., but usually they are most concerned that my approach won't "alienate anyone," "open a can of worms, etc. That's fine, but usually when they say "anyone" they aren't talking about Colored folk. Many times, when the workshop starts, I get a few folk who, from jump street, ask why they have to be there and in one form or another let me know they think this is a waste of time. They are either openly disagreeable or passive aggressive, *booing* behavior like I said. After the workshops, it's not unusual that someone(s) of those booers will go to their supervisor and complain about the workshop. Usually they are upset about either something that was said by me or someone else or act like it was a waste of time for them to attend. In general they get pug ugly about the whole workshop experience. Too many times, the supervisors will waffle in their commitment to see the process all the way through, tell me I alienated some folk and talk about how to avoid that in future sessions. I tell them it is inevitable that the people who need it most are going to complain the most and that it may happen again in the next workshop. In some cases, the supervisors even cancel future workshops regardless if the majority of participants got something out of it.

So in other words, the very people who are narrow–minded need to work on their race relations and tend to deny any problems, are the very ones to whose complaints the supervisors respond, and often use them as the gauge for whether to continue such training. Well those narrowed-minded folks in my life have short-circuited a lot of learning for themselves and others, and, on a selfish note, have cost me some straight up cash! Talkin my livelihood here, so it's personal plus.

And this kind of thing happens not just in my little workshops, but in society at large. A lot of folk would speak up for what is right, but know that somehow it will alienate some narrow-minded person who can influence their future, so they keep their mouth shut.

The saving grace is that I find caring people in my workshops as well, Caucasians and folk of African descent. They will purposely take extra time to greet me and thank me for coming; some actually apologize for their peers' "booing," and some simply share what they are trying in order to create fairness and better relationships between the races. They often share that many of their colleagues try to block their efforts or simply marginalize them or don't support them, so they tell me they have to be cautious in talking about it. Frankly those comments come from mostly White folks about their same-hued colleagues. I encourage them to keep trying. Also had folks tell me things like that the workshop changed their lives, now they understand. They say they felt good they could talk honestly, be respected and heard. They were glad they learned what they learned and it would help them in the future. Some tell me that kind of thing. These are the folks that inspire me to keep hope alive.

One Caucasian man said something very moving that I will never forget. He said, and he was talkin to the Colored folks in the workshop, "I want you to know I have prejudices, but I also want you to know that is **not all that I am**." His statement hit me right where I live, because I know sometimes, if I think someone is prejudiced, I just think in my own head, without consciously expressing it, that indeed "that's all they are." I guess folk aren't all one thing or another. Don't know what to make of all that, but I know it is part of the whole truth. Plus it gave me something to reflect on related to my own shortcomings. Hard as I try I know I'm not free of sexist behavior. If women catch me being sexist I wonder if they write me off as just being sexist. No doubt I am still sexist to some degree, but that's not all that I am.

I love the workshops I do with young folk. They usually have no place to talk about all this stuff outside of these kinds of workshops. They ask all kinds of questions, make a lot of "statements of fact" as they see it, yet are often ready to hear truth or another view that doesn't fit theirs. And sometimes just being presented with the facts makes them start seeing things different. In one session a bunch of kids said the race prejudice was not too bad in their school. Very outspoken

146

blond-haired, blued-eyed exchange student from Germany stood up quick and told them when she arrived in the school district, folk told her right off to avoid Black people and to be careful about socializing with them too much. For sure, she continued, she was cautioned not to date African Americans. What she said took a lot of students a back for a minute, but they were open to hearing it and addressing it.

Young people give me *cause* for hope and also make me *pause* in dismay at times. Some really, really get it and are ready to move past this stuff. But still too many have no sense of the history of race relations and end up spouting what they've heard from the media or friends and family. At such a young age, how can they be so narrow in their thinking? What worries me is that I can tell a lot of these youngins, are bound for leadership roles. But overall the young give me hope. It is not unbounded as yet, but it is hope. People say, "leave it to young folk, they will change it," and I say, yes, they will change it faster if more of us change. So I say, "leave it to all of us."

I learn a lot about race relations in these workshops. Since I have worked all over the country for almost twenty-five years, my workshops strike me as a microcosm of the larger society. They give me a reality check as to where things stand, what has changed and what hasn't. We've come far, thank the Lord (or whoever you thank), but we still have promises to keep and miles to go before we sleep.

Please be clear. The reason I am bringing these workshops up is because I find way too many of my lighter-hued brothers and sisters unwilling to budge, notwithstanding the ones who are trying hard. As a microcosm of the greater society, that is cause for concern. So I celebrate heartily the progress I see and so should you, White and Black. I am however, realistic about what it will take to continue that progress. It simply can't be left to chance or time. Martin Luther King would always say that folk of ill will often use time more creatively than those of good will.

I remember, I heard a statement that was reportedly made to a group of slaves who had just arrived at a place of temporary freedom. It goes something like this: "So sing, shout and dance tonight for tomorrow the journey continues. We've crossed a river and now we've got to cross the sea."

Chapter 14

Trying to Stay Positive, Relying on God, Faith and Religion through Stereotypes and All

My challenge, and the challenge for many CNBAAPA folk, is to avoid letting all the negative energy make us bitter. It is vital and healthy that we don't focus on insensitive or hard-headed lighter-hued brothers. We need to focus on those sincere Whites who are willing to go the distance or at least try or we'll go crazy while makin everyone around us crazy at the same time.

Fact of the matter is, once you've had enough personal negative experiences with a group of people and folk who look like you have had the same experiences, it's easy to notice when those people do bad things and not tune in to the good things. That's human nature and somethin African American folk have to continue to be wary of. We have to focus on *tunin in to the good*. My favorite prayer says it like this:

> O God! Refresh and gladden my spirit. Purify my heart. Illumine my powers. I lay all my affairs in Thy hand. Thou art my Guide and my Refuge. I will no longer be sorrowful and grieved; I will be a happy and joyful being. O God! I will no longer be full of anxiety, nor will I let trouble harass me. I will not dwell on the unpleasant things of life. Oh God thou art more friend to me than I am to myself. I dedicate myself to Thee, O Lord. ('Abdu'l-Bahá, 1991, p. 150)

I say that prayer many a day and night. "I will not dwell on the unpleasant things of life," is my refrain.

Some time back I figured a way to work on my "tunin into the good" process. I've been takin time to add up all the good experiences I've had with Caucasian folk either personally or what I hear about or even see on TV, instead of dwelling on the bad ones. I mean, really takin a minute to reflect on them on a daily basis and let them soak in. Let me tell you, it helps a whole lot because I have a lot of good ones that are addin up. I think this can help Caucasians and African Americans if we both do that. Add up good experiences you have with your lighter or darker-hued brothers and sisters and just let that soak in.

Another thing and really the *main* thing that helps me is using religion and spirituality within to keep me strong. When things get bad or I'm dealing with some undesirable person or situation in terms of race, I try this: if a person has one good quality and ten bad ones, I try to focus on the one good quality and ignore the ten. Someone made a joke one time and said, "What if you can't find the one good quality, then what do you do?" Makes me smile because don't we all feel that way at times? If you try, you will no doubt come up with at least one.

Also, oftentimes when a person's behavior bothers you, instead of focusing on them, think about what lesson you might learn about yourself from their behavior. That doesn't mean you shouldn't address the issue, but first think about whether you might sometimes act in the same way toward other folk or just toward some folk; maybe not exactly the same, but a version of it. Maybe it's with a spouse, friend, significant other or even another culture, gender or class. Many times I find, when I focus on what I can learn about myself from their behavior, I find something I need to work on as well, which humbles me a bit. I still address stuff, but the energy in which I address it changes. Sometimes if it feels like it is not worth addressing, I might just pray for the person. My high road self kicks in and keeps me sane. My view is that folk come into your life

150

for a reason and often for more than one. If I get too worked up, I might miss my lesson. This is part of the practicality of spirituality.

Point is, we all got an ego that kicks in when we get upset about someone else's behavior or attitude, and we all get indignant, or feel superior and sometimes get way up on a high horse, because we now have just cause to come at someone with all our venom. Part of it is justified, but sometimes the offending party gets the entire wrath from whatever ails us; all the feelings we might have been sittin on forever. Plus it feels good to focus on someone else's faults for awhile. It gets tiring lookin at our own stuff all the time. Well, I got news for me and you: ego causes folk to complain, find fault, overreact, seek revenge, separate from others and paint them with a broad negative stroke. Also causes folk to react, bringing in all bad experiences, to somethin a person says or does. Ego generally just messes life up, usually not resulting in anything too fruitful. Call it our low road self or ego, whichever works for you. Personally, I find if my ego reacts to someone else's ego-related insensitivities, then I end up getting nowhere, except makin their ego madder so they can make mine even madder. Ego gets in the way of my sanity most times.

When I kick my high road spiritual self in gear, my energy changes. I feel more in control, and I emit a different vibe. I do believe you appeal to the best in others by bringing that good vibe to the table. The energy I put out when I get myself in that space is powerful. It changes things and many times sweetens up my nature and the other person's. If it doesn't work, then at least I don't feel like I lost my dignity. I didn't let anyone rock my day. Since I'm only responsible for my stuff, I say Amen, I'm gonna keep trying to check my ego at the door. I'm convinced if egos keep winning the battle everyone loses. So many of my respected ancestors had the kind of spiritual strength I'm talking about, and it is spiritual strength that's gonna get us through this and out the other side. Least I can do to honor their dignity is to try and follow their example. You may say this is hard to do in the moment, and I say again and hear me clearly. Don't underestimate the power of a few deep breaths at the right time. Breathe in and breathe out, slow yourself for a minute, center yourself in your dignity space before you speak. That space is the space of unending strength.

I recall our oldest granddaughter, Ananda, when she was four or five years, keepin my wife and I in check about what our focus should be, as only a child can. She was sitting in the back seat of the car listening to my wife and I talk about something that, in her mind, had clearly upset us. As we were talkin, probably thinkin she was not payin any attention, we heard her quiet voice, from the back seat, share something she had memorized from the Bahá'í Scriptures.

> Love the creatures for the sake of God and not for themselves. You will never become angry or impatient if you love them for the sake of God. Humanity is not perfect. There are imperfections in every human being, and you will always become unhappy if you look toward the people themselves. But if you look toward God, you will love them and be kind to them, for the world of God is the world of perfection and complete mercy. Therefore, do not look at the shortcomings of anybody; see with the sight of forgiveness. The imperfect eye beholds imperfections. The eye that covers faults looks toward the Creator of souls. ('Abdu'l-Bahá, 1982, p. 92)

My wife and I sort of smiled at her as if to acknowledge how cute and smart she was. She looked at us with a solemn expression and said somethin like, "Grandma, Grandpa, don't laugh, it's important." She was right, and she was cute at the same time!

152

Relying on faith, religion and spirituality is what CNBAAPA folk been doin since slavery and before. I think it kept us from becoming bitter, and it is somethin we gotta keep doing because bitterness can be right on the other side of faith, separated only by a thin veil. I don't like it, but I know it's still gonna take more time for things to get better. If we can walk with faith and spirit *during the time it takes for things to get better, we won't get bitter*. I'm not saying we just sit back and do nothing, because moving with faith and certitude is part of the proccss. I'm just saying, we gotta move with spirit and integrity because that's who we are. Besides, I hear too much anger is bad for the liver. Also I heard forgivin people helps your head and health. So taking the high road with your spirit self, is not only right, but it's healthy; hard but healthy.

I heard a speech by a powerful woman. Her name is Mpho Tutu. She is a reverend and the daughter of the famous and great Desmond Tutu. I took a lot of notes. She was talkin about how they tried to pull things together in South Africa and tried to reconcile Blacks and Whites after Apartheid. She talked about the importance of forgiveness in the reconciliation process and said it this way: forgiveness is *unhitching the chain that hooks perpetrator and victim*. As long as forgiveness does not take place, the perpetrator's deeds and misdeeds *yank upon that chain*. She went on to say forgiveness frees the heart and lack of forgiveness is what allows *"the perpetrator to live rent free in your psychic space"* (Tutu, 2007). Whew, somethin to think about, I'd say!

So do what's right, I tell myself, and White folk have told me and continue to tell me, "Treat each person as an individual and don't judge our whole race because of some bad apples." Yes, indeed I agree, but I wonder if the folk who say that know how many bad apples Negroes my age have had to taste in this life. Makes it a bit hard to treat each White person as an individual and not prejudge. But, like I said, my religion and my

153

oldest granddaughter are keeping me on the right track. I say if we're gonna solve this thing everyone is going to have to "get religion" in a real spiritual way. Being truly honest, I mean real honest, I sometimes want to make it all about White folk fixin this thing cuz I'd rather sit back and say "you started this mess, you end it." That's my ego, my side that's tired out—it grabs me sometimes and doesn't want to let go. My spiritual, my noble side knows that, victim or not, I have responsibility too. My spiritual side tells me it is not about who got it wrong the first time(s) around but rather whose gonna get it right this time around. Regardless of what anyone else does, my job is to seek justice on the noble path. Just like I, and most of us, have told our own children a million times, "just because someone else might act up doesn't mean you have to." That's on them, so don't make them your enemy. Speak up and speak out, but follow the noble path, the spirit path. May sound preachy, but it's the truth and a tall order indeed.

In fact, sometimes it is such a tall order for me, I use sort of a mantra to remind myself of my dignity and who I am and let hope take me to that space again and again. My mantra comes from the Bahá'í Scriptures. You can feel free to use it or find your own. I will not only take a breath or two, but in my head or out loud, depending on the situation, I will say "Noble have I created thee," and I may need to say it more than once (Bahá'u'lláh, 1954, # 22, first section). If I'm really struggling during the day I say this: "Armed with the power of Thy name, nothing can ever hurt me, and with Thy love in my heart all the worlds afflictions can in no wise alarm me" (Bahá'u'lláh, 1991, p. 127). I meditate on this or something like this to start my day and end my day and whenever I need it in between.

I've got more than a few mantras like that, but let me share one I really find powerful: "Turn thy sight unto thyself, that thou mayest find me, standing within thee, mighty, powerful and self subsisting" (Bahá'u'lláh, 1954, # 22, first section). Man, do I get juiced and calmed with that one. If you don't believe in God, I hope you believe that within you, there is a place of profound depth and capacity, if tapped, can allow you to transcend average every day emotion/ego responses.

The Past and Present Can be the Same

I'm thinkin and wonderin again if my White brothers and sisters realize this race thing is not about holding them to blame for what their ancestors did, but it's about what they inherited from their ancestors and haven't fixed yet. Said this earlier but am revisiting it because it's a big thing for White folks. Colored folks often get accused of living in the past and blaming Whites for their ancestor's behavior. I'm not sure White folk realize that, as one article recently said: half the CNBAAPA folk interviewed have experienced discrimination in the last thirty days of their time wakin up Black in the US of America. So the past is the present for a lot of folk. Yet I will hear so many folk say how fed up they are with hearing about the *past* race problems of Colored folk.

That goes down hard for me. I'm not sure why those folk who say we dwell on past can't acknowledge that the past and the present are part of the same reality. And for some of us, the past and the present feel real similar. Far too many of my White brothers and sisters act like Black folk are supposed to keep our mouths shut and do all the *suffering* and exercise all the *patience*. I hope my Caucasian family will realize that suffering is a part of the struggle and that they personally and White folk generally have to suffer too. Sometimes they may get accused unfairly of being prejudiced but they have to hang in there and just keep tryin to be fair and patient like they advise Afro-Americans to do. They gotta realize that we may not always be right, but we're definitely not always wrong.

155

Dear White brothers and sisters, you will no doubt have to be spiritually and emotionally prepared to hear about race as long as race is an issue for me, you and us. I say it again; White and Black are two halves of the whole so we're stuck with each other "in sickness and in health" for as long as we both shall live. Amen. Hopin there'll be a honeymoon in our future and soon.

So many Caucasians tell me they are tired of constantly being hammered about prejudice, or hearing that the system is not fair for CNBAAPA folk because of them. I understand their frustration, I really do. Even if you might need to change some things (in this case White folk working on their prejudices) or are willing to entertain that thought, no one likes to feel like they are being beaten over the head, time and again, with something; or like things are being rammed down their throat. On my low road days I want to say, "just don't let it bother you" or "get over it" like so many tell me. But I don't, because I understand and don't want to be sarcastic. I also understand that their feelings are no excuse for throwin in the towel. Suffer with me, I say, because it's the only way to a new day!

I hope White folk who feel "beat up," put down, and chastised by Blacks will stop to think for a minute that if they're tired of it all, how past tired of it Black folk must be. Without dwellin or yellin about the past, the system created by the majority population had its way with us for 350 plus years. If you're tired of dealing with race, that tiredness has not and could not have been around for that long. I'm still not denying you're tired, but if you're tired, we've got the right to be exhausted, long as we've been at it. Many of us are. Give us our props for hangin in and not hangin it up.

Like I said, I think some folk expect that the patience and loving business has to be one-sided and that they can sit on the sidelines unscathed. Well, I am here to say that none of us are gonna go through this race thing unscathed or unhurt. I hope White folk will acknowledge the part they have to play, dig in and accept that they are going to get hurt and get angry and exhausted too. No one can stay on the sidelines observing and making judgments about folk. It's the stone cold truth, if you're not part of the solution; you're part of the problem.... I say if you're not part of the solution, you are the problem! On that count, the same holds true for us darker folk.

Don't expect me to suffer in silence and just smile like everything is okay while you stand on the sidelines tryin to keep your feet out of this murky, scary water. "Jump in!" I say, "Get wet!" That's what I want to say to my White fiftieth cousins. Jump in and learn, listen, humbly share your thoughts with us as we share ours with you, and let us all create a "new dance" in America where everyone is an equal partner. Work on this issue with us, toe to toe and side by side. Draw on your spirit self. We have that in common and that's a good thing.

Whites and Bad Behavior: Is It Because They're White?

And while I'm on a roll, can those of you who like ramblin on about all the problems we have in "our" (Black) community stop it? Just stop it, because "your" (Caucasian) community has more than its fair share too. (This is what Tim Wise was saying in the article cited earlier.) Only your problems don't get smattered all over the news in such a way to suggest that somehow your problems are connected to your "Whiteness." Challenges Black folk have, one way or another, somehow get connected in folks' minds to our "Blackness" like being Black carries with it some kind of pathology (CNBAAPA-ness). I'm comin out strong on this because it's straight up painful and anger-producing, constantly feeling your community is being assaulted with pathological-type descriptions while the same standard is not applied to the White community. Who wants to feel like they are considered part of a pathological community?

Here is what I mean: when you hear about government political corruption, fraud, mortgage schemes, banking and other serious business and accounting shenanigans, drug use in suburbia, a continuous flow of violent and decadent movies (CNBAAPA folk don't run Hollywood), violent video games, violent mass killings (Columbine type stuff), cronyism, certain promiscuous behaviors and many other moral or criminal issues that involve a significant percentage of Whites, what you hear is that we need to address these social problems in our "society" or that we need to get tougher on this type of crime or stop this or that behavior. There's no reference to the color of those misbehaving, implicitly or explicitly. By the way, I realize African Americans are involved in some of these crimes, but by and large not so. They're not usually bank presidents, mortgage company heads or CEOs of large companies, Hollywood moguls etc., so by virtue of the positions it takes to commit many of these types of crimes, they are not committed by Black folk.

When big wigs in the music industry helped pollute *some* of the hip hop music to make a financial killing and destroy its original positive and powerful cross-over messages, not only did no one White get labeled as deviant for their "White behavior," but Black folk got/get blamed for polluting America. It was a sick White/Black marriage to money that polluted America but again "Blackness" was seen as the problem. When problems like drugs involve Whites, you hear things like there are increasing drug problems in the suburbs or in "America." You rarely, if ever, get the impression the drug problem in the suburbs is related to how many White folks are there, how they behave, and how they raise their children. In other words their problems don't get connected to their "Whiteness."

158

In a hot minute, you will hear about drug problems in the "Black community" or in "urban America" (meanin Black and/or Hispanic usually), and the problems quickly get *equated and related* to color. When White folk are involved you will hear things about problems in "middle America" and vague references to mainstream America which could mean anyone depending on how it is used. In the article I cited earlier by Tim Wise, it is clear White folk have as many problems as CNBAAPA folk, and definitely White folk use drugs as much as Colored folk, and in some cases more. But again their problems do *not get equated or related* to their "Whiteness" even such cases as those almost exclusively White male CEOs and CFOs indicted for funny financial business all over America. Folk still don't relate it to them being White and then start lumping White CEOs in some type of socially depraved, pathological "Caucasian" category.

Adding insult to injury, those CEOs and other White collar type criminals often ruin thousands of lives with their callous and malicious criminal behavior, but most of them, if they even get a stiff sentence, just get sent off to some cushy prison. When they get out, someone is usually willing to hire them. Small-time felons get out of prison and can't, for the life of them, get a job. No ex-felon or other kind of stigma attached to CEOs and other "White collar" criminals. Some even end up celebrities making more money than before—regardless of how many lives they ruined. Small-time Black felons often are ruined for life.

Saw a picture in the paper sometime (sometime after Tim Wise made his point in his article) back that showed all those boys who have done things similar to Columbine. Yet again the article said these killers did not all fit a clear profile type, even though ninety-five of the boys they showed were White. Not equated and related to their Whiteness. Who finances all those drugs coming into this country? It's mostly White folk, but again no White stigma. Not stigmatized till the drugs reach the Black community, and then it's time to crack down; not on those bringing it in, but rather on those in the community sellin and takin it. Now I'm not the smartest person in the world, but I know if you really wanna stop something you have to cut out the source, and the source of drugs is not Black folk.

I ask you, who is studyin the "pathology" of White folks? Where are the academicians and other folk who are observing, analyzing, dissecting and maligning the "White" pathological behavioral patterns? True enough, their racial attitudes get analyzed fully, but what about the rest of the patterns. I'm here to ask for equal opportunity for all. I ask that White misbehavior be studied on an equal basis with that of Negro folk and that it be equated and related, both subtly and overtly, to their Whiteness. Maybe add that to the duties and responsibilities of the Office of Equal Opportunity. You heard it here first! The Black and White communities need equal opportunities to be maligned for their color at all levels of society! I don't really mean that, but the point is clear. Be fair and just and look at all of the US of America when we study social and moral problems. I will be the first to admit Black folk got a lot of big issues, and in the same breath I will say, so do White folk.

CNBAAPA folk been studied and surveyed so much that all kinds of stereotypes and bad generalizations have stuck to us like glue, and the results are humiliating. We're often perceived as less intelligent, more criminal, more likely to prefer welfare, lazier than other ethnic groups. Usually African Americans come out at the bottom of the heap in these surveys. In other words, a whole bunch of U.S. Americans view Colored folk as the ethnic group containing the most negative traits. That's a hard pill to swallow. CNBAAPA folk aren't mostly lazy or mostly criminal. Most of us want what White folk want—just an even chance—no more and no less.

I say it's time to take a long hard look at the accuracy of those stereotypes and maybe start studying the "hard-working" qualities of Black folk. An honest U.S American needs to look no further than the maids cleaning hotels (both young and old), to the men riding around collecting garbage, to short-order cooks in restaurants, to the bus boys in so many places. (Not to mention the fact that Black folk still too often have to work twice as hard and be twice as good, behavior wise and competence wise to make it in the US of America.) A lot of these folk are CBNAAPA and other People of Color that surely don't get paid their just due. How can anyone look at all those folk and at the same time hold the image that CNBAAPA folk are lazier than most other folk? Where are honor, dignity, and respect for a people who do so much of the "grunt" work in the US of America?

When I drive by or stay in motels and I see all those women of color in their blue work outfits working or going to work cleaning up the rooms, scrubbing floors and cleaning toilets I often pause. I look and see the advanced age of some of them and *I'm sad and proud at the same time*. When I know of African American women and men who get up at the crack of dawn so they can go two hours or more to work for minimum wage while their children have to see themselves off to school, I wonder at the concept of laziness. Many of them work two jobs. When I think of my mother, who walked a mile to the bus stop in the dead of bitter cold Minnesota winters, to ride for miles to go to work and for what I now know was very little money, I marvel. I marvel at my dad working two jobs and going back to school at the same time while in his thirties. So I bristle at those surveys that conclude CNBAAPA folk are seen as lazier, more criminal and more likely to want to be on welfare than other U.S. Americans. I've been reading that stuff for most of my life and it's a tough pill for this Negro to swallow, real tough.

So my day dream at this moment, on this day, is that together we envision a new US of America without stereotyping. US Americans of whatever ilk can be like pioneers, forging a new frontier, going where no humans have gone before. We can call the new frontier "the Unified Peoples of America," and all the cousins of light and dark hue are invited. First order of business is to create that new dance I told you about. I say it like this to my cousins of greater and lesser color: "***Embrace Your Race: Your Whole Race***." No doubt; no doubt we can do this. Chief Arvol Looking Horse put it this way, "Each of us is put here in this time and this place to personally decide the future of humankind. Did you think the Creator would create unnecessary people in a time of such terrible danger? Know that you are essential to this world. Believe that! Understand both the blessing and the burden of that. You are desperately needed to save the soul of this world. Did you think you were put here for something less?" (The My Hero Project, 2001).

Get carried away at times I know, but that's my life. Get excited and hopeful one minute and discouraged the next waking up Black in US of America. But I do get excited when I think of the possibilities. I like the dance idea, and I can't even dance. One more stereotype dispelled.

Do You Feel What I Feel?

This morning, all this has got me thinking real strongly, what a great big advantage it is not to have to deal with being stereotyped your whole life. I remember sometime back, a White woman professor named Peggy McIntosh wrote out a bunch of questions on life experiences of people in the US of America. She was trying to help Caucasian folk understand some of their advantages, or what she called privileges, that come from not having to face certain kinds of prejudice stuff. It was her attempt to create awareness for the subtle things

162

African American folk experience on a daily basis that White folk may never have thought about or had to think about. Thought she did a pretty good job. Here are some, not necessarily verbatim examples of the kind of things she would ask. If you apply for credit, can you be pretty sure your race will not work against you? Then you're supposed to think about that statement and answer yes or no. If you get stopped by the police, you can be pretty sure it has nothing to do with your race? Yes or no? When you speak about race do you worry that you have to represent your whole race when you speak? Are you pretty sure the school curriculum will reinforce a positive identity for the cultural and racial background of your children? Do you think about being followed in stores when you shop? Can you arrange your activities so that for the most part you will never have to experience feelings of rejection owing to your race? When you are told about "our" national heritage or about "civilization," are you shown that people of your color made it what it is (McIntosh, 1988)? These types of questions and statements are intended to lead to insights that all Americans don't have the same relationship to daily life or the same advantages. The point is that we should all have the same advantages. It isn't bad that some folks have them; it's only bad that all folks don't.

I remember a book by a guy named Andrew Hacker entitled *Two Nations*. Hacker shared the response of White college students who were given a scenario for response. Students were told they were born White by mistake and at midnight they would turn Black as was intended. The fictitious scenario went on to say that they would remain the same person inside but outside they would be Black. They were told they could receive compensation for this mistake and for turning Black. They were asked how much they felt it was reasonable to receive to live for at least fifty more years as an Afro-American. According to Hacker they said a million dollars; not a million dollars total but a million dollars a year—fifty million total and mostly, he surmised, from the class, so they could shield themselves from the impact of discrimination (Hacker, 1995). Not sure what that all means because I was not in Hacker's class to hear the discussions, but it feels to me, deep down folk know there's a big difference growing up White in the US of America and growing up Black. But they just can't bring themselves to say it out loud.

So what's my point? We've got to understand it's the difference that makes the difference and if we deny that, we not only miss the boat, we miss the whole ocean. In my race workshops, to make the point, I ask a Black and White person to stand up side by side and look at the rest of the participants. I ask the group if they think that these two people would have differing life experiences growing up in whatever city we happen to be in, just based on their race. I say, "other factors would influence their experiences but I am just asking about race at this point." Ninety-five percent of all the participants say yes, they would have differing experiences just based on race. I then ask the person of African descent if they understand what it would be like to grow up White. Most say, no. I ask the White person if they know what it would be like to grow up Black. Again most say, no. A lot of smiles appear during those questions. I then ask the group what I consider to be the key question: "Whose life experience represents truth?" At that point almost everyone says, "both." I then ask the whole group, "How can they learn about each other's truth, given that neither has a clue what it would be like to grow up as a member of the other race?" They say something like, "Guess they'd have to hear each other out." Finally I ask, "Are you willing to do that?"

I must say I think this is a good way to make a point. Some folks in my workshop are willing to do that and others aren't; even the ones who acknowledge the life experience would be different often simply shut down one way or another. Once the real dialogue starts, it's as if they forgot what they just agreed to; that indeed folk have differing life experiences. Not being negative, but that's just how it works. So I try to focus on the folk that want to move forward and leave it at that.

Before movin on I gotta tell you I can't help but thinkin about that one million dollar a year compensation for Whites turning Black. Wishing I could get a piece of that action. I wonder if anyone has asked the question to Black folk. How much would you need to get compensated to turn White? I've been Colored fifty plus years now, and I don't have an answer to that one.

Back to issue of advantage. Here's a big one. Many of us are thinkin about Barack's run for president, exhilarated about the possibility of a Black President of the entire US of America. Right beside that exhilaration is deep anxiety wondering if someone will try to do something awful to him. Most of my darker-hued friends are tryin not to give that thought much energy, but threats on his life are off the charts, as is the size of his security detail. By the way, no headline will ever read: *Threats from Whites to Kill President Elect Obama at Record Number*. We will simply read that threats have been made on his life, as if it is a general phenomenon. Though it probably can't be substantiated, I mean *proof positive substantiated,* no doubt, it is not a generalized phenomenon, but a lighter-hued one.

I know I harped on this point before and even though it is not my main point now, I feel compelled to say if there were a bunch of Black folk in groups or as individuals threatening or plotting to kill a White President of the US and it was at record numbers, I'm thinking the fact they were Afro-Americans would somehow seep out in a few headlines and talk shows and the color "Black" would be equated and related to the would-be perpetrators. You see how this thing is so insidious?

That's my point in bringing it up again. You've got to be clear on the challenge if you want to resolve it.

Not sure White folk worry and have anxiety when electing a President that looks like them that enough Black folk are going to hate him because of his color and one of them might do something awful to him. Or that an organized group of Blacks might do it. Or that Black young people are going to be shouting in schools about how he should get assassinated. So the time of the greatest joy for many African Americans is right beside the time of the greatest apprehension. It has been quite a ride for many of us having to juggle these feelings about the election of a President of African descent and what might happen to him. It's not because we're negative, not because we like dwelling on the past, it's because it is a part of the way it is. Many of us are praying over him big time and not just folk of my hue.

Now that you read this last paragraph please only send positive energy to the Obama family and think only good thoughts about how he will be treated. Don't want the stuff I just related to linger in the universe any more time than it takes to read it and think on it a minute. I just felt I needed to make this point.

Admitting to having advantages in the US of America doesn't necessarily mean White folk got it easy in life. I know boat loads that have a very rough go of it. It does mean there's a whole bunch of stuff they don't have to deal with and a bunch of other things they get the best crack at because of their hue. Admit that and we can move forward and figure out how to make sure I get what you get and that I don't have to deal with what you don't have to deal with. Then we can all be fast friends. Sounds good to me! How bout to you? My soft side may be comin out, but I do believe in my heart that we truly

166

are better together. United we stand, divided we fall, I say, or at least someone said, and I'm repeating it.

Chapter 15

Finishing Breakfast and Going to Work

Now I really am back to my breakfast and finishing up reading my newspaper. Truly, I'm gettin ready to start my work day. Always try to read the comics last. I like to end my reading with a smile on my face, not having to dwell on anything too serious. I did notice they have more dark skinned folk in the comic strips than they used to. "Things they are a-changin."

I know I'm late startin work, but I remind you, I work for myself, so it's all right. I'm not quite ready to fire myself just yet. Besides, I'll be hittin the road in a little while to do some out-of-town work. My office manager and part time consultant, we'll call her Briana, who is just twenty-two, is giving a talk at a high school a couple hours from here. She will be speaking to a gym full of high school students about race issues. It's part of a program my daughter Angela and I started several years back to bring about greater unity between the races in high schools. My daughter got very upset about the aftermath of a racial incident and wanted to do something about it. That's my long rationalization for startin work late. Knowing we won't be leavin town for a bit allowed me to ease into my day slower than usual. Party over, here comes Briana, so I guess I can finally fold up this paper and get on with it.

Briana and I spend many an hour on these trips talkin and prayin and trying to unravel some of these race issues. The reason I mentioned she is twenty-two is because it's helpful for me to see how someone views issues of race who is less than half my age and bi-racial but seen as Black. I like to find out if she sees the same things I am seein or if I am just old and jaded. According to our discussions, we see a bunch of things pretty much the same way. There are some differences, but a lot of the same nuances and complexities about this thing called race. That doesn't answer the question of whether I'm old and jaded, does it? Partly I think I am, and partly I think I see things as they really are.

On our way up to give her talk, we converse about cornrows—you know, the way Black folk wear their hair in real tight braids close to their scalp. She shares opinions of White folk she's heard who associate Black males in cornrows with being thuggish and sometimes feel the same about those wearing braids. I think of cornrows as a powerful and beautiful expression of culture. My daughter used to spend some serious time braiding her husband's hair. I thought the young brother looked good. Thinkin of him bein perceived as a thug because of his hairstyle is out there to me. He is a brilliant and loving young man, great husband and father to his three daughters and because of his hair could be considered dangerous. I'll tell you something: I just cannot believe folk think that way. I believe what she is telling me, but I'm going to have to check that out some more. She told me some Colored folk think the same way. I know we don't all think alike, but I just never imagined cornrows or braids being related to thuggery. Must be I am out of touch with some things. But I guess if people are going to think I'm "real Black" because I wear clothing from parts of Africa, it's not too far-fetched that some would think something about cornrows and braids. Anyway I'm gonna let that go.

NEWS FLASH

My son in law Karim, told me he was walking home from the train on the opposite side of the street from a White fella who got off the train at the same time. Karim crossed the street so he could start walking toward his home and ended up walking behind this White fella. Guy keep turning around to glance back at Karim. Finally Karim said, "you okay man?" He said, "no offense but I don't like people following me, nothing personal it's just that there's been a lot of "shady shit" going down in this city." Karim said he was having a good day till then but it had been awhile since he'd felt like folk saw him "as a big scary Negro." He said his vision of himself is much more of a "fatherly/avuncular" sort with three girls of his own and a bunch of kids he teaches in school. "I just haven't felt like the gorilla in a long time. I mean, I was in flip flops, you know? How can you scare somebody in flip flops?" Well, the upside is that he hadn't been treated that way in awhile. The downside is that race based stuff is never far away. (Mind you, Karim is the same guy whose experience is that he can't get a cab to stop for him.) Well, this White fella pushed Karim's button and Karim had a few words for him letting him know that this newly gentrified neighborhood was his home too. Karim said in retrospect he might have handled it better. Maybe so, but so could have the White guy. When he said "shady shit" the gut level translation is that shady shit means me! We gotta work together on this stuff folks!

NEWS FLASH OVER

Reparations and Repairin

We also spoke about the ongoing push for reparations. That conversation has come up in the African American community in a serious way and even has been put forward by some Congressmen and -women of African descent. The thinking is that Colored folk should be compensated for slavery, lost income and related oppressive practices. It could amount to trillions of dollars by some calculations and seems to be a real sore spot with a whole lot 'a folk. Many Whites say emphatically, "No way; I was not a slave owner." On the other hand, whether folk owned slaves or not, many profited directly and indirectly from free and forced labor; so did some big companies that news sources have been naming lately. Some of these companies are being sued. Let me say that these same folks who were not slave owners were also not responsible for puttin Japanese Americans in internment camps, but Japanese survivors or their children got reparations. Wasn't a whole lot I heard and surely not enough to compensate for what they went through, but they got an apology and some cold cash. "Why not us?" many Black folk are saying, "We're long overdue." Briana and I kicked this around for quite some time and got a little testy about it too. Not so much that Caucasian folk and some Negroes didn't agree with reparations, but that so many react as if such a thought is absurd. Forget the fact that much of the economic strength of this country was built by our forced labor and without benefit to us.

Maybe we could start reparations by repairing the textbooks and making sure they tell the whole truth. Perhaps some extra targeted resources could be directed into poor Black schools. Another option would be to target African American inmates who have an excellent chance of rehabilitation and focus resources in that direction. That could prove to be a tremendous boost to the Black community and to the US of America. Some have suggested that no direct cash be given but instead educational scholarships. Those are some thoughts off the top of my head for "repairing" or reparating (though I don't think "reparating" is a word).

To be honest, I am not sure about how I fully feel about reparations, but I can tell you one thing I'm sure of: I'm sure that at least *considering* reparations in some serious way, form or fashion is not absurd! The fact is, that as a people, we were held in bondage year after year, lynched, mocked, mutilated, scorned, disenfranchised and belittled for most of our country's history. Millions, not hundreds, millions died in the middle passage coming across the Atlantic. Inventions were stolen from us as we could not even patent what we invented. We were prevented from learning to read and educate ourselves and some who managed to do so often had to hide the fact. Our families were separated, maligned and humiliated to keep us in place. We could fight for our country, but even in the wars we were segregated, and in many cases not wanted. When we came home from wars across the water, we were still not accepted and were in many places re-segregated and had tough times getting decent jobs and education. In Viet Nam we were sent to the front lines and came home to the back of the line.

To put it mildly, the US of America got way off "on the wrong foot" with CNBAAPA folk. Yet when folk of African descent suggest that the government and/or the companies in the US of America—who sanctioned and benefited from slavery and post-slavery practices (that continued into the mid-twentieth century) or did little to prevent such abuse—need to somehow compensate for these injustices, many folk get downright indignant. Families in the US of America get compensated for all kinds of past tragedies, from school shootings to gettin burned by hot coffee from a fast food restaurant. I say, literally and figuratively, a whole race of people got burned with hot coffee and shot up needlessly.

Well, *some* African American folk are saying, to create a level playing field, there needs to be some form of compensation. Whether this is the best way or not, the notion of compensation and reparation is simply ***not absurd!***

NEWS FLASH

This may be the most personally devastating one for me to write about. This **NEWS FLASH** did not exactly come up in this order but I'm putting it here because it fits best. I was listening to a White fella on the Tavis Smiley program named Douglas Blackmon. He wrote a book called *Slavery by Another Name*. He located documents from to courthouses throughout the South that identified a system of slavery in practice well after 1865 and the thirteenth Amendment. Turns out, after slavery, *Black codes* were enforced in various forms until WWII and in a most horrific manner. Black codes were set up to control the lives of Black folks after slavery and virtually circumscribed their every move. Though declared illegal by Congress, Southerners found other ways to restrict and constrain the very movement of Black men from place to place and criminalized all sorts of behavior to further their control. Blacks could be arrested for almost no reason. They'd be arrested for vagrancy, charged a bail they could not afford, or convicted for such crimes as loud talk, then *leased or sold* to cotton farmers, coal mine owners or to work in factories. Literally tens of thousands of Blacks suffered this fate after slavery "ended." Their treatment was oppressive and brutal and working conditions horrendous. The whip was used again as a main source of enforcement. Many could not survive the working conditions, the diseases and the inhumane treatment. Those who died were often thrown into oven furnaces near coal mines or buried in mass graves.

In addition to Blacks being arrested for such violations as traveling without a White person's permission or letter or for changing jobs without a White employer's permission, Black men in certain states were literally snatched off the street and forced and sold into labor camps of one form or another. All this was done with the collusion of politicians, law enforcement, the judicial system and major companies. This amounted, according to Blackmon, to thousands and thousands of Black men, not even being convicted on trumped up charges, but essentially kidnapped off the street and sold or leased into servitude.

According to Blackmon, companies made millions of dollars from this forced inhumane practice and several Southern states added millions to their coffers on the backs of these men. For almost eighty years, from 1865 to WWII, these "free" Black men were terrorized and brutalized into submission. And what was the response to the revelation of such criminal behavior?

> Most ominous was how plainly the record showed that in the face of the rising southern White assault on Black independence—even as Black leaders increasingly expressed profound despair and hundreds of aching requests for help poured into federal agencies in Washington, DC—the vast majority of White Americans, exhausted from the long debates over the role of Blacks in U.S. society, conceded that the descendants of slaves in the South would have to accept the end of freedom. (Blackmon, 2008, p. 8)

I share this section with anguish, as the whole account of this wicked time period is more heinous and wrenching than can be described in these few paragraphs. I knew about sharecropping and I knew about Jim Crow, but somewhere I missed the gravity of this despicable and shameful piece of U.S American history. You may want to pause a minute on this one.

Tavis Smiley said that he was on an airplane discussing this book with another Black man and both agreed the book was vital. They noted however that Black scholars had been trying to get this information out for years with very little attention and now that a Caucasian was sharing the story, it was getting a lot of attention. What can I say?

This was genuinely a tough one for me; I mean, really tough.

I had to sit with that quietly for some time and then slowly ease back into my day. I was so moved, so humbled by the sacrifice of yet another several generations of Black men. I felt more committed than ever to make my life count. Those were my feelings as I recall them. The "delete, delete" didn't kick in at all. I also remember thinkin that reparations indeed are far, far from absurd. I mean, far from it!

Because of life experiences like this, for folk like me, the road to reconciliation is going to take superhuman effort. My, oh my, I think Mpho Tutu so eloquently said what it takes for such pain to be transcended and transformed into reconciliation. Here's how she put it, and again I paraphrase from the notes I took at her speech 2007:

First and foremost is the desire to achieve reconciliation. It is not a place we reach, oh, by the way. We have to be aiming for it. It is an opportunity to create society on different terms. It takes truly courageous leadership. Courage has lost its true meaning in the pop culture of our society. We say such things as "it took courage to change my hairstyle." We need courage to move forward regardless of public opinion, the end product being a society that serves all its citizens, courage to continue when the direction is not always obvious. Nelson Mandela, of course, conveyed this as he emerged from prison after twenty-seven years, not as an embittered man asking for revenge, but rather asking for reconciliation. Reconciliation does not come CHEAP! It comes when people are willing to lay down what they consider righteous demands in favor of the creative community, to let go of factions so we can create a community we all desire to live in. What am I willing to give up to create that world? *Reconciliation is not a shortcut to anywhere; it has to be renewed day by day* (Tutu, 2007). I say to all that, "Amen."

So who will respond to that noble call? Who will reach out, who will give up a righteous demand for the sake of unity and justice? Who's going to take the next step? Who will move to the intersection and out of their comfort space?

NEWS FLASH OVER

Stand Up and Say Yes!

I know I was talkin to you all about my trip with Briana, but this thing about Black men being kidnapped and brutalized is stayin with me. I'm thinkin and feeling after trying to absorb all of what I just told you, it sure would be nice if some high-powered Caucasians would stand up and admit that what our country did to Black folk was real wrong, and we're not done fixin that wrong yet. Then they could tell Americans we all need to work together for justice and play our part to make sure justice happens. It would be nice if some "higher ups" would set that example and on some level *acknowledge* there is still work to be done.

Well, I got myself a big shock from an unexpected corner. Someone important did stand up and say many of the things I hoped they would say and in a real eloquent way. It got said, of all places in Senegal, at Goree Island, where so many free Africans got enslaved, put on boats and brought to this side of the Atlantic. Speech was very moving, but the problem was the message never seemed to make its way across the middle passage. I'll tell you who gave the speech after you read it.

> Mr. President and Madam First Lady, distinguished guests and residents of Goree Island, citizens of Senegal, I'm honored to begin my visit to Africa in your beautiful country.

For hundreds of years on this island, peoples of different continents met in fear and cruelty. Today we gather in respect and friendship, mindful of past wrongs and dedicated to the advance of human liberty.

At this place, liberty and life were stolen and sold. Human beings were delivered and sorted, and weighed, and branded with the marks of commercial enterprises, and loaded as cargo on a voyage without return. One of the largest migrations of history was also one of the greatest crimes of history.

Below the decks, the middle passage was a hot, narrow, sunless nightmare; weeks and months of confinement and abuse and confusion on a strange and lonely sea. Some refused to eat, preferring death to any future their captors might prepare for them. Some who were sick were thrown over the side. Some rose up in violent rebellion, delivering the closest thing to justice on a slave ship. Many acts of defiance and bravery are recorded. Countless others, we will never know.

Those who lived to see land again were displayed, examined, and sold at auctions across nations in the Western Hemisphere. They entered societies indifferent to their anguish and made prosperous by their unpaid labor. There was a time in my country's history when one in every seven human beings was the property of another. In law, they were regarded only as articles of commerce, having no right to travel, or to marry, or to own possessions. Because families were often separated, many denied even the comfort of suffering together.

For 250 years the captives endured an assault on their culture and their dignity. The spirit of Africans in

177

America did not break. Yet the spirit of their captors was corrupted. Small men took on the powers and airs of tyrants and masters. Years of unpunished brutality and bullying and rape produced a dullness and hardness of conscience. Christian men and women became blind to the clearest commands of their faith and added hypocrisy to injustice. A republic founded on equality for all became a prison for millions. And yet in the words of the African proverb, "no fist is big enough to hide the sky." All the generations of oppression under the laws of man could not crush the hope of freedom and defeat the purposes of God.

In America, enslaved Africans learned the story of the exodus from Egypt and set their own hearts on a promised land of freedom. Enslaved Africans discovered a suffering Savior and found he was more like themselves than their masters. Enslaved Africans heard the ringing promises of the Declaration of Independence and asked the self-evident question, then why not me?

In the year of America's founding, a man named Olaudah Equiano was taken in bondage to the New World. He witnessed all of slavery's cruelties, the ruthless and the petty. He also saw beyond the slave-holding piety of the time to a higher standard of humanity. "God tells us," wrote Equiano, 'that the oppressor and the oppressed are both in His hands. And if these are not the poor, the broken-hearted, the blind, the captive, the bruised which our Savior speaks of, who are they?'

Down through the years, African Americans have upheld the ideals of America by exposing laws and habits contradicting those ideals. The rights of African

Americans were not the gift of those in authority. Those rights were granted by the Author of Life, and regained by the persistence and courage of African Americans, themselves.

Among those Americans was Phyllis Wheatley, who was dragged from her home here in West Africa in 1761, at the age of seven. In my country, she became a poet, and the first noted Black author in our nation's history. Phyllis Wheatley said, "In every human breast, God has implanted a principle which we call love of freedom. It is impatient of oppression and pants for deliverance."

That deliverance was demanded by escaped slaves named Frederick Douglas and Sojourner Truth, educators named Booker T. Washington and W. E. B. DuBois, and ministers of the Gospel named Leon Sullivan and Martin Luther King, Jr. At every turn, the struggle for equality was resisted by many of the powerful. And some have said we should not judge their failures by the standards of a later time. Yet, in every time, there were men and women who clearly saw this sin and called it by name.

We can fairly judge the past by the standards of President John Adams, who called slavery "an evil of colossal magnitude." We can discern eternal standards in the deeds of William Wilberforce and John Quincy Adams, and Harriet Beecher Stowe, and Abraham Lincoln. These men and women, Black and White, burned with a zeal for freedom, and they left behind a different and better nation. Their moral vision caused Americans to examine our hearts, to correct our Constitution, and to teach our children the dignity and equality of every person of every race. By a plan known only to Providence, the stolen sons and daughters of Africa helped to awaken the conscience of America. The very people traded into slavery helped to set America free.

My nation's journey toward justice has not been easy and it is not over. The racial bigotry fed by slavery did not end with slavery or with segregation. And many of the issues that still trouble America have roots in the bitter experience of other times. But however long the journey, our destination is set: liberty and justice for all.

In the struggle of the centuries, America learned that freedom is not the possession of one race. We know with equal certainty that freedom is not the possession of one nation. This belief in the natural rights of man, this conviction that justice should reach wherever the sun passes leads America into the world. (Bush, 2003; emphasis added)

Well I say George W. Bush gave one heck of a speech, and I have to say I am touched deeply every time I reread it. This was the kind of straight talk about slavery that needs to be spoken. Some say Bush didn't mean what he said, that it was all politics. I don't claim he did or didn't mean it, but those are touching words that need to be made more public in the US of America. Really wish that speech would be repeated on this side of the Atlantic and then backed up with some real action. I would be somewhat disingenuous if I neglected to say that many folk, in the area of Senegal where President Bush spoke, were treated with tremendous disrespect in the process of securing the area. That does not nullify the significance of the words spoken but it does reinforce that words have to be supported by deeds.

Barack Obama gave a banner talk on race too. Some say it was a classic for the ages. I say it was a challenge and a call to action. Put George's speech with Barack's and there's a true message. It would be the kind of message, if reinforced, that could keep us moving closer to unity or at least real healing; something that is yet to happen. We didn't do it after slavery, after reconstruction ended, after the Black codes, after Jim Crow, after WWII as we learned from Blackmon, and we didn't do it after the sixties' Civil Rights Movement. We passed laws but we never reconciled or healed in a collective way. Even legal redress was begrudgingly granted and far too many wanted African Americans to be satisfied with just a slice of the "American Dream"; so healing is still necessary. The Barack Obama phenomenon has helped create a renewed spirit, but it's also merely feeding into what a lot of people are ready for, even seem to be yearning for. Change is in the air and it's a desire for true unity; however, it won't just happen.

A friend of mine and I were talking about the challenges we've seen in so many marriages and realized there were some parallels with the emotional chasm between Blacks and Whites. We said it's like a husband and wife who've had a lot of big ugly fights. There is a primary initiator and a primary victim and this has been going on for years and life between them is tense. They can't just get a set of rules imposed on them to keep their marriage going. Rules may work to a point, but if the hearts aren't healed and the bully remains arrogant and the spouse keeps feelin put down and dominated, no real healing is going to take place. Living in close proximity with each other, they're going to continue to get under each other's skin; distrust and resentment will deepen, and the wounds will fester. They will fester until everything gets festered and they won't even know where to start to heal after a while.

Well we figured Blacks and Whites need to do what a husband and wife would do if they wanted to make a healthy marriage, if they really want a marriage that was beyond just living under the same roof, barely keepin the lid on. The major wrongdoer in the fight would have to get real humble, and, because their heart tells them to do so, look in their spouse's eyes and say, "I'm sorry; I was wrong, real wrong and will you forgive me?" Even if the wrongdoer doesn't think they're the same person as they once were, they realize there's a lot to make up for and they care enough about the marriage to step up. If the spouse is able to let go of the pain and forgive immediately, more power to them. But chances are, the issue is going to be tender for awhile until trust can be restored or built; so some patience and effort will be required on both parts. But bottom line, without a heartfelt acknowledgement of what went wrong and some forgiveness, it's gonna keep creeping back and rippin at the marriage. With an acknowl-edgement, chances are that sooner or later they will be able to give each other a genuine hug and say, "never again" and really mean it. Well in my view that's what has to take place in the US of America between Whites and Blacks. Some seri-ous acknowledgement, some serious sorry for what happened, some patience and real effort that hopefully will lead one day to, as my friend put it, a big "national hug." Then true recon-ciliation and unity building can begin. Would that really be so hard? If we really believed the future of the US of America was at stake, we'd do it. I say it is. Some think we can get along without such healing—maybe so, maybe not, but in my view a much bigger "maybe not."

NEWS FLASH

This just came in: I had lunch with a friend of mine the other day. Let's call her Teanna. Almost forgot to tell you all about this. She's another brilliant young mind and a soul-filled sister. She tends to ask probing questions that keep a brother on his toes. She said, "Who is the audience for this book?" I knew but had to reflect a minute because a half-baked answer wouldn't satisfy her. "One audience is CNBAAPA folk," I told her. "I'm tired of seeing us denigrated as if we are somehow more immoral or less honorable than other U.S. Americans. I want us to realize that our race struggles are real and not in our heads and that they have impacted our social and economic progress big time. I also want to make clear that regardless, we have to take the high road, the spiritual path and focus on who we are as a people and our proud heritage of beating the odds." Before she could say anything, I went on, "I want White folk to read this book too and feel the heart and truth in it. I want those White folk who are 'in the choir' to sing louder, the less engaged to get more engaged and the silent to step up and step out. I'm aiming at those Caucasians and am not at all worried about touching the extremists, though I am open to them changing too. I want White folk to feel the hope and faith I have in them and also understand the frustration I and many darker-hued folk have."

Just like I expected, Teanna probed some more. "Tell me more about this issue of White folk thinking we're less moral than other folk. Haven't a lot of them always thought that?" "I'm thinkin so," I told her. "But over the past several years I've heard this concept insidiously seepin into the dialogue more loudly, as if it were fact. That can only damage an already damaged self-esteem of Colored folk, and we don't need more generations of children growin up thinking they're somehow naturally immoral. That will be lethal." I told her, "White folk are just as dysfunctional and functional as we are, no better and no worse. I know you know that, but I'm just sayin it out loud. In my view, dysfunction for White folk just shows up in different ways and doesn't have the same *obvious* life-threatening consequences as our dysfunction does. Theirs is ultimately soul-threatening and life-threatening as well. Point being, as a people, Black folk lack the financial and social resources to cover up our dysfunction, and plus we get studied all the time so that makes us appear worse!" She sat with that a minute and made her point: "In a sense, the immediate life-threatening devastation our dysfunction is having in some of our communities makes our problem worse. We're not worse but our problems are worse, at least on the surface." "Yes," I confirmed, "the immediate consequences are worse, but not the dysfunction."

Then we talked about how this reminded us of the miner's canary. In the old days, miners used to put a canary in the mine with them, because canaries have a sensitive respiratory system. Since the mines released undetectable poisonous gases, the canary was a life-saving necessity. When the canary died, the miners knew it was time to get out!

She said, "So what do you see as the poisonous gases in our society?" I rattled off the ones that immediately came to my head: "Greed, materialism, excessive individualism, immorality and unethical behaviors, racism and sexism, all that and much more," I said. "Those gases impact the most vulnerable in society first, just like the canary, and Negroes are the canaries in the US of America. Gases are killin 'some' African American communities in a hard, rough and obvious way. Look close and you'll see it's killin all communities, but again we seem to be the first and worst," I told her emphatically. "Give you a simple example. Greedy folk have to have money so they use folk to get it. They hire them for minimum wage or as little as possible while they're taking home record amounts of money. (Chris Rock said minimum wage is another way of bosses saying, 'I'm paying you what I have to and if I could, I'd pay you less.) Those hired are already poor or lower income so they have to take the jobs they can get. Those folk stay poor so education can be poor for them and their kids. Their health suffers because health costs are out of sight in part based on greed. Recession comes along in large part due to greed. Who gets hurt the worst and first? The poorest and often the darkest do, at least percentage-wise. But guess what? All that 'greed gas' is hurtin others and sooner or later creeps up and in on lots of middle income folks. Killing me (them) softly, you might say."

"So," she said, "you're saying these gases are impacting other folk all along, but if they're not the most vulnerable they will *just die slower*, so to speak." "Bottom line," I said, "these gases, if not taken care of, will ultimately spread *and poison* everyone." "So," she said, "I guess your point would also be we can't blame the canary for dying? The canary is not the problem, the gases are. That's the point isn't it?" she said. "Indeed," I said, "and Negroes are surely not totally responsible for all the gases that found their way through the cracks in our communities."

"Teanna," I said, "What really bothers me is that some White folk are lookin down on us even more these days. They're talkin stuff like 'even their own people (Bill Cosby and others) are sayin Black folk are more dysfunctional than other folk.' That means racism is off the hook cuz it's our entire fault now, and never mind the racist practices of the past and present in the US of America." I paused for a minute and waited. Finally she responded, "Agreed, but I don't think Cosby and others are saying we're more dysfunctional than anyone else. I think they're just hot because they care and they see the damage we're doing to our own communities. They acknowledge the consequences of racism, and still say we have to start fixin the US of America by taking personal responsibility, making good choices and fixing our own communities."

I fully agreed, but said, "The US of America in large part created the race and poverty problems over several hundred years and if that same US of America doesn't kick in as well and continue to uncreate what it helped create, then long term change is dead in the water."

I went on to share my thoughts on why the 1964 Civil Rights Act and other legislation only got enforced with "teeth" for such a short period of time. I told her that twelve or so years after the passage of the 1964 Civil Rights Act, Caucasians started talking about reverse discrimination, or as I say when I'm feeling a tad sarcastic, they started "playin the reverse discrimination card." Things steadily went downhill after that. Told her I remembered an article I had read, that shared how the same thing happened one hundred years earlier. In 1865, after the Civil War, reconstruction took place for about twelve years till 1877. A hue and cry went out sayin things like, "We've done enough for Black folk" and now Whites are suffering discrimination. That was in the 1870s! Different words, same argument, same results.

"Anyway," I said to Teanna, "that same government that 'put us down' must *partly* be responsible for lifting us up and it might take more than a minute. It needs to meet us halfway for real change to take place." "Sure," I said, "Black folk gotta stay in school, we got to stop killin each other, stop having babies out of wedlock, stop drugs, stop using the 'N'-word and those violent lyrics about women and all that God-awful stuff. But if we're growing up in communities with significant dysfunction that this country helped to create, then this country has to help do the *uncreatin*; not by a handout but by a 'help out.' Man named, Charles King, former head of the Urban Crisis Center in Atlanta said somethin like, 'You can't cripple a man and then complain about the way that he walks.' Man, at least give the brother a cane," I say, "Meet him half way. Help a brother out."

Told her I was reading that only three percent of kids who qualify for such a program as Head Start actually are able to participate because of lack of funding. "That's a program that some say works for a lot of kids, by helping them keep up, so they don't get disillusioned with school. Helps them feel like they're as smart as anyone else. I don't know politics but I say why not give money to that kind of program? That's not a *handout,* that's a *help* out. Maybe it's not all that simple because money alone doesn't ensure a good education for all. I also told her there are programs helping folk of color all over the US of A, but they simply don't have enough funding. We seem to be more willing to send folk to prisons than fund programs that would keep them out. But Teanna," I said, "that's not my point, my point is government and the people *both* have responsibility."

Teana said, "The government isn't going to do anything near as dramatic as in the 60s because the people back then were pushin the issue, marchin and protestin and the government responded. So," she said, "if change is going to come, communities have to organize, do their part and make their voices heard." I responded and said, "The reason that approach was so effective in the 60s was because the middle class kicked in big time along with poor folk, and there were national leaders like King and others pushin this. Presently many poor communities and middle class folk are too strapped day to day to organize effectively, thus makin this go around much more complex than in the 60s. Middle class folk I know, or a lot of them, are one check away from the poor house, and so instead of lookin around, they're lookin straight ahead, and when their day is done, straight ahead is in the bed. Next day they gotta do it all over again."

Barely takin a breath I said, "If poor Black folk, (many of which are workin poor) have to support themselves and their kids, to fight against drugs in their community, against violence, drop-outs, stop outs, opt-outs, hold a job or two, and keep up a home, it's a pipe dream to expect their vision, hope, perseverance, independence or capacity to increase in any substantive way. That's especially true when, too often, we're talkin generational poverty and all those psychological and

187

social consequences. There'll always be individual success stories, but the masses will continue to suffer. And we sure can't think these folks have time to organize and rally."

She asked me if I really thought the middle class were too strangled with their own challenges to substantively reach out to the poor and help create a movement in sustained and meaningful ways and in mass. We both pondered this and felt like, indeed it had a lot of merit to it. Doesn't mean nobody is doing anything, just means the miner's canary is up on them as they are now the vulnerable ones as well

We ended up agreeing on a lot and definitely agreed on one big thing: the system of materialism that was perfected through the institution of slavery, which relegated Black people to the function of objects for material gain, is the same sickness that is starting to strangle the middle class in all demographic categories. Not like slavery but it's the same greed that is stretchin the middle class folk to the hilt. Exorbitant prices and profits while too many companies lay off, pay off and close up shop headin for cheap labor in other lands, without regard for folks they're puttin out of work or puttin to work. Same greed that disregarded Blacks is disregarding the White working class and middle class. The root is materialistic self-interest that drives **everything** at the expense of **everyone**.

Have to revisit a point here: Black and White are both getting strangled by this greed. But remember the difference makes the difference. Two people being laid off, one Black and one White, with equal qualifications, who will most likely find another job first, all things being equal, so to speak? You know the answer, and don't say, "it just depends," unless you say, "by and large it will depend on color." Not trying to rub this in, but it is important to share clear examples. So here is a clear example based on a powerful research study with the following result: a white man with a known felony conviction was more likely to be called back for a second job interview than an equally qualified Black applicant without criminal record. According to the researcher, the study was done in Milwaukee because its demographics are representative of many urban areas across the country (Pager, 2003). And by the way, the applicants were sent to 350 places of employment and the researcher, a White female who at the beginning of her research, thought a criminal record would trump race, won a research honor, in part, for the thorough nature of her analysis.

A similar study was conducted in New York City several years later by the same researcher with very similar results. So I say to myself," folk would rather hire someone with a criminal record than hire me with no record." Believe me, I'm all for givin folk a criminal a second chance but I gotta say allowing race to trump a criminal record is a crime of human humiliation.

I'm tellin you all this stuff, not to rub it in or to say, "I gotcha." I'm tellin you because it's part of wakin up Black in America for me; dealin with ugly stereotypes and their consequences and tryin to figure out how to remain that loving human being my parents tried to teach me to be. I'm not the only Person of Color wrestling with this either.

So my friends, particularly of lighter hue, one thing you can do is when you hear that Black people are always *playing the race card* or that the reason we don't have jobs is because we don't try hard enough, speak up. Say, "it ain't so!" When you hear folk saying some form of affirmative action may still be necessary don't be so quick to disagree. That's a start.

Well Teanna and I went at this conversation hard and like all our conversations, it left me with a lot to think about. Like I said she keeps me on my toes.

NEWS FLASH OVER

Before I leave this subject, I will tell you one thing that is plain as day. Then I want to tell you about a second related thing. First, Afro-Americans aren't just runnin their mouth talkin about racism and waitin on folk to give them something. All over this country they are volunteering as mentors, big brothers and sisters, care givers, academic supporters and the like to help our young folk. They are startin non-profits to address every issue under the sun in African American communities. You name the service and there are folk of African descent in the communities doing it and gettin little pay or none to help lift folk up that need a hand liftin themselves. Colored folk do more than just talk about how bad racism is. They are reaching up and reaching out to help themselves and each other.

Secondly, I need to throw a word in about two of the Revs in the African American community. Reverend Al and Reverend Jesse get pot shots thrown at them all the time for speaking up everywhere and anywhere for Black folk and even White folk sometimes. I remember when Rev. Jesse was up in Minnesota speakin out for a bunch of farmers, none of whom shared his complexion.

Anyway the Revs get a lot of grief for actin like they speak for all Colored folk and for supposedly blamin everything on racism. My view is that they don't seem to be claimin to speak for all Black people, but chances are they're speakin for some, nor do they blame racism for everything. Media sets it up that they talk for all Negroes, even though everyone knows that it's not possible for one or even two people to speak for an entire race. Here's what happens when the Revs talk about the needs of Black Americans or about some instance they see as racism. First the media makes them out as Black spokesmen, like I said. Then some White folk jump on them for blamin race for everything. Some Black folk answer, "They're not speaking for me," like they need to defend themselves so the Revs won't reflect on them. "No need!" I say. Let the Revs say what they want and let folk think what they want, but please don't act like you have to defend yourself "against" them or make sure you get a comfortable distance from them. You're free to agree with some things and disagree with others like you would with anyone else speakin out publically. Black folks should be free to have opinions like White folks.

Most White folk don't feel the need to defend their race to Black people, every time someone White says stuff. I don't think it's assumed that there are just a few White leaders who speak for all Whites like it is for Blacks. I say, "Relax my brothers and sisters," and let folk be who they are with all of their strengths and weaknesses and pray God leads them to do the next right thing. Don't shoot the messenger, shoot the message if you don't like it, and let the messenger live to speak another day. Who knows when it might be you that needs speakin for?

More importantly than all that is this: whether I agree or disagree with the Revs, I know if they weren't out hollerin for this or that right, or against this or that injustice, I bet you my left big toe (or my right one), a whole lot more stuff would go unreported, unsolved and unrecognized. I mean swept under the carpet big time. I also bet many of the folk they're standin up for and givin a voice to are glad someone is hearin them. I'm guessin the Revs feel like, if they don't make noise and are all quiet and nonchalant about stuff, no one will pay attention. I have to say that, sadly in many cases, it's true. Squeaky wheel often does get the oil or at least the attention and some things need attention brought to them. Are the Revs right all the time? "No!" I say, "Introduce me to that person who is."

Finally in listening to the two Revs, I'm hearin 'em talk about racism a whole lot, but I am also hearin them talk about Afro-

Americans cleanin up their own act. Just because the news chooses to put them on TV only when they are fightin against racism, doesn't mean that's all they stand for. Fact is most Black "leaders" who deal with race, on the big stage or on the small stage, talk about self-help and responsibility right alongside racism. So I thank the Revs for fightin the fight in the way they think they're supposed to, and I pray God will continue to lead them on their path.

Chapter 16

Is It Racism or Just Blacks Misbehavin?

(By the way, I am easing back into my trip with Briana.)

I told you before, dealin with racism sure doesn't negate the importance of Blacks dealing with personal responsibility and vice versa. So it's true that some Colored folk gotta start takin responsibility for themselves in a big way. (By the way, White folk got a lot of house cleaning to do too; did I mention that?) Most of the problems of drugs and violence are comin primarily from poorer *segments* of the Negro community. Those *segments* not only have had to deal with racism, the very condition in which they find themselves is, in *part*, due to past and current racism. Bottom line is that over time, the problems of past racism got meshed with the consequent and subsequent behavior of those on the receiving end and became so intertwined it's impossible to say what is causing what at this point. It's best to simply realize both past and present racism and personal responsibility need to be addressed simultaneously and in very significant ways.

Either way, Black folk gotta step up and stop doing things that are inexcusable. Like I always say, "There are a lot of good reasons for messin up, but no good excuses." I can understand the reason for many of the dysfunctional behaviors exhibited by some of my Black brothers and sisters and empathize, but I can't allow those reasons to be long-term excuses for bad behavior. If we want to see heaven in our own faces and the faces of other brothers and sisters, some of us really have to stop the madness and earn it. Similarly, I can understand the challenges many Whites folks have in facing the prejudice and racism that exists within themselves and in society. I can understand the reasons behind the fear, anxiety and even frustration about their role in eliminating discrimination and racism. However, the reasons are no excuse for abdicating responsibility. They too have to earn their stripes as conscientious and interconnected citizens of the US of America.

Another thing though; it's not just poor Negroes dealin with racism either. Middle and upper income Colored folk are also dealing with racism while they are raisin *their* kids, working hard and payin taxes. Study came out recently asking a lot of questions about why there are problems in the Black community. Middle income and poor Colored folk saw it different as to the reasons, but the one thing they agreed on was that racism is still a big issue for *any* Black person. What's my point? Point is when racism comes up, most folk start talking about how Black folk have to take responsibility and then life will be fine. I have to say, it's truly "out'ta lunch" to suggest the only issue of race in America is that Blacks in lower-income areas aren't actin right, and if they would just act right, racism wouldn't be much of a factor in the US of America. Many high, middle and lower income folks are "actin right" and these actin right African American folk still have race prejudice nippin at their heels; just ask them. Then ask yourself, what earthly reason would a person, who is financially makin it in the US of America, have for saying racism is still a problem for them unless it was true? Who needs the headache? One reason might be, makin it is more than makin money. They're still experiencing racism and prejudice and they still want to feel a sense of honor and dignity, in their own country. Folk have pride!

Even in my diversity workshops, participants more and more have been trying to *race away from race*. It happens most often this way: when folk talk about race with any fervor or at any length, someone shoots their hand up and says with earnestness and often with irritation, "Diversity means more than race; it's a lot of things." Then a whole bunch of folk start

194

nodding their head in agreement and rattlin off everything under the sun about what diversity is. They say it's gender, age, personality, class, sexuality, temperament, education level, two-parent or one-parent families, military background, occupation and some even say it's about who is left-handed or right-handed, actin somehow as if they all have the same import. In effect, that shuts down any meaningful talk about race and dilutes the whole discussion by introducing so many factors that you can't even remember what's all included in diversity. Folk conclude since we all have so many differences of so many kinds, we're all in the same boat.

Of course diversity is more than race! But it's still race at the core in the US of America, and if we think we can get away with spreading it out like all diversity factors carry the same emotional explosiveness, then we're in a world of hurt, playin a dangerous game. If you want to fix a disease you gotta get at the core of it, and the core got poisoned early on with racism and materialism acting like two wings of a vulture, ravishing everything in its path. I care about everyone's pain, so I am not suggestin that other kinds of diversity aren't important. I'm saying if the core is rotten with racism, we got to focus on that big time, and not act like it's just another thing.

I know this is a touchy subject, I mean, tryin not to leave any-one out of the fairness picture. However I have learned a few things in my day that I think apply. One is that focus does not mean exclusion; it just means focus. Focusin on race does not entail excluding other kinds of diversity. Secondly, when you focus on something, it can often spread and impact other as-pects you are not focusing on, like a magnifying glass focuses the light of the sun on a spot and then a fire starts and impacts everything around it. The Civil Rights days of the 60s initially focused on rights for Blacks, but eventually impacted many folks including Caucasians. We're gonna need some serious help from the Almighty to create the right spirit and balance so we can more forward without leaving out anyone.

The Flipside: The US of America Needs a "Racial Facial"

Speaking of history and healing (which is not exactly what I was speakin of), I forgot to tell you, before I closed the newspaper, and after I read the comics, I caught an article about the mayor of Charleston, South Carolina, proposing to build the biggest slave monument in the United States. It would be built right in Charleston, South Carolina, and it will tell the whole story of slavery like it has not been told. He is a White fella and I congratulate him on his vision and hope he can follow through on it. This could produce some real healing if it's done right. Someone said somethin about it being like the Holocaust Museum in Washington, DC. I haven't been, but I heard it is a deeply moving human experience and makes you really stop and feel.

Getting back to my time with Briana, I thought about that slavery museum because I was sharing with her something I read in the paper just before I read the comics. It was taking place in a Southern city close to where I lived at the time. Article was about this old Confederate ship that sunk during the Civil War and how some folk found it way down under and were pulling it up from the ocean floor and restoring it. Many Southern Caucasians seemed excited about it. In that same city, folk of African descent were excited about tryin to get a monument built for Denmark Vesey, a former slave who laid a big plot to overthrow some slave owners and set a whole bunch of Colored folk free, back in the slave days. He was betrayed as I recall it, and got caught and hanged. Blacks see him as a hero that deserves to be saluted.

Now, like I said, both the restoration of the Confederate ship and the efforts to get a monument built for Vesey were occurring at the same time in that same Southern city. All depends on how you see things and what life you have lived as it relates to how you view these two events. To many Caucasian folk, Vesey was a criminal conspirator and potential killer. Then a whole lot of Negroes look at that Confederate ship and view the folk on that ship, not as heroes, but as traitors to America and exploiters of Black folk. So where is the truth in all this? As the article says, the truth is shaped by "whoever has the microphone at the time" (Brinson, 2001). If I had the microphone at the time you know what I'd say: "How can you compare a monument for someone fighting for freedom for enslaved people to someone wanting to honor and restore a ship that was a tool for preventing freedom?" But then that's just my view.

You see, the problem with the race discussions is that they are so personal and so emotional. And with all that feeling, everyone needs to be allowed a voice; everyone must be heard. A lot of folk, includin myself, at times, wish we were the only ones to have a voice about some things. So I try hard to listen, but I react instinctively at times. "Heritage, not hate," is what I'm told regarding such things as this Confederate ship. I say, "I'm glad you don't hate me anymore, but now can you stop slappin me in the face." Well that's an instinctive response, and sometimes it's good for things to come out that way, but sometimes it does damage. Takes a lot of fortitude to stay at the table when we start talking from "instinct," but the reality is that it's just going to happen sometimes and we've all got to stay at the table. Tricky business this race stuff. Bahá'í Writings state this about the challenges that remain on this journey to justice: "A long and thorny road, beset with pitfalls still remains untraveled..." (Effendi, 1937, p. 54). The terms "thorny" and "pitfalls" tell the story.

One way or another there's polarizing issues like this all over the US of America. What choice do we have but to start listenin, hearin and feelin each other? Remember, listening with the heart is not a wimpy response. It opens up possibilities that stay closed when minds and hearts are clogged up. Friend of mine, who trained me in mediation skills, said folks have dropped huge law suits amountin to millions of dollars in some cases, just because someone said they were sorry. They felt heard, they felt acknowledged. Seen it many times, when folk are thinkin money can fix something. I find what folk really want is for someone to care in word and deed. It often starts with genuine words.

Same friend said she worked on a suicide hotline. She spent most of her time just listening, acknowledging and makin folk feel heard. Many times that single response prevented them from carrying out the act. Over and over I have heard people being asked what they wanted after some tragedy, and invariably they will say something like, "I just want someone to come here and say they are sorry," or "I just want someone who will listen to me and give me a real response." Another thing I hear: "No ones seems to care what happened." I say carin and connecting can lead to correcting. That deep carin can only come from a transformed mind and heart.

Thinking about all this race business made us both a little bit tired on our drive up for Briana to give her talk. We sure don't want to assume all those Caucasian folk who want to restore that ship are prejudiced and don't like Black folk. That's the easy way out, to just paint everyone with a broad brush … as being prejudiced. "Can't let ourselves do that," we say to each other, because we don't want that broad brush labeling Negroes either.

So what goes through both of our heads is real similar. We still wonder if White folk go through all these changes. Does being fair mean that much to them? Do they put the kind of effort into being fair that many of us do? Or do they just write us off when we talk about this stuff? Do they think about their behavior and action on a daily basis as it relates to how folk of African descent are treated and dealt with in this society? Do they think about their role in makin things better; how they can be just in their views on race? Do they even think about having a role to play? Our conclusion is that some do and some don't, but we can't place a number on either group. That is a cause of concern for both of us. These are things we wonder about, think about, talk about and get tired about during an otherwise beautiful day for a drive.

Here I am again, wearin myself out with another friend, trying to sort all this through. I said it before, but I'll say it again. "I'm gettin older; so energy is a big thing in my life and today I'm runnin low." And also repeatin myself is becoming a way of life. As my mom says, "Of all the things I ever lost, I miss my mind the most."

Thinkin what we need in the US of America is a *"racial facial."* We, with a little help from above, need to change the face of race—need to see it all together different than we have in the past. That's exactly what we need, a complete and total *racial facial*! Can you imagine that all this human diversity was created for any other reason but to mix and blend in harmony and bring out the best in each other? That's the new *face of race.*

A White Man Spreading Some Light

Where was I? Oh, with my office manager, Briana, arriving at the school. By the way she is very passionate, smart as a whip and can sing too! She's a bit petite, but when she opens her mouth to sing, the room vibrates like she's ten feet tall. Not sure how that all works. I know it has to do with the diaphragm and vocal cords, but I still get amazed at how something so beautiful and vibrant can come from one so small. She also uses that voice to give real good speeches and she gave a very inspiring talk on race relations to a gymnasium full of high school students. It really seemed to hit home with a lot of them, that I could see anyway. It's no small feat to keep a gym full of high school students interested.

The program ran late because, not only did Briana speak, but there was music and all sorts of things to bring home the point that race unity is important. Some of the teachers were gettin antsy to get back to class. Their students had just missed one class to sit in the gym and hear about race relations and now were about to miss another one if this program didn't stop and stop quick! I saw the principal, who happened to be a White fella, headin straight for the microphone because the program was runnin over time. Thought to myself he was going to cut things off and be real polite about what a good program this was and talk about how important it was that we all be nice to each other. Then he'd tell those students to get their hind parts movin and high tail it back to class and "don't be late!" I was already gatherin my things, so we could get to our car ahead of the rush of students racin back to class. Well I was dead wrong. Just as he got to the microphone, he pulled a piece of paper out of his pocket where he had taken some notes. He looked out at the audience with a kind, calm and sincere expression on his face and thanked everyone for a wonderful program. Then he asked them to settle back down because he had some things to say. He proceeded, thoughtfully and earnestly, looking at his notes and telling everyone how important this day had been. And that learning to get along with each other and bein brave enough to come out of our comfort zones was real important and that neither race could ignore this challenge. He made something like eight different important points about the need to deal with race and make things fair. Everyone was paying attention as he was talkin very *humanely and sanely.*

He talked about ten minutes or so, maybe longer, and didn't mention anything about students and teachers needin to rush back to class. Briana and I were impressed. After his talk, I recalled that when I first walked into the gym I saw this White fella, around my age, kickin it around with four Black male students, who looked like they were, what we used to call "hip." They all seemed very relaxed and having a playful time with each other. This caught my eye because I'm still not used to seein that kind of comfort level between White men his age in a suit and tie and young, hip-lookin brothers. Well turned out this man was the principal and it's lookin like he was tryin to practice what he preached. I asked a few teachers about him on the way out and they said that's just how he is.

Remember, when I said Briana and I wondered if White folk thought they had a role to play in makin things better between the races, and we thought some are dos and some are don'ts? Well I think this man was a doer and it sure ended our few hours in the gym on the upbeat.

It's powerful for African American folk to see Caucasian folk stand up, in front of God and everyone, and say clearly and with conviction that how we treat each other across races is important and back it up with action. To some, his effort may seem small, but I know where that school was located. It's in an area where race is no joke and folk can make your life hell if they want to. Briana and I talked about this on the way back home, agreeing with each other that such talk and action lifts a burden from our hearts, at least for awhile—almost like a spiritual connection takes place. We also agreed that people who are in a leadership role, like a principal, can make a huge difference. If he had just closed the program or rushed everyone back to class, that would've sent a message that this was just another program to sit through. Leadership has to lead, and he led. We smiled a lot on the way home. "Keep hope alive," as Rev Jesse would say. I heard motivational speaker Les Brown say something like, "Stand up for what you believe because you can fall for anything. In life you're either sayin hello or goodbye. If you're not on the way, you're in the way." Les can fire up a crowd too.

Chapter 17

From Hope to Hurt and Hurt Back to Hope

'Bout the time I was feeling happy and touched by that principal, I got a call from my brother the actor. After talkin for a minute he sort of "went off" about a major movie award ceremony program. Talked bout how few CNBAAPA were represented, nominated, or even present at the ceremony. I told him about an article I read in the paper that said the reason more People of Color or CNBAAPA folk don't receive those kinds of awards is that the same full-blown opportunities just don't exist for Colored folk in Hollywood; in front or behind the camera. Went on to say there probably would be no change in this in the near future. This wasn't some Colored person saying that, to my recollection, it was a Caucasian man who was some sort of Hollywood insider. He talked about how Hollywood honchos put folks in stereotypic roles. Maybe the article was correct, maybe not, but that's what it said, and that's what I've seen with a very few exceptions.

Well, I told my brother to try not to let it bother him too much, though I acknowledged that it bothered me. Bothers him more because he is an actor and has witnessed this stuff up close and personal. He was on a soap opera for a while and took the risk of talking to his producers about some racial and cultural dynamics he felt needed to be considered. One of his concerns was that all the writers were White and they often wrote parts for Black actors in stereotypic ways or without taking into consideration the cultural context of how Black people relate and interact with each other. Producers acknowledged his points and said they were going to do something about it. In this case they did nothing. He has never been sure if that backfired on his career and if somehow the word got out that he was a "troublemaker." Overall he felt it did some damage.

203

I recall watching another award show around the time of the conversation with my brother. I didn't see a CNBAAPA person for almost forty minutes, and I have to say I got a little peeved. I mean I did not see a brother or sister on stage, back stage, in the audience, anywhere. I said to myself, "Where have all the Negroes gone?

Like I said, we have some Colored folk in the movies, but I watch those award shows and see what I see and don't see what I don't see. And if you accuse me of perhaps missing some Black folk, then I still say, if I missed just a few, I rest my case. Too often Negroes are expected to be satisfied with just a taste of the American dream and grateful for just "bein in the game." Well, I'm grateful for a whole lot of things in the US of America, but bein in the game is only the start, not the finish.

Believe it or not, I worked my way up to watching one of the 2008 major award programs. Try again, I told myself. Except Oprah and a very few others, whoa, what can I say, but the Colored folk were way gone! And by the way, now that they have DVD's you can watch special features that show how the movie was made and who was involved in the making of the movie. Unless it is a movie with a Black director nary a Black person is to be seen even behind the scenes.

Race Prejudice Finds Me without Me Looking for It

Some might suggest I'm just lookin for things to rumble and grumble about; I'd say, I didn't have to look for things—things found me, and in this case they were all White … or mostly. What I was actually "lookin for" was to enjoy the awards program and relax a little; that's what I was really looking for. Same when I watch DVD's. I just want some enjoyment and sometimes just an escape from day to day life. Anyway my brother and I talked a while and then I told him I had to go. He said he was fine and that he just needed to get that out of his system.

Briana kept glancing over at me during the conversation with my brother. After I hung up she looked at me as if to say, "What's up?" Told her I'd tell her later, and we went back to talkin about our time at the school. That's how it goes sometimes. Race can just find you during any day without you lookin for it. It can be real sweet like at the high school or real sour like the conversation with my brother.

NEWS FLASH

Oh no, this can't be happenin again! Radio has a sad and tragic story on the news. Turns out a young unarmed Black man got shot and killed by a policeman. Young man had a bunch of outstanding parking tickets or something like that. He was running away when the cops saw him. They caught him and said they thought he was goin for a gun. They shot and killed him. *Turned out there was no gun.* Radio is saying that the police have shot and killed several Black folk in that city in the last ten plus years. You guessed it; no white folks have met a similar fate. It sounds like Black leaders have been all over the city to look into these killings, but are feeling like very little is happening. So inevitably riots started, angry people emerged, a sad mother cried, and CBNAAPA leaders everywhere wanted answers. Black Panthers were on the scene saying they wanted to change things by any *divine means necessary.* Of course the mayor is calling for calm. Oh my, I'm speechless. This stuff messes with my head and heart. Don't worry I 'm gonna wait till the full story comes out to decide what I think. Either way this has gotta stop!

Police killed a guy in another city recently, shot him so many times I can't remember. I guess they were found not guilty on that one. Our Black brother is still real dead, and he was not a crook of any kind according to reports. It was just a *mistake*, folk were told. A lot of CNBAAPA folk been killed in similar circumstances over the years and whatever happens in this case, another young Black person is dead and it appears, though he had troubles in his life, he was no kind of awful kid. Like I said, I think policeman have a tough job so I'm not down on them as a group, but they need to come out and admit they have some prejudiced apples in their crowd, and they got to get them out! Have to make a mission out of doing it. Talk about fair, that's fair! Cops need to take measures to weed out the rotten eggs from the police force, just like Black folk are told to do. We are told we have to control our community better, and we need to take more responsibility for the bad apples in our communities. I say to the police, "you have to control your 'community' too and take more responsibility for bad apples in it."

This is makin me think of a friend of mine, we'll call Chris, tryin to return a product he bought from a major discount store. Apparently some items like what he was returnin had been stolen in recent days. So the police told him he was going to have to come back to the manager's office and have a talk. Actually put handcuffs on him and paraded him across the store in plain sight of everyone. Now this is the town where he owns a business and where he does a whole lot of work. They figured out he made a legitimate purchase of the items. They let him go; damage done, humiliation complete. This has been a huge heartache for Chris, even had trouble sleepin for awhile. Why did they have to handcuff him and walk him across the store? What about all those folks who saw him? I gotta get off this subject.

I hope God hears my prayers loud and clear tonight because I need help. The inexplicable shootin, killin and beatin of African American folk, young and old, happens far too often.

NEWS FLASH OVER

Not so fast, I guess. **NEW FLASHING** again—In fact, three flashes involving friends, family and me and all with the police. All of them just happened in like a forty-eight-hour period. All this served as another reminder to me that, indeed, I'm not crazy for feeling what I feel about the complexity of race in the US of America.

> 1. I asked a young Black mechanic acquaintance to come by and look at a problem with my car. We'll call him Jimmy—tryin to support Jimmy's up and coming business. Jimmy comes by, and I'm in the house and don't know he's outside workin on my car. Apparently he started to put a jack on my car and a policeman, well call Jorge, drives by, stops, gets out and asks him for his name and ID (happened to be a Latino police-man). Jimmy gets real upset and tells the cop he's not doing anything but changing my tire. Jorge tells him the tire doesn't look flat to him. Jimmy gets testy with him, and Jorge gets testy right back. Jimmy calls me on the phone and asks me to come outside. I come out-side and Jorge, who I recognized and who I had a lot of friendly discussions with in the past, tells me his ver-sion of what happened. Meanwhile Jimmy, who has had some bad experiences with the police, is sayin if he had been White this wouldn't have happened. Jorge said he'd have asked anyone the same question. Told him it's against the law to work on cars in the street. Jimmy just kept getting hotter.... I put my two cents worth in, tellin Jimmy that we've had a lot of robberies

in the neighborhood lately and our neighborhood association had asked the police to be particularly alert to anything that could be suspicious. I also told him I totally understood his feelings given his and some of his friends' experiences with cops. Made that real clear, but also told him, I would have wanted Jorge to ask him what he was doing with my car. I asked him if he could understand that. He sort of nodded reluctantly as if to say I understand, but I'm still mad. I asked Jorge if he could understand how Jimmy felt. He said yes and that he knew some cops who were like that, but he was not one of them. Well, they still went at it for a while longer, and Jorge told Jimmy that he didn't like the fact that he was getting all up in his face because he was just doing his job. Jimmy couldn't seem to let it go. Jorge was pretty patient, finally sayin he was going to leave and let it go because he knew me. After he left, Jimmy and I talked some more. Both of us agreed this is tough emotionally on Blacks because it's humiliating when you're just makin your livin and have to justify it. On the other hand, we said, cops deal all day long with people denyin, lyin and tryin to get over, so cops get conditioned to be suspicious. Person can be drivin seventy miles an hour in a thirty mile an hour zone and they'll still make up some kind of excuse and get in a cop's face. Can't *totally* blame the cops, even though we know some of them are profilin.

I told Jimmy we got to heal these rifts because if we just let them go, they end up lockin in an almost irreversible tension. Told him I would like it if he would sit down with Jorge and talk this through. He said he would. I went and found Jorge and asked the same thing. Told him when things go wrong we can't just walk away with a bad taste in our mouths. Jorge said he'd be glad to talk with Jimmy. I tried to arrange it, but it never worked out. It was the right idea though.

2. Picked up my son-in-law Karim from school to give him and my granddaughter a ride home. I told him the story I just told you, and he had one to tell me. Told me he and his wife, Angela (my daughter), and their youngest daughter, Zaynab, were ridin home after they'd purchased a car. They didn't have tags on the car yet. The police stopped them. He said three cops basically surrounded the car, one on each side and one in the rear. One was talkin to Angela while another one was talkin to him at the same time. I guess this is a tactic to make sure no one is under duress. Karim was very nervous, but my daughter was mostly okay. Bottom line is Karim and Angela were technically in the wrong for not having tags and drivin, but at the same time needed to get the car home. Police were no doubt especially alert and cautious because there had been some car jackings and shootings that night. Karim said he was anxious even after he got home. Lot of scary thoughts went through his head when the car was being surrounded. Easy to flash back on bad experiences you and others like you have had. Can feel like life-or-death. May have felt like a simple traffic stop to lighter-hued folk, but not to him.

3. On my way to a meeting that night I was telling another young Black male friend, Neil, these two stories. By way of background, he is like an uncle to my granddaughters. He told me of an experience he'd had the day before. He had taken my granddaughters and his daughter to the park. He was playing with them and all of a sudden, three policemen came up on him

and told him to get/sit on the ground. He was upset and confused, but he did it. He was agitated and asked them what he was doing wrong. They said that some lady had called and said there was a man "watching" young children at the park. He said, "I'm watching them because they're my children." He said the policemen were pretty nice after he explained, as it became obvious they were all together. Said he could not help but think that, if he were a White man watching his children at the park, no one would have called the cops; or, if the cops had come, he wondered if they'd have ordered him to the ground. He felt like they were doing their job but at the same time he was upset about the way they did it. The main thing he said bothered him was the accusation of whoever called the police assuming he must be up to something because he was with children. My question is why the three policemen couldn't have just had a conversation with him before ordering him to the ground?

Neil and I spoke about this later and he said when he is in that park now, lighter-hued and darker-hued people are sort of distant and, by their non-verbal communication, act like they are wondering the same thing. What is he doing with these children? He's not sure what's up with that. Is it because the children are all girls? Is it about wondering what a Black male is doing with four children who all look like they have different parents, because of their different shades of brown? He said he's not sure, but something is bothering them about his Black male self bein with these children.

Neil is the same young man who has been randomly stopped by the police coast to coast. He's a great guy, not a trouble-maker of any kind, just trying to live life.

NEWS FLASH

I just called Neil in LA to ask him about a shirt he had given to my son-in-law. I really liked it and wanted to see if he could find one for me. He said it was a one of a kind. I messed with him for not givin the shirt to me and for givin it to my son-in-law instead. As he was about to hang up, he asked me how my book was coming. I told him fine. He said "I got stopped again." I asked him why. He told me in California you have to have a light that illuminates your back license plate, and he got stopped for not having his illuminated. He got a ticket. Only problem was, his was illuminated. He went to the precinct to protest. The cop's word against his, so guess who lost? Some of you still gotta be thinking what's with this guy? He must be doing something wrong to attract all this attention. I'll say it again; Neil is just a good guy period. Not a saint, just a good guy!

NEWS FLASH OVER

All three of these scenarios came my way in the same forty-eight hours. The police were "just doing their job" (still say there was no reason to make Neil get down on the ground), and the young men were essentially just living their life. History and hurt created the reactions of everyone. So who is going to make all of this right? Who is going to step up and help break these patterns, this historical and debilitating cycle?

TRIPLE NEWS FLASH OVER but I might as well tell you that, as I was proofreading this book it happened again. A friend of mine, we'll call him Jimmy, was in a bar one night with his brother, whom we'll call John, and another guy, whom we'll call Thomas. Thomas had a few too many and was being obnoxious, so the two brothers decided to leave because they didn't want any part of that. Well, Thomas left too and the brothers tried to avoid him. All of sudden, Jimmy felt a hand on his shoulder, and he pushed it off and turned around. Turned out it was a policeman. The police started beatin Jimmy up and at least two other policeman joined in. One used a taser gun on Jimmy. John saw his brother getting beat so he jumped in. Well, they got arrested and now are in a heap of trouble. They had charges for assaulting a police officer filed against them.

I tried to look at this from all angles and seemed to me it could have been avoided. One thing I know is that you don't walk up behind someone at night and put a hand on their shoulder! It makes no sense. Again I was not there, so I can't vouch for all this. I met Jimmy over the phone because he's working on a project for me and the mother of his girlfriend recommended him. Seemed like a quiet kid and very respectful too. His girlfriend's mother, whom I fully trust, tells me he is a very good kid. He's trying to get an art career off the ground and keep his life right.

Jimmy and John can't afford a lawyer, and for some reason they're saying the court won't appoint one. I'm gonna keep an eye on this and help him in any way I can. I can't take all these young brothers bein carted off to jail or having their life ruined especially over something like this. It's easy to think John should have never jumped in. Well, I'll tell you all something: I try to be a morally and ethically high-minded person who definitely does not get in fights, but if I saw a bunch 'a cops beatin up my brother, I know it would be hard to just stand by and watch; maybe impossible. Just don't know if I could do it; that's my flesh and blood. Not sure you could either.

If I heard that some cops pulled over my college-aged, responsible son and his friend , out in the middle of nowhere and for no reason whatsoever, and then, with their guns drawn, made them get on their knees, taunted them and threatened to kill them, not sure, as a parent or family member what I would do. If my son had a gun pulled on him by a cop at a traffic stop— if he was doing nothing wrong in the first place—and told to "get out of here before I kill you," not sure what I would do. And if my brother had a gun put to his head by a cop and threatened for no reason, I'm not sure I wouldn't be tempted to do something about it. All these instances are true, no exaggeration and all for no reason. All were done to law-abiding citizens who are Black, with degrees, jobs and intelligence and all done to people I am close friends with or related to. (I mention degrees and jobs because there is a perception that this kind of thing happens only to poor Blacks who may "look suspicious.")

Wakin up Black in the US of America and wakin up White are not the same, folks. The rotten apples gotta go. Whew! Whose gonna stop the madness! W*e all are—we all have to pay attention!! Not just White folk, not just Black folk, not just the police, not just the activists, everyone.*

Well, as always, God, the universe or however you want to see it, sends me a little something good to help take some of the edge off, and it comes right on time. He gives me just enough so I can come back to some sanity and humanity. I got a call from a chief of police from a small town who was a White fella. He asked me to conduct diversity training for his police officers because he felt they needed it to better serve. He seemed like a genuine enough fella. Those kinds of calls help me through the day. When you're getting hit with a lot of emotional race stuff you need to feel, preferably up close and personal, there are White folk who care about this stuff. It's good to see this fella puttin his money where his mouth is and even better puttin his money where my mouth is and none too soon either.

NEWS FLASHES REALLY OVER

Chapter 18

Joy, Sorrow and More Joy

Anyway, I am more than relieved and grateful we got back in town (Columbia, South Carolina, my former residence) in time to go to the program being held on the state capitol grounds. I am attending this wondrous event with my friend Briana to round out our day. I can't tell you how much my heart was moved to be going to this dedication of a monument in honor of African Americans. It is the first such monument dedicated on state house grounds in the US of America. Perfect, this is happening in South Carolina, as Charleston was the major port of entry for a large percentage of the Africans made slaves in the United States. We ran into a dear African American friend, who is in her late seventies. My first thought was how moved she must be to see this happen in her lifetime; after all she must have seen and experienced wakin up Black in the US of America.

One of the major participants on the program was a White fella who was also a supporter for keepin the Confederate flag flying above the state capitol dome. He later supported a *compromise* to bring it down and put it in another place on the grounds of the state house. He worked on the Confederate stuff, at the same time he was supporting the African American monument and working on a committee for that. Folk are complicated, complex and sometimes just plain political; definitely not just one-sided.

The event itself was so very poignant. CNBAAPA folk and White folk attended in large numbers in the pouring rain. Speakers spoke with passion and the poems and music touched my soul. I remember the words of one of the poets who spoke so eloquently and reminded us that who was brought to America were *free men and women,* and they were made slaves. A country based on freedom stole theirs. She talked about the beauty of so many of these folks and the strength they had to have just to survive the middle passage. Hard to think about all this on the one hand and yet it was pride-producing at the same time. What superhuman fortitude and courage they had and what an inhumane trauma they must have experienced. Black folk have a lot of strong and mixed feelings about life in the US of America, and they can all come up in the same moment in the same emotional space.

Somethin about the way this poet was sayin all this touched me. As she was speaking I started reflecting on all those beautiful dark-skinned souls that ended up in South Carolina, probably petrified. Thought of all their achievements in spite of all and realized that out of all the previous monuments on these state house grounds, there was not one dedicated to any Black person before this one. Reflected on that for a minute and decided not to let it spoil the moment. No need to get testy on me for pointin that out, and please don't remind me how important it is to dwell on the positive. That's exactly what I did, but I told you before, I wish I didn't have to see what I see, know what I know and feel what I feel. I would have to be deaf, dumb, and fully blind not to notice that of the hundreds and thousands of Black folk who helped shape and build up the riches of the state of South Carolina, none was worthy of a monument on the state house grounds before this time. "Try not to think about that," I said to myself, and I let that go. That's past, I thought to myself; if I don't look right or left, I don't have to see any of that. So I looked straight ahead at the speakers and stayed in the moment.

I didn't let these thoughts bother me to the point that I could not soak in the beauty, elegance, and profound nature of the unveiling of this monument. Thank God, I got to see, feel, and experience this occasion. I even got to touch rocks that came

216

from the very places in Africa that my honored ancestors came from. I got to see physically sculpted representations of 300 years of African American history in South Carolina. Black and White teachers brought their students from all backgrounds to this event. Tourists were everywhere too. How sweet it was!

NEWS FLASH

Excuse me; I have to break in to my story to tell you about what I'm hearing at this moment on TV as I'm writing this book. It is about a small town in Florida that apparently is still segregated. A Black man, who was a former resident of this town, came back to visit. *He was trying to get a drink at a bar and was asked to go to the back where Colored folk are served.* It turns out everything in that town remains segregated. Both Black folk and White folk suggest that things are just that way and folk are too afraid to try and change it. I'll just leave that alone, but as I heard it while writing this book, I thought I should put it in. Wasn't lookin for race trouble, it found me.

NEWS FLASH OVER

It's About DIGNITY

The poet who spoke at the monument dedication, talked about how important it was for Black folk to feel **appreciated, acknowledged and recognized**. What she said there is profoundly real and accurate. At the heart of all of the hurt, pain, anger, and frustration that most Colored folk experience are issues of dignity, honor, respect, acknowledgement, and recognition. When the death of so many African American children, youth, and adults seems to be accepted as normal and nothing to really consider outside of the Black community, it appears folk don't really care. Where is the acknowledgement? Where is the dignity? When Colored men and women are targeted, then arrested, then thrown in jail for minimal offenses, sentenced longer, to the point of decimating their communities and destroying their family structure, where is the outcry that we have a problem in the US of America that we all have to face? When the poverty of children and particularly Children of Color is skyrocketing, where is the concern for these children? When folk of Color are still denied loans unfairly, are too often paid less for similar work, still largely ignored in terms of their history and contributions, have to put up with nooses as a joke, I ask myself, where is the dignity in all that; the sense that others respect and care for us as worthy human beings? When we are maligned for simply bringing up race as a factor in our lives what should we make of that?

When White folk are held up as national heroes, yet we know they despised people like us, how are we supposed to feel about being fully accepted U.S. Americans? (Yeah, I know I said that already but I'm on a roll and that one really irks me.) At the same time you know full well, if a Black person hated or degraded White folk but were somehow successful in their field or public service, they would not be memorialized by the US of America. They'd be on the demagogue list. Where is the honor for Black folk in that? When you can dominate a sport as an athlete, yet people who look like you are still considered as unfit to coach that sport and efforts to improve the situation with affirmative action are resented, what's up with that? The message is, "You don't matter," "You don't count," "You are dispensable." Where is any sense of recognition? Where is respect for CNBAAPA folk as human beings with aspirations and feelings with dreams and hopes and abilities?

When I have knowledge that folk with my complexion, male and female, were lynched in a party atmosphere the lynchings were often advertised ahead of time like a sporting event, yeah, I get angry. This of course was done or supported by the good citizens in the community, the reputable ones. Oh, and it's not so distant a time in history. I learned long ago the last recorded lynching in the US was in 1968. Some say 1998, with a Black man in Texas being dragged to death behind a truck. We're told these perpetrators were just a product of "the times." Come on now, burnin, hangin and butcherin people for sport and for no reason other than their color is pathological in any "time."

Knowing that the same mentality exists in its own form in too many parts of the US and is still minimized makes "the past" hard to forget. How can I feel darker-hued people are valued and not devalued in this country? How can I feel respected and safe, when I'm now hearing that some Black folk are havin classes for young African American males about how they should handle themselves if they ever get stopped by the police, so they don't get shot? How can I not feel folk of African descent are belittled, and dehumanized? Tell me and other Colored folk that our dignity and honor as human beings is not still under attack and assault.

Yes, I agree we've made great progress in race relations in the US of America. I already acknowledged that. At the same time, the consequences of our history of racism manifests itself in ways that cannot be ignored, cannot be relegated to simplistic notions of "hang in there," "get over it," "be positive and just try harder," "don't blame me, I never enslaved you," "what's past is past," and "don't play the race card."

This whole thing or much of it is about affording human beings a sense of dignity, nobility, honor, and recognition. That is what CNBAAPA folk want in America, and we don't want to be further humiliated by feeling like we have to beg for it or "shuffle" for it. Most of us won't, and if some of us end up

219

feelin we have to go along to get along, we'll resent it, resent you and probably not feel too great about ourselves. Who's that gonna help?

Please don't focus on some one point you disagree with to negate everything I'm saying. If there is something you disagree with, that's fine, but understands the overall point. I read this statement one day and it summed up what I'm trying to say:

> It is entirely human to fail if that which is the most important to people's self perception is denied them—namely, the dignity they derive from a genuine regard by others for their stature as human beings. No educational, economic, or political plan can take the place of this essential human need: it is not a need that businesses and schools, or even governments, can provide in isolation from the supportive attitude of society as a whole. (National Spiritual Assembly of the Bahá'ís of the United States, 1991)

Beautifully stated I'd say.

I guess my trip to that first African American monument brought out a lot of feelings and thoughts. Thanks for listening. One reason I think we all have to honestly get together about this stuff is because it's easy to get all clogged up inside and not be able to see anything else. When I get with folk who really care about this and aren't out to just shoot me down and we talk, I can see things more clearly and love more deeply. I can hear you too, if you're willing to talk with me and not dictate to me. I will if you will!

NEWS FLASH

When I am not in my dignified place, centered and spiritual, I can let my mood dictate my "race space." This was one of those times. I was in a cafe the other day havin a *bad race day* (some folk have bad hair days, I have bad race days). I was waitin to have lunch with a friend. I saw this Caucasian man in a suit and tie, and he was fiddlin with some things on the shelf. An item fell to the floor close to my feet. Normally I would have bent down to pick it up but on this day I was feelin a bit sensitive about race stuff and it flashed in my head, "Why should I stoop to pick this up for him?" In that moment of hesitation he bent down and picked it up. Within a few seconds I started feeling bad, knowin that I was runnin an "old tape" in my head. Tape clicked in when Blacks had to do everything for White folk. If I picked it up it would *feel* like I was shuffling as Colored folk had to do in the old days to show deference. At that moment, in my bad race day state of mind, if I'd picked up the item, it would've felt like I was saying the equivalent of "here you go, boss." All that sort of flashed through my head in a moment. Sounds crazy but on a low road day I can see the "White man" as trouble and allow myself to react to old experiences and old tapes. Like I said, I was havin "a bad race day." I didn't know the guy from Adam, but on this day I automatically reacted to him based on what my tapes told me he represented.

Well, I got a second chance when he was trying to put the thing he dropped back on the shelf and several more things fell down. I immediately bent over and side by side we were both picking up the items. He thanked me and made a joke about how clumsy he was, and we both laughed and had a nice light moment together. Thought about this afterward and realized again, it's about reaching out, whether it be with a smile or a helping hand. White folk have to do the same. Reach out, reach out, reach out, and pay attention to what goes on with that little voice in your head when you're dealing with Colored folk. Pay attention to your attitudes and behavior, be willing to go out of your way to make overtures and admit when you're wrong. I'll admit when I'm wrong too. (That might come as a shock to my wife.)

NEWS FLASH OVER

In my life, God makes me practice what I preach. One day I was thinkin deeply about this race stuff trying to get past some of the tapes that run in my head. Around that time I was traveling a lot, flyin all over the US of America and to distant lands. I started to notice that when a Person of Color would sit in the seat next to me, I would strike up a conversation within a few minutes. If it was a White person, I was much more content to just be polite, say "hi," and go back to readin my book or newspaper, or just snooze till the plane landed. I wasn't mean or anything, just not as open to the fact that he or she might want to talk to me.

As usual my prayer was answered in a different way than I expected. Before I knew it, about ninety percent of the folk sitting next to me on airplanes were Caucasian males. I noticed my ambivalence, so I starting focusin on my attitude. I started to be more welcoming instead of just being polite. I learned a lot from those experiences. I had many very engaging and genuine conversations, some not so good and others that just never panned out because one of us had work to do or we were just plain too tired to talk. It was a small thing, but it helped me to be more open and helped me realize, not from theory, but from practice that you cannot tell a book by its cover.

It is important to be frank here. One of the experiences I've had with too many White men in my life is that it often feels like I have to make the first overture of friendliness. Then, instead of just interacting with me, too often I'd end up feeling like they were doing some kind of evaluation on me; sort of seeing if I measure up to some kind of unspoken standard. In my spiritual race space I reach out regardless and am not concerned about who initiates the gesture, but on other days I get that "why the hell should I always have to reach out" attitude and why should I submit myself to feeling like I'm being evaluated. Doesn't last long, but it reminds me that I still have strong feelings. I find that even in my faith community, I am sometimes more cautious with the White males than females but I have higher expectations there, since the pivotal principle of the Bahá'í Faith is the oneness of humankind. I have had many good experiences in and out of my faith community with White males and females. But I still have that edge, that on-guard part of me because the bad experiences still happen and if I let them or am having a bad race day, they can be like salt in a wound. An African American friend of mine who is struggling with her racial treatment told me that lately she fears one more thing is just going to make her snap. Anyway as I reflect a minute, I am feeling that I sense more initiation of friendliness from my White male brothers than I used to, and so it is improving. "Focus on the good, Tod, focus on the good." Hope it keeps improving before my friend snaps, because she is hurtin bad.

Tellin you all this because I think White and Black folk got to do stuff like finding ways to reach out, purposefully and often regardless of fear and past experience. If you're a praying person, pray about the race challenge and ask God to give you opportunities to do something about it, and then keep your heart wide open. If you're not the praying type, do whatever it takes to help you find those opportunities to go out of your way. I always say you have to be *uncomfortable* before you can be *comfortable*. Have to put yourself in situations that you normally wouldn't and hang in there long enough to bring the discomfort to comfort. Black folk have had to do that all along and we have to keep it up and White folk; more of you have to join us. This is something I have full confidence "we the people" can do!

CNBAAPA Can Stand Proud of So Much

To be honest, I was happy with myself and sort of proud for stickin with my *reach out to more of my White brothers* airplane plan. Have to say the Bahá'í Scriptures motivate me when I get lazy about all this. They remind me that if we're gonna solve this issue, we all have to take advantage of everyday opportunities to get rid of our prejudices, and we have to do it *deliberately* and *consistently*. I reread those passages quite often when I get discouraged or lazy. It's easy to give up or get sidetracked, forgetting the importance of reaching out. Truth be told, I am proud of Black folk in a whole lot of ways! So I'm feeling a little proud of myself today for stayin the course. Sometimes we all have to encourage our own selves so I'm doing that today.

Truth of the matter, is I'm proud of my "peeps" in general. Allow me to be proud with you all for a minute. I'm proud of my dad and mom, my daughters, granddaughters, my brother, my sister, my sister-in-law and son-and-law and so many beautiful Black folk. I truly see heaven in the face of Black folk. We got love in our hearts, creativity in our bones, spirit in our souls, perseverance in our genes, and resilience in our gut. We got intellect, common sense, street smarts and people smarts. Some of us are hard-headed. I mention that because it has served us well at times; not so well at other times. Most of us believe in a higher power and spirituality.

A trip to the barbershop or the neighborhood mechanic can become a social occasion in a hot minute full of laughter, joy, dissin and dismissin, politickin and plain talkin smack.

Love the way we use laughter to get through life's pain—may not even be totally aware we're doing it, but some of that laughter goes so deep it serves as a healing balm. Laughter is just a part of who we are, how we connect and how we love. We can laugh at each other and with each other; laugh at our challenges while at the same time acknowledging their reality, without missing a beat.

And oh my, what can't we create? Soul food came from left-overs we got from White folk back in the day. We made chitlins out of pig intestines to survive. Can't stand 'em myself, but a whole lot a folk love them. We created jazz, blues and R&B, hip hop and rap. Music seems to be part of our DNA. We bring creative expression to all the sports we play, from high fives to back flips in the end zone after a touchdown. The fist pump in golf, fashion queens in tennis, superhuman dunks in basket-ball, and the in-the-air chest bump, are all part of a unique flair. We've come up with hundreds of inventions from the dust pan, to the stop light, to refrigeration, to the preservation of blood plasma. We helped lay out the plans for our nation's capitol and were slave carpenters helping to build the White House. We come up with the best and funniest slogans and slangs and all kind of ways to strut, step, talk and dress. In my day, "bad" meant "good." Later "dope" meant "cool." "You go, girl," has become almost universal. Wearing our caps backwards, once shunned, is a norm along with high fiving and the fist bump greeting. I love the three part hand shake endin with a half hug or the snappin of the fingers

We can conjure up all kinds of creative names for children. Some say those names can make things hard on our kids later but regardless, creativity abounds. We can preach up a storm and many have the gift of gab. We can adamantly disagree with each other and walk away laughing. Can talk trash on the basketball court or on any court, play the dozens, and then go have lunch together.

We can love so deeply and feel so fully. I remember my brother, the actor, in one of his plays, quoting Descartes with vigor saying, "I think, therefore I am," and then going on to say about himself with even more vigor, "I feel, baby, therefore I am!" We're a true feeling, relationship and connection culture. That's why in so many traditional Black churches you see the minister and congregation in a call-and-response mode. It's about connection, "feelin and feedin off each other." I think that's partly why we come up with so many different ways to shake hands. It's connection with flair. Seems like we can bring a rhythm and verve to almost anything we do.

We still have extended family too. Folk in the South go to funerals of their fourth cousins and being an "auntie" doesn't mean you're a blood relative. We care about how we're perceived and how we act. Every time we hear about some sort of crazy crime, in our head we say, "Man, I hope that wasn't someone Black." We say that because we know it will end up reflecting on all of us in the US of America, and we say it because we feel connected. We're so proud of seeing one of us rise high in a particular field, profession or in service. Icing on the cake is how so many of us have made a way outa no way. For all that and more I see a lot of heaven in the face of so many Black folk. Not braggin; just taken a moment to share part of what I experience as the joyful part of wakin up Black in the US of America, the proud part.

And finally, speaking of proud, my mom and dad came to visit me the other day. My wife and I took them to the African monument so we could experience it together. We witnessed again those of all backgrounds conversing and being moved and educated by the monument. Friends of mine went to visit the monument at 1:00 am and said there was a crowd even then! On that day I was proud of my entire human family of all hues. My, my, perhaps we are making progress.

Comparin Apples and Oranges Doesn't Work

I know some people still wonderin why Colored folk can't do what *other "minorities"* have done to make it. I've heard that one too many times in my workshops and in general conversation about race. Not sure when folk talk about that, if they're talkin about Latino folk who have made some inroads but have some big-time struggles. Latinos come from many different places and some do well and some don't. Could be talkin about Asians who some have called the *model minority*, wondering why *us folks* can't be like *them folks*. Some Asians don't much like being thought of that way, as they got issues too. And folk forget, Asians come from a bunch of countries, and some of them are really struggling too with education, poverty, as well as with gangs and such. I know folk are lumpin them all together when they call them the model minority, wondering why we can't be like them. Folk could be talkin about White immigrants too.

In reading the real history of US of America, I have come to see how a bunch of White immigrant groups came to escape persecution or bad conditions in their countries. I have seen how many tried to assimilate but were still discriminated against. A lot of them tried to give up their accents real quick so no would know where they were from. Some cities had riots on large and small scales where folk got killed or beat up. White folk got discriminated against, but over a few generations no one knew where they were from, and their color began to work *for* them. You can change an accent but you can't change your color. Not tryin to make this a history lesson, but the "why can't we be like them" folks have to realize their ancestors came here with their family structure and culture intact. Black folk got separated from their families, their ethnic groups, their cultural groups, got prevented from learning to read and write for years and then after slavery, got "Jim Crowed," Black coded, sharecropped, then got segregated without Crow, then got prevented from entering the mainstream, then got desegregated but never integrated. Built our own businesses in many cases, but integration took its toll on our communities, and White folk didn't support our businesses, and some of us got brainwashed to act in a similar way. Since we never got integrated, we got spread out all over the place trying to fit into other neighborhoods and workplaces, leavin many of the communities behind to struggle. We often felt isolated in our new neighborhoods without our roots. In some ways it felt like we had to choose; try to fit into new communities, with higher property values but less camaraderie, etc., and *move up,* or stay in communities with less apparent and real resources and *stay down.* Since we were expected to be the integrators, many Negroes felt pressured to *openly* give up bein Black when they moved out of their communities and into the new. Meanwhile, as we tried to move up the ladder and get what White folks got, we got separated from our poorer brothers and sisters, and, sadly, too many of us left the Black neighborhood to fend for itself. Well, we "misplaced" a lot during integration days, but especially a strong sense of community and identity and unfortunately some of our pride. Still got it, but it's not manifesting itself like before. Shouldn't ever say we lost it. Should say some of it has gone underground. I fully believe we can tap into it again.

Bottom line is, comparing different experiences of People of Color in this country can sometimes be like comparing apples and oranges. We can't just over-simplify things instead of dealing with the nuances of the whole picture. Even in a family, two children growing up in the same circumstances don't

228

always turn out the same way. Far as I've experienced, sayin to one, "why can't you be like your brother/sister" doesn't provide much motivation. Fact is trying to make one like the other just creates "push back" and resentment and becomes part of the problem. Tryin to make or expect folk to be like other folk doesn't work in a family, and it doesn't work in the US of America.

The "why can't you be more like them" syndrome really needs some reconsideration. White folk simply are not the standard bearer for acceptable behavior and for deciding who should be like whom. We all got improving to do, so the mirror is the place to look first, for all of us. Finally like in a family, encouragement and support work a lot better than comparing and criticizing.

Women Leading the Way out

Since we're talking about apples and oranges, let me slip something in about women and men, two different human fruits (that one made me smile). Glad I'm windin out because I'm thinkin this might make some folks hot too.

One thing I've been thinkin for a while, progress not with-standing, is that we're sort of stuck between second and third gear on this race problem. Then I got to thinkin, lightly at first, then more deeply. One of the problems with this whole race thing is male testosterone, close to the word testy. Seems like discussion on this issue gets testosterone-filled (testy) al-most before it gets started. Don't get me wrong, some women can be real testy too, but men seem to have the edge on them when it comes to "patterns" of testiness. From sports to poli-tics, board rooms to bars, husband and wife discussions and disagreements, and everything in between men seem to talk over, talk at, cut off, give advice, correct, attempt to dominate,

229

act superior, struggle to listen and empathize and state opinion as fact as a *pattern* more than women and sometimes try to make women be that way to fit in.

That kind of acting and reacting makes this race issue impossible to talk about and more impossible to resolve. Big generalization you might say. I say, I agree, but one thing I know is that force has ruled the roost for many a year in this world and things are changing. Folk still need to be strong, true enough. Way I see it though, strength comes in many forms and nothing is stronger or more important than bein flexible, thoughtful, reflective, empathetic and sympathetic when appropriate, intuitive and knowing how to create connection and disagree without dissin and dismissin. I think women, *overall,* got a better handle on these things than men, and to get us over the hump on this race disgrace issue, we're goin need a lot of those qualities and quick.

I'm in hot water with some of ya'all now for sure, but hear me out. If you took a hundred men and hundred women, I'd bet you a chunk of change that the hundred women would exhibit those qualities more often than the hundred men. Don't get me wrong, I love bein a man, testosterone and all and love what we can offer, but as Clint Eastwood said in the movie *Magnum Force,* "A man's got to know his limitations." Point is, I think women are going to have to jump in the lead on this race issue if we are going to get it solved. Even with the historical challenges between lighter- and darker-hued women, I can't back off that one. They seem to have the capacity and have demonstrated the ability to create a more conciliatory climate and atmosphere.

Chapter 19

Windin up to Wind down but Not without a Word about Native Americans

Thinkin I better start tryin to close this part of the book out now. Not finished yet but startin to wind it down.

This *color* prejudice has America all twisted up in a way that defies rational explanation. Let me tell you that one of the craziest examples of this entire race disgrace is the light-skinned/dark-skinned phenomenon. I still find many folk are more nervous and uncomfortable with dark-skinned Negroes than they are with light-skinned ones. Some folk from all different backgrounds seem to share that *nervous affliction*. All that got started during slavery when the White slave owners took the light-skinned Black folk to work in "the big house." (A lot of light-skinned Negroes came from Black women being exploited by the slave master.) White folk were more comfortable with the light-skinned ones who also might now be the kinfolk of the master; so the dark ones got left in the field for the more painful work. Divide and conquer at its worst and it somehow clung and stung and still stings today.

Light skin seems preferred in many other parts of the world as well and in many cultures, according to what folk from many places tell me and what I read. Without creating a **NEWS FLASH** here, I just talked to a dark skinned African American friend who recently returned from a European country that I will not name. She was devastated by the overt racism she experienced. It is taking her some time to emotionally recover, particularly as initially she had been so excited about her trip. I've talked to other dark-skinned brothers and sisters, and they have stories to tell; everything from children being scared or nervous around them to comments from their own folk about preferring light-skinned sisters or brothers. See lots of magazines with folk *shinin* on the light-skinned brothers and sisters. So some folk not only have to deal with wakin up Black in the US of America, but also wakin up dark and Black. That's double jeopardy and the true essence of adding insult to injury and some of it even comes from other Black folk. Poison is poison, and when it gets circulated it poisons everyone. In other words light-skinned preference jammed up some Black folks' minds as well.

So what am I tryin to say in my wakin up Black in the US of America story? I'll say it again here. To bring greater unity and justice a big step is that more and more White folk have to understand that wakin up Black in the US of America is STILL very different than waking up White. That difference has to be accounted for, addressed, undressed and redressed. Caucasian folk and CNBAAPA folk gotta fight that fight together.

Being White still carries with it a whole bunch of advantages that need to be everyone's or no one's. If you think about it deeply, the battle we gotta fight is the battle to save the soul of the US of America. That's exactly what it is!! Our soul got lost almost before it got found. Declaration of Independence was about life, liberty and the pursuit of happiness and Constitution was about forming a more perfect union and about justice. Well, since that did not include us, and "We the people" was not all of us as full U.S. Americans, the heart of these documents never made it fully into the *soul* of the US of America. So when I say it is a battle for the soul of the US of America, I mean just that. Just like what was true in the Iroquois confederacy, everyone has to be in the mix and fully represented for this country to have and save its "soul." "Soul brothers and soul sisters" have to be fully included and without playing favorites.

Mentioning the Iroquois confederacy and the soul of the US of America got me reflecting on a parallel and deeply troubling challenge all U.S. Americans must face—same cause, different symptoms. I said this book is about Black and White, but I can't help but say something about my Native American brothers and sisters. If there was ever a forgotten group in the US of America, it is the Native people. Been in touch with several of my Native brothers and sisters across the US of America lately, and I'm hearing their stories. Both pride and distress abound, but bottom line is, the rest of the US of America needs them, and they need the rest of the US of America. Just think about what you know of the many traditional qualities that are a part of so many of their tribal heritages. I will just mention one. What would our country and the world be like if we had learned to live in harmony with nature? Who could have best brought that gift to the table and still can? That's just one thing we missed out on, and look at the consequences of that gaping hole.

My brothers and sisters, it does not take a whole lot to figure out that if you leave the original inhabitants of a country out of the evolving culture of that country, that country is going to be missing something. Well, that's what we did and are doing in the US of America. The very people who still have some of the answers, that can rescue us all, are not invited to the table. What moral, ethical, practical or spiritual sense does that make?

The circle of unity will remain incomplete till Native folk are included. The spiritual laws of the universe demand inclusion. How do I know that, you ask? Same way you do, if you stop and think about it. Remember the human body analogy. If part of the body is not fully functioning or somehow is marginalized or not working in harmony with the rest for whatever reason, ultimately the whole body will break down.

But let's just cut to the chase with some plain talk. You and I know full well we simply cannot marginalize the group in this country that really formed its foundation and somehow just skate by. Deep down we all have a soul and that soul responds to right and wrong. I am convinced that nine out of ten times when any of us think of the plight of Native Americans in this country, that soul knows what the US of America did and is doing regarding Native Americans was and is wrong. Yet the mind can dismiss what the soul knows, so life can go own. You might think you/we can move on, but if we don't find ways to be more inclusive of *them,* it's only a matter of time before what has happened to *them* happens to all of us. The same greed and callousness that took land from the Native people and continues to marginalize them, is definitely in a Wal-mart near you and in its current manifestation it's called recession. In very straight language with not a hint of malice intended, we all know in our hearts, what goes around eventually comes around. That's another one of those spiritual laws of the universe. A friend of mine from the Lakota tribe told me that in a very short time there may be only a dozen Native languages left in the US. Language is at the core of culture and when they are lost, you lose a whole lot.

Another Lakota friend told me there had been twenty four suicides among his people in about a month period. Said unemployment is as high as ninety-five percent in some areas. Poverty can be up to eighty percent and homelessness around ninety percent. Broke my heart in half when he said he had come to DC to meet with some politicians to raise awareness and support for some promising efforts on the reservation. While he was here his grandson hung himself. What precipitated him coming in the first place was that he found a sixteen-year-old girl who had hung herself near his house. His own son hung himself several years ago.

234

Both of these men are working hard to improve conditions and insist that there is hope and that they don't want to complain, but at the same time awareness is critical. Who of us could respond with such nobility in the face of this kind of circumstance? What are we, the body of humanity, losing when we lose so many from such a rich cultural heritage? What must it be like for the children and young people growing up in such conditions? This is all of our issue.

Deep down, we know oneness and unity are the key. We may not have the guts to live oneness, talk about it out loud, but deep down we know oneness, unity and justice are the key principles. Don't make it more complicated than that, because in practice, once we agree on the principles, it is going to take all of our collective juices to operationalize them. Pay attention and act on what your soul and heart are telling you. If we leave Native people out of the unity picture, and that is who I am talkin about at this minute, our country will have a longer and more painful journey to its ultimate destiny. Fact is we may never get there. As they say, "if you do what you've always done, you'll get what you've always got." That's more than a slogan. I want to say to my Native brothers and sisters, "the US of America needs you. I pray you can maintain those spiritual and cultural values your country needs so badly. I salute you!"

Up and Leavin the US of America

I recently met one African American brother who is fed up with the hypocrisy he sees all around him. We'll call him Joseph, and Joseph told me he is up and leavin the US of America. When he first told me he was "quitting America," as he put it, I thought maybe he was a little over the edge, but I have learned long ago that it pays to listen and learn. He started talkin about the conditions he saw in this country, the conditions for Black folk across the board and why he felt he needed to do something significant to make the case, and I finally understood his point. Joseph is a very smart fella, well-read, thoughtful and humane. He got a website with a letter on it asking for *political asylum from this country*. Gave up some good money and good wealth and has had to practically live out of his car for months till he could get his paperwork done so he could "quit America." The man is courageous enough to put all this on the line to make his point. Agree with him or not, a thoughtful person should reflect on why a sane man of public standing who'd been living a life of comfort would feel like this is the choice he *must* make.

I remember some years back a lawyer and activist, Randall Robinson, did something like that as well. I hope too many others don't reach that point of disillusionment. I must say "quittin America" is not my choice of activism, but I am totally inspired by anyone who cares so deeply about humanity that they will sacrifice their life of comfort tryin to take a stand.

Deciding Who We Are

Joseph called African American folk, "the people of America." I think I understand what he is trying to say but regardless, we still don't know how we fit. The reason we can't decide if we are Colored, Negro, Black, Afro-American, African American or a Person of Color or a person of African descent (CNBAAPA) is that we are still struggling *to feel* like, be perceived like, and be accepted like true blue U.S. Americans. We want to be accepted without having to give up who we are as a people. We are still trying to find our place of dignity in this country. So many White folk keep wondering why we can't make up our minds what we are and why we have to be hyphenated Americans. Why can't we just be "American," they ask. In part, I say, we are hyphenated Americans because *that's what we really are* to many folk. We are not totally acceptable and accepted as U.S. Americans, so some of us remain or at least feel hyphenated. Others of us just like the idea of being connected to Africa.

(Now if you go on YouTube and listen to Smokey Robinson talk about being Black in America you'll see he has another view, which is also worthy of consideration.)

Most folk, if they were honest, they'd admit that when they conjure up a picture of a U.S. American in their head, that picture is not of our hue. But let me tell you something: I'm a US of African-American citizen like God made me, and that's good enough for me. My ancestors are from one or more of those fifty-three countries in Africa, and I'm now living in America. I am thinking the Lord likes my color and a whole lot of my culture(s) just fine. Thinkin, the Almighty likes all colors since he made it so we could travel the continents till some of us got dark and some stayed light. If the Creator made me what I am, then I feel just fine acknowledging it. Lord made us in his image, helped us become different cultures and colors, and in my view, wanted those different cultures and colors to intersect and explode with creativity and joy; so I intersect with Africa and the US of America and I'm proud of bein both. I like all kinds of flowers in my garden, hybrid included.

A fella in one of my diversity workshops didn't agree. I was giving the example of the diverse flower garden and how that diversity makes it beautiful. He'd been sitting stoically during the whole workshop but his hand shot up. I called on him and he said matter of factly, "what about purity?" I said something like "pardon me?" He said, "what about purity?" He went on to try and explain how you can dilute something pure, by adding another color and the offshoots will be impure. Well, that was his view, so what can I say? But it made me a bit nervous because my co-presenter pointed out to me that when he shot up his hand it was more in the form of a Nazi salute than it was a raised hand. I reflected on that, and sure enough, that was exactly what it was. Why did I tell you that? Not sure, it just came to me, but I do know some folk don't like the concept of the colorful flower garden.

Well, I like the different colors in flowers. Folks say if we would just emphasize our similarities we could get rid of these problems. I say we can emphasize similarities to build bonds of trust and a deep sense of a common humanity. I also say, looking deeply at our differences can bring unity, if we view differences as something to draw on to make us all stronger instead of weaker. What if we thought of diversity as naturally and lovingly created dissimilarity?

The thing to do is to reframe how we see differences instead of pretending that we have no differences. Some say, celebrate the differences. That's great, but I think we're gonna have to try our best to understand them too, sorta like what husband and wife have to do. Sometimes I don't have a clue why my wife responds to certain things the way she does and she feels the same about me. I just get frustrated, and so does she, if I try to change or belittle her perspective, approach or ideas, or try to make her think like me. Things go much better when I step back and try to understand what she's saying and likewise if she does the same. Men and women have a lot in common but, at the same time and very often, think and communicate differently. When I step back long enough to see her point, a lot of times it broadens mine or gives me new knowledge. Sometimes I still disagree, but I usually get her point. Can't say I am always ready to celebrate all of our differences but I'm getting closer to that. Bottom line is it takes work to understand, appreciate and capitalize on diversity, and marriage or close relationships provide great training ground.

238

I'm comin back to a point I was makin before. Callin yourself African American doesn't mean you want to divide from other folk or you're not happy bein a U.S American. Being proud of where you come from does not mean you think you're better than anyone else either, it just means you're proud of where you are and where your ancestors came from. The only problem comes if you change pride into a feeling of superiority. Seems to me that's reasonable, but some folk are just lookin to make something outa nothin. Well, I guess I shouldn't say that, because they may have a reason for thinkin the way they do. I often have to remind myself, because something someone thinks makes no sense to me in my life experience, the same may not hold true for their life experience. What may seem absurd and out of touch to me may not be to them. Tell you one thing; it's hard to keep reminding myself other people can have a point too! Whew!

Okay, I still gotta say there's some hypocrisy in what you're "allowed" to call yourself without gettin grief. Where I used to live in the South, seems to me folk were proud to be Southerners, not just Americans, and they made a big thing about it. They didn't define themselves simply as Americans but as Southerners and in their minds they are still patriotic U.S. Americans. They certainly didn't see themselves as divisive though many of them loudly and proudly proclaimed their dislike for Northerners. Read a bumper sticker shortly after moving to South Carolina that said, "I don't give a damn how you did it up north."

I love many things about the South and about Southern culture. In my view, Southerners often get a bad rep. On the other hand, in a discussion with some of my Southern brothers, I was told my comparison of the use of the term "Southerners" and the use of the term "African Americans" didn't hold water because Southerners are still referring to themselves within the borders of this country or some such thing. If we're all

Americans why do we need to bring Africa or Mexico or other things into it? Well, I ask them why they think they can set the acceptable range of ways to refer to oneself in the US of America. There was no real response to that question.

Seems to me like some folk think they're the *deciders* and *definers* about what constitutes a loyal, patriotic U.S. American. Too often folk state their view as if it were fact. If we want to set some guidelines for something, then we need to do it together or not at all. Can you imagine what would happen if a bunch of Black folk started going around questioning the patriotism of Southerners because of what they call themselves and then acted like we had the right to define for them what qualified them as true U.S. Americans?

We don't need to go down the "who is patriotic and who is not" road anymore, do we? With all due respect, Southern states seceded from the Union of the US of America, so who would have a better case for patriotism? Most Black folk fought on the side of the US of America and continued to fight for freedom in US of America's wars, even though we weren't free in our own country or were treated as second-class citizens. That's patriotism in my view! Not trying to make a case here against Southerners or anyone else referring to their culture or ethnicity any way they want to; I'm just saying folk gotta stop the madness on all this. As I often say, "don't major in the minors." We have bigger fish to fry in this race thing.

However we define ourselves it is how we understand each other's experience that will make the ultimate difference. In the movie, The *Color of Fear* (Wah, 1994) one scene powerfully illustrates this point. Eight men of different ethnicities spent a weekend talking about race and its impact. All weekend long folks were tellin their stories about discrimination and what they faced in the US of America. One of the White men would not accept the truth of their experiences. Finally

240

the facilitator asked him what kept him from believin their stories. He said in essence, "if these things are true, and I don't want to believe they could be, it would mean there is a sad state of affairs for some people in the US of America." Then the facilitator said to the White fella, "If what these men are saying is true what would that mean for you? What would that mean for your life?"

Good question, I think, don't you? If what I am saying in this story is true, what does that mean for you and your life? I am talking to my White brothers and sisters for a minute now. If what I'm saying in this story is a lot of truth, what does it mean for you and your life? What might you do differently or more of to build a new unity with your brothers and sisters of Color? Correspondingly, I say to my Black brothers and sisters, what does it mean for your life? You got your own wakin up Black in the US of America story to tell, but what does my story mean for your life? I hope it means something, helps something or triggers some reflection. What do you need to do to bridge the gap, to continue to work for unity and justice in the right spirit to keep on keepin on with dignity and grace? I say this to you as I say it louder to myself. It is my own heart and soul I need to continually strengthen. I suggest that is the case for all of us.

Chapter 20

The End of My Story, But Not My Journey

Understand again why I took all this time and energy to tell this part of my story. Was it all about "woe is me?" No, indeed, it wasn't. Took all this time because it matters to me what happens in the US of America and because I love my culture, my country and I love the vision of what Whites and Blacks can achieve if we choose to. Love is who we are and what we have to be. I remember my brother doing his one person play about the life of Muhammad Ali. He ended the play quoting Ali. "Love; everything else is just illusion." Hope you felt my love in this book because truly it was a labor of love for a non-writer to write a book and try to make it worth reading.

Last story now, I mostly promise. Man in one of my diversity workshops came up to talk to me just before lunch break. He was standin in line behind some other folk who wanted to talk to me, steadily and angrily tapping his foot and staring hard into my eyes. When it came his turn I knew I was I was in for it. He said he had something to say and he was gonna tell me straight because I had encouraged everyone to be open and honest. I invited him to go ahead, though I don't really think he was waitin for my permission. He got real emphatic and animated. He said, "*I am sick and tired* of being blamed for all the problems Black people have, for all the poverty in your communities, all the drugs, for what my ancestors did, for folk of African descent not having jobs and gettin promotions, getting discriminated against, etc., etc. I am sick and tired of hearing that it is all because of what White people have done!!" He didn't say "etc.," but he did go on to pound the podium with his fist a time or two. I was feelin real spiritual that day (havin a good race day) and after he finished talking, I calmly thanked him for sharing his version of truth with me. I meant it too. I looked back at him and said, "Now can I tell you what I am sick and tired of?" He hesitated a minute and got a bit uneasy, but he said yes. I got a little animated myself although I didn't pound the podium. I told him I was sick and tired of folk seeing Black men as criminals, of being stereotyped in TV shows, of seeing environmental waste being dumped in our communities, of people thinking we want handouts and prefer to be on welfare, of being mistreated just trying to get waited on, of people thinkin we're lazy and can only get ahead through affirmative action, of being followed in stores just tryin to shop, etc. I didn't really say "etc." either, but I did go on just like he did. I took a breath and then I told him, "Now I know what you're sick and tired of and you know what I'm sick and tired of." I looked him straight in the eye and said: "What do you want to do now"? I waited a bit before I answered my own question. I told him we could talk a tad more, and I could listen to him and try to understand why he felt what he felt, and he could listen to me and try to understand what I feel. Then if we keep lookin, we might figure out where the truth lies. Told him we can't resolve all this in a hot minute but we can lay the groundwork. Or I could walk away mad and he could do the same. I could go talk about him and about other White folk to my Black friends, and he could go talk about me and other Black folk to his White friends. I told him we could either talk *to* each other or run off and talk *about* each other. I asked him what he wanted to do. We had an uneasy moment together. Then we started to talk about a couple things that came up in the workshop that tripped his trigger, real stuff for him and where his head was at. I think, he listened to me, and I listened to him. Instead of moving further apart, I think we moved a little closer together, maybe just an inch. (I heard Les Brown say "inch by inch, anything's a cinch.") If I saw him again, I truly think we could talk again and make more headway. Talk from better understanding; most importantly we could talk out of some mutual respect.

This was no love story where we embraced and sang Kumbaya. We didn't become bosom buddies in those few short minutes, but we did move those few inches closer together. More importantly, the moral of this incident and part of the moral of this whole book is, if we are honest with each other and hear each other, with our spiritual heart, our higher natures, then we have the chance to discard some emotional baggage. Who knows, we might be able to move closer together in our agreement or even in our disagreement.

So I didn't alienate this guy, and he didn't alienate me, and the universe is a better place. I really believe that. Alienation and estrangement are ugly things because they cause us to dehumanize and demonize folk and that leads to all kinds of things, none of them good. Unity is the key even if we disagree on the facts (like me and this fella did). That takes a level of self-transformation, self-discipline and a spiritual perspective that, thus far as a whole, we've been unable to achieve. We can only make progress if we build bonds of unity based on our many commonalities. Building on those bonds means slowly gaining trust that breaks down our defenses and in that spirit of unity we can address our differences. The goal is not to just tolerate but to capitalize on and even embrace diversity. If we can't do all that, sometimes just understanding why we see things the way we do can lead to progress. We can do this as U.S. Americans if we don't cut and run every time the fire gets a little warm or when real truth is being told.

You've heard this kind of thing a million times, right? I mean how important it is that we talk to and listen to each other. Even been called cowards by U.S. Attorney General Holder because we don't talk about this stuff. So what is Tod Ewing saying that's new in this book? What's new is that most of the work is spiritual work, not emotional work, not social work, but spiritual work. It has to be done in our soul first, with the focus on who I am, what I do, how I say what I say, my

244

motives, my energy, my intent. Focus is not on fixin the other person or group, because you can't fix or change anyone else, but you can influence everything and everyone by the sincerity, conviction and earnestness of your own example and spirit. Spirit and energy are real forces.

That is the key and it applies to institutional change as well. People run institutions and if policies and practices are going to change, people have to change and the systems then have to follow suit. Individual change is not enough. The mentality that created these systems came from the low road side of our natures that objectified human beings, that defined life's ultimate purpose as owning and possessing and that sanctioned unconscionable behaviors if they made money or retained power. Collective institutional changes must complement individual change. Individual and collective transformational change will reinforce one another, uplifting everyone and reinforcing moral and ethical behavior.

Back to the Future and Our Common Spiritual Roots

You can see I'm getting back to spirituality and religion again to close this out, because that's a big part of resolving this whole thing as far as I am concerned. I am windin out of the challenges part of the book and lockin down on the solutions part, though I have offered some already that I'm sure you are taking to heart.

The Almighty knows, I know and you know that a lot of ugly things have been done in the name of religion and spirituality, but a lot of good things too. Not to compare the two, but a whole lot of ugly things have also been done in the name of money, yet most folks know we need it but also need to keep its purpose in perspective. Same is true with spirituality and religion. If we use it to belittle and minimize others we've lost it purpose but if we use it to lift ourselves and others it can be a mighty instrument to wield. Black folk have survived and thrived in large part due to their spirituality and faith in God. White folk have too. But too often both have adopted a narrow view in terms of their beliefs and practices. Instead of using the inspiration of spirituality to motivate and bond, it has been used to hide, divide and collide. You're with us or against us kind of thing. Not just White folk, but Black folk too. The very thing the Creator sent to unite us we've used to divide us. I'm saying we can use spirituality to break down barriers instead of building them up. If we don't use it for that, what good is it? (Check back in the Preface for the definition of spirituality if you need to, pp. iii–iv)

Why do I think spirituality is so vital, you might or might not ask? Earlier on I said, I believe, it is "emotionally impossible and spiritually possible" to solve the race problem. My experience is that our feelings have gotten so thick around all this; an almost impenetrable emotional wall has been created between the races. The wall is so thick we can't blast through it unless we can tap that spirit force from within that will allow us to transcend and transform some of the pain, guilt, shame, anger into a power the motivates us to unify on the high ground of hope, love, honor and dignity.

Some say we have to work through the emotional pain, and I say we have to transcend and transform it, call on deeper powers. Our emotions have been so jacked up, jacked around and high-jacked; all they do is set us off, sometimes way off, into bitterness, badness and sadness. My experience has been that I have emotionally discharged my anger and frustration over and over about this race stuff and that helps temporarily but also wears me out. Wears me out in part because once I do that, I feel emotionally vulnerable, and sooner or later someone's gonna pierce that wound with some action that triggers the anger and hurt all over. The wedge then goes deeper. Emotions around race tap such deep feelings in folk that we just keep bumpin heads and hearts.

So I'm working on the transcendence piece and so far so good. Trying to transcend does not mean denying the real problems, it just moves me to a *place* and *space* where it's easier to see the spiritual approaches to change all this, to appeal to the best in others. "When deep speaks to deep, deep responds." Higher vibration states can overcome lower vibration states. Dr. King used to say it like this, "We shall match your capacity to inflict suffering by our capacity to endure suffering. We shall meet your physical force with soul force. Do to us what you will, and we shall continue to love you.... One day we shall win freedom but not only for ourselves. We shall so appeal to your heart and conscience that we shall win you in the process and our victory will be a double victory" (Oates, 1994, p. 236).

It is that spirit that Black and White must fully embrace if we are to move forward. We must be willing to suffer for each other, hopefully not inflicting any more undue suffering. But if so, we'll be willing to endure for each other; for our first, eighth and fiftieth cousins or whichever ones. It is the power of spirituality that can engender this unique perspective and capacity. It is the capacity that so many of the leaders we revere draw upon. *It is the capacity we so admire in others yet often fail to choose for ourselves. It is time to choose it.*

Golden Rule

Spirituality is necessary because the universe is as governed by spiritual laws as it is by physical laws, and they are just as essential. Spiritual laws are as binding as physical laws such as, say, gravity. Gravity is a powerful force but you can't touch, see or feel it. You better know about it though, know it exists and how it works. The same is true for spiritual laws.

247

Can't see, touch or feel them, but life will work better if we know they are there and how to work in harmony with them. I have asked many people how they feel when they do some service or act of kindness for others. No one has ever said, I feel bad. Everyone says they feel good. Such service often requires going out of our way for others. So why is it that we feel good? Could it be because we are made up that way and that it is a spiritual law that, if we serve others, we feel better about ourselves? In schools I've worked in I have seen those children who are troubled and hate school perk up and change totally when they are allowed to work with and assist children who have disabilities. This is quite common. Something feels good about this type of giving to others. The converse must also be true. If you do ugly things to others, it does not make you feel better, except on a superficial egotistical level. Kindness and doing for others is a premise of every major religion and is demonstrated by the fact that they all contain a golden rule:

Hinduism

Do not to others what ye do not wish done to yourself, and wish for others too what ye desire and long for, for yourself.

Judaism

What is hateful to you, do not do to your fellow man. That is the entire Law; all the rest is commentary.

Zoroastrianism

What is disagreeable to yourself do not do unto others.

Buddhism

Hurt not others in ways that you yourself would find hurtful.

Christianity

And as ye would that men should do to you, do ye also to them likewise.

Islam

None of you truly believes until he wishes for his brother what he wishes for himself.

Bahá'í Faith

And if thine eyes be turned towards justice, choose thou for thy neighbor that which thou choosest for thyself.

Even if you don't believe in God, the golden rule stands tall and represents a certain quality of spirit that most people can accept as a fundamental moral premise. That rule alone, if we internalize it and accept it as a law of the universe, helps us remember there is *no right way to do the wrong thing*. It gives us a foundation for conscience and consciousness, helps us persevere in goodness when we wanna quit, gives us the strength to forgive when we'd rather not. It can help us look for good qualities in folk instead of focusin on the bad, to work it out instead of taking it out (on someone), to let go of the anger we're holdin on to. Importantly it gives us courage to do what we think is right, in spite of ridicule and rejection.

Great example: who'd ever thought a Black man named Barack Hussein Obama would be a contender for president? Many White folk have shown courage to vote their conscience, not their fears. Win or lose, it's created a new day with new possibilities undreamt of by many even a few shorts years go. Campaign trail exposed and surfaced old racial battles, but also provided hope, if we view it right.

Whether he's your candidate or not, something is happening in the hearts of enough U.S. Americans to make his election possible. Some may say, "well, things had gotten so bad in the US of America; White folk figured they couldn't get any worse, so why not give a Black man a try." Here's what I say: in my life sometimes things have to get real bad before my spiritual faculties wake up and blast through my ignorance and sloppiness. So yeah, maybe some folk woke up because they felt the US of America was going down, but I'm not at all concerned about what caused the awakening; probably some combination of politics, pragmatism, principles and spirit. I'm more concerned about building on it, realizing we are not yet "post-racial." Gotta keep pushin the envelope so one day a woman and Black running for President won't even make us blink or think.

Even science is coming out proving the merit of ideals, attitudes and behaviors, spiritual and common religious principles have long propounded. I mean basic stuff that hardly anyone could argue with, whether spiritually oriented or not. Just like science proved the law of gravity, it is now turning itself to deeper matters. I'm no scientist, but let me share a few snippet examples I've come across lately.

There are so many seemingly simplistic expressions about kindness such as "don't repay kindness, pass it on." A popular movie titled *Pay it Forward* seemed trite to some however it inspired other folk, all over the globe, to adopt and adapt its premise of giving to others in ways that require some sacrifice. Turns out, kindness has profound implications. Read about one study that said kindness releases a chemical in the brain which leads to feelings of well-being and happiness. Said that kindness showed by one to another causes that chemical release in the person who is being kind, the person receiving the kindness and the people watching the act of kindness (Dyer, 2004, p. 25). I know that's true for me, when I am kind and receive kindness something happens to make me feel better, just didn't know it was partly chemical. I don't think that's an exclusively White chemical or a Black chemical that gets released either.

What about all this seemingly over-simplistic talk about the need to connect and that fact that we are all interconnected. Some "poo poo" the simplicity of those notions and view them as naïve or at best secondary to the business of achievement and success Well another study I mentioned earlier concluded youth are "hardwired to connect." Said a bunch of problems related to depression, suicide, alienation and the like are related to the inability of youth to feel connected. "Hardwired" to me means built in, a part of who they are. It also said young folk are hardwired to seek deeper spiritual meaning. A summary of the study states it this way: "In large measure, what's causing this crisis of American childhood is a lack of connectedness. We mean two kinds of connectedness—close connections to other people and deep connections to moral and spiritual meaning" (Commission on Children at Risk, 2003). Study acknowledged spirituality is a sensitive topic but said we better not avoid it or we might leave a whole lot of young people feelin empty and disconnected. Study was conducted by thirty-three different experts from across the board including Linda Spear, Alvin Pouissant, and James Comer and may be a first of its kind to suggest the spiritual needs of our children and youth require serious consideration. "For what may be the first time, a diverse group of scientists and other experts on children's health is publicly recommending that our society pay considerably more attention to young people's moral, spiritual, and religious needs" (Commission on Children at Risk, 2003).

Round about the time I read about the importance of connection I started hearing and reading about Quantum Physics and how our thoughts and energy affect everyone else's thoughts

251

and energy. I learned that we can actually change molecular structure with our thoughts. Read about energy having higher or lower vibrational qualities meaning the energy from love and courage vibrates at higher levels than energy from guilt, shame and fear. Some of this came from a profound educational-type movie titled, *What the Bleep Do We Know* (Arntz, 2004). Quantum physics is a complex field but these folks are making it palatable for common folk.

Science is now simply telling us in greater depth what many of us have experienced in our interactions with others but could not explain. The explanations from science sure fit with what religion and spirituality teach us about our thoughts, actions and behavior.

Forgiveness is another spiritual law so to speak and has been a part of the spiritual teachings of most religions. Already mentioned that folk are saying forgiveness is good for us psychologically, mentally, physically and spiritually. Not sure if I told you anger can mess with your liver or one such organ, but also the heart and gallbladder.

I gotta throw this last one in too. Long time ago I read a book called *God Loves Laughter*. It's a great title for a book and a great book. Much later I read that different kinds of laughter actually strengthen different organs in the body. How great is that? Personally, laughter helps me stay on the spiritual path because sometimes it's like a balm for the pain and anguish. Plus, I truly do believe God does love laughter.

This one is big for me. Read that being acknowledged recognized, or receiving recognition is one of the highest needs humans have. Prejudice and racism are the antithesis of all this and destroy perpetrator and victim alike, destroy connection, recognition and acknowledgement. In one of his speeches, Dr. King referred to these elements as the *vitamin A* of life.

I remember shortly after listening to the vitamin A speech, I walked into my bank and the manager or teller says, "Hello, Mr. Ewing." I remember sort of perkin up a bit. Thought about it later and realized it was because someone acknowledged Tod Ewing. It was a form of recognition, appreciation, connection—small but significant. I was also impressed because I personally can't remember folks' names for the life of me.

On a more profound level, I remember discussing the importance of acknowledgment with a friend of mine. She told me a touching story. She was walking down the street and saw a homeless man with a cap on, head down and pushing a shopping cart full of his stuff. She said hello to him and kept walking. He looked up, tipped his cap and said thanks for speaking to me; put his head back down and walked on.

Just showing acts of kindness toward each other, acknowledgement, a willingness to forgive and genuine regard across racial/cultural lines can create a spirit connection that we can build on to solve this race problem. Not saying it's just that simple, but those elements are a huge piece of the collective puzzle. They can help create a new climate across seemingly intractable boundaries, so we can get to the deep stuff. The current climate is still way too chilly in a lot of ways. I don't know about you, but when I'm feelin chilly, all I'm worried about is keepin myself warm.

Indeed, a lot of information is coming out from science explaining how we work best as connected and loving human beings, and it is supporting the spiritual laws, which came about long before science discovered their physical corollaries. All this stuff is coming out at just the right time. There's a new energy afoot and it's almost palpable. Don't know how long it will last, but it feels like souls are experiencing a starvation to connect and reconnect to each other and not just the youngins either. It feels like folks are yearning and desiring to come together. The Obama experience has demonstrated people can and want to cross boundaries. We need to put some "pep in our step" because this upsurge won't last forever. Last time this fifty-something Negro felt this kind of energy was in the 60s.

Connecting, uniting, forgiving, acknowledging and loving are what spirituality is all about, so let me tell you some about where my main spiritual inspiration comes from. I get my main spiritual inspiration and beliefs from the Teachings of Bahá'u'lláh and the Bahá'í Faith, like I told you way back in the beginning of this book. I want to say that straight up because I'm not trying to hide, divide, or collide. I want to share it to connect. Bahá'u'lláh is the Messenger or Manifestation of God for the Bahá'í Faith, in the same way as there are Messengers or Manifestations of God for religions such as Hinduism, Buddhism, Judaism, Christianity, Islam and others. No doubt many of you receive your inspiration from one or more of these spiritual sources. Point is, the Bahá'í Faith teaches that the core and central focus of all the spiritual teachings offered by these religions is one. Always made sense to me; if there is only one God, then there must be a unity and oneness of the religions. Religion is about helping people become and realize their spirituality. If we use them right, they can motivate us to transcend and transform.

> The fundamental purpose animating the Faith of God and His Religion is to safeguard the interests and pro- mote the unity of the human race, and to foster the spirit of love and fellowship amongst men. Suffer it not to become a source of dissension and discord, of hate and enmity. This is the straight Path, the fixed and immovable foundation. (Bahá'u'lláh, 1971, p. 215)

That purpose is a common foundation of religion and its man- ifestation is what spirituality is all about. However words are not enough. "The essence of faith is fewness of words and abundance of deeds; he whose words exceed his deeds, know verily his death is better than his life" (Bahá'u'lláh, 1988, p. 156). Amen to that and praise the Lord. There's a funny recollection I associate with this last passage. A young man in a meeting I attended was trying to recite it from memory. He said: "He whose words exceed his deeds is better off dead." He cracked me up. Either version makes the point.

Religious talk can be touchy, but I say it's time we all realize, truth is truth. A rose is a rose, so don't worry about the garden (religion) it comes from. If you feel something is true, take it and if not, don't. No need to hate the Messenger or the followers! Young folk say, or at least the used to: "Why you gotta hate?"

So I need to share some of what the Bahá'í teachings suggest about approaching all this and see if it doesn't jive with much of what your religion, spirituality and whatever other "goodness" philosophies teach you. I also cite Dr. Martin Luther King Jr. in this section, not because he was on the same order as Jesus or the other religious founders, but because, by his own admission, he did his best to apply the *spirit* of the teachings of Christianity to the many racial problems he gave his life to solve. Outside of the Bahá'í teachings, I'm most familiar with Christianity, which is why I am making reference to it at this point. However I want to reiterate unequivocally my belief in the oneness of religion. Now stay with me.

Bahá'í religion, like many others, states clearly that we need prayer and meditation to stay centered in our spiritual self so we can stay centered in justice:

> The best beloved of all things in My sight is Justice; turn not away therefrom if thou desirest Me, and neglect it not that I may confide in thee. By its aid thou

shalt see with thine own eyes and not through the eyes of others, and shalt know of thine own knowledge and not through the knowledge of thy neighbor. Ponder this in thy heart; how it behooveth thee to be. Verily justice is My gift to thee and the sign of My loving-kindness. Set it then before thine eyes. (Bahá'u'lláh, 1954, p. 2).

In the US of America, in so many cases, we need to see with our own eyes and not through the eyes of the media. It's no joke that it takes a lot of prayer and centering not to get snatched up by the emotion-laden sound bites and stereotypic depictions.

Whether you pray or not, meditation is becoming a common practice for folk from all backgrounds to keep "centered." Whatever name it's called, folk are trying to be centered in a higher or spiritual self. I never heard anyone say they want to meditate deeply so they can get centered in their ego.

In that centered space, it is possible to understand the impact of racism without finger-pointing, blaming or defensiveness. Throughout our day, week, month, year we all have to con-tinuously find ways to bring ourselves back to that center. It is in that space where we'll be more concerned about how we can achieve justice than we are about who's to blame. In that space, we are capable of taking to heart the truth of such statements as the following: "Racism, one of the most baneful and persistent evils, is a major barrier to peace. Its prac-tice perpetrates too outrageous a violation of the dignity of human beings to be countenanced under any pretext. Racism retards the unfoldment of the boundless potentialities of its victims, corrupts its perpetrators, and blights human progress. Recognition of the oneness of mankind, implemented by ap-propriate legal measures, must be universally upheld if this problem is to be overcome" (The Universal House of Justice, 1985, p. 3).

In that spiritual space, it will feel difficult to ignore prejudices, because in that space we want to be connected to others. This space can be called the "grace space." That is the spirit of it. In that space, we realize that the manner in which we address racism must mirror the outcome we want to achieve. Dr. King, in the aforementioned speech about the power of *soul force*, also stated the following:

> Second, we must recognize that the evil deed of the enemy-neighbor, the thing that hurts, never quite expresses all that he is. An element of goodness may be found even in our worst enemy. Each of us has something of a schizophrenic personality, tragically divided against ourselves. A persistent civil war rages within all of our lives. Something within us causes us to lament with Ovid, the Latin poet, "I see and approve the better things, but follow worse" or to agree with Plato that "human personality is like a charioteer having two headstrong horses, each wanting to go in a different direction," or to repeat with the Apostle Paul, "The good that I would I do not: but the evil which I would not, that I do."
>
> This simply means that there is some good in the worst of us and some evil in the best of us. When we discover this, we are less prone to hate our enemies. When we look beneath the surface, beneath the impulsive evil deed, we see within our enemy-neighbor a measure of goodness and know that the viciousness and evilness of his acts are not quite representative of all that he is. We see him in a new light. We recognize that his hate grows out of fear, pride, ignorance, prejudice, and misunderstanding, but in spite of this, we know God's image is ineffably etched in being. Then we love our enemies by realizing that they are not totally bad and

that they are not beyond the reach of God's redemptive love. (Borris-Dunchunstang, 2009)

Dr. King is calling on the best in the Christian spiritual tradition and letting us know love has a real power. He often reminded us that love is a verb and not just a romantic or sentimental notion.

Still not easy and not necessarily a "one-an-done" proposition for this striving brother; talking about myself here. Looking past the ego-centered racism in others and tryin to zero in on their true reality is no easy task for me. Trying to stay focused on what I can do to change myself is challenging, because as I said it'd be easier and less work to focus on changing others. Likewise it is not an easy task for White folk to hear and deal with the word racism when it feels like an attack on them or to stay on the job 24/7 when they can easily just go home and not have to think about it.

Only way I can do my piece is if I am in touch with my true reality. Can't explain it, but when I stay there, I feel like I can handle anything, White, Black or other. It's like I'm operating from another dimension of myself; my transpersonal (beyond personality) or spiritual self. So that's my goal, to deal spiritually with the practical manifestations of racism. Also it keeps me trying to focus more on what I'm for than what I'm against. I'm for racial justice and unity, and that's the vision I keep in my head trying not to look at just what I'm against, which is injustice and racism. Focus more on the light than the dark, I'm able tell myself. In my spiritual space, I'm clear that no matter how dark the room is, a candle will lighten it, and no amount of darkness can overcome that light. And if I/we burn brighter the dark will disappear.

Spirituality, by its very nature, requires us to reach in and reach out, in a sort of rhythmic process similar to the heart, contracting and relaxing, or the lungs breathing in and breathing out. It's all really one thing. If we do too much breathing in without breathing out, we die. If we do too much relaxing of the heart, we die; and with too much contracting we get weary and die just as well. As we grow in our understanding, we will see that the essential oneness of loving and strengthening ourselves and loving and serving others is like breathing in and breathing out. As we love and serve ourselves and focus on our own growth, we likewise have to love and serve others and work to improve their lives as well. I can't help others without helping myself and I can't help myself without helping others. This is the spirit in which we will solve the race problem, the spirit that will bring about a creative explosion at the intersection of Black and White.

Sounds a little pie-in-the–sky, but it's real. Mandela tried his best to respond to his higher self and set the tone on the world stage. Rwanda's Hutus and Tutsis have made bold efforts toward genuine reconciliation. Had they come at this from only the emotional space, there would have been no hope. In Rwanda they chose higher ground, not focusing so much on what happened but more on what must happen if there was to be any future for anyone. South Africa continues to struggle but tries to do the same. It could have been a blood bath. Neither place has reached Nirvana, but what an effort!!! Effort counts, effort provides energy and hope. Effort can be built upon. *Truly it is indeed that spirit we admire in others yet so often fail to choose for ourselves.*

We have everything we need in this country to get the job done, but we need the will, the humility, the drive and the spiritual fortitude to get it done. A new kind of leadership is within all of us and our national leaders can help by setting the tone. I'm not just talkin about politicians; I am talking about everyone who is in that role or cast in that role. Me, I'm not waiting for anyone to lead me. I'm goin for it myself, but higher ups can help us all.

No religion teaches that only people of a certain color were created in the image and likeness of God and we should only do unto others of the same color what we would want done unto us. All religions I know of tell us to sacrifice for our brothers and sisters without regard to hue, to feed the hungry as hunger has no color; clothe the naked—and it doesn't just say clothe those of the right color. Now we all know this, but these aren't just words. In my humble opinion, these guidelines are spiritual laws. Can't play with truth and can't play with the Almighty, as the quote by Thomas Jefferson alluded to earlier. I'm remembering a speech of Dr. King's that I refer to as one of his "out of body," transported to another spiritual plane, speeches. What he said sounded like a Providential warning though he never claimed it to be so. He got that glistening look in his eyes and said, "God has a way of standing before the nations with judgment, and it seems that I can hear God saying to America, 'You're too arrogant! And if you don't change your ways, I will rise up and break the backbone of your power, and I'll place it in the hands of a nation that doesn't even know my name. Be still and know that I'm God.'" (King, 1967). That last sentence is a clear reference to Psalms 46:10 in the Bible. Guess this was King's way of saying God doesn't play about serious business. King got jacked up by a lot of high-powered U.S. Americans for sayin that. What he was saying, in my view, is that we'd better take some time for reflectin, introspectin and correctin, and that all of us can get big-headed sometimes; both individuals and nations and that we'd better check ourselves before we get checkmated.

I have personally learned the hard way in the "school of hard knocks," you can't fool the laws of the universe. They come under the motto, *pay me now or pay me later*. The Almighty created a world that is supposed to be just, fair and loving.

Do it right now or you're gonna have to do it right bye and bye. Only if you put if off, it might just get harder to accomplish. I find that to be evident in my life as well. If I deny and lie to myself for too long, fixin whatever problem just gets harder. It's not like a punishment from above; it's me doin it to myself by not paying attention. Sounds a little like fire and brimstone, but if you can read all this without conjuring up that hell-fire image, you'll feel the truth of what I'm saying. A lot of the problems we have, personal and collective, we cause ourselves. God and the Universe don't have to do a thing.

I'm a witness to folk drawing on spirit to deal with this race stuff. Black folk have had to and White folk have too, when they've decided to take a stand. It is a beautiful thing to watch a human being draw on that spirit and come from a position of nobility and integrity. Blacks and Whites both have that nobility within. When Whites do so, as I said, it gives me hope. Let me share a few common folk stories.

I remember one White lady; we'll call Lily, who grew up in a small Southern town thinkin it was such an idyllic place to be. She didn't think African Americans had it so bad in her town. She got elected to the town council and on one vote she happened to vote the same way the Black members did. The vote had nothing to do with race. In the days after that vote, she got a bunch of threatening calls, folks boycotted the store she owned and in general made her life miserable. This was an awakening for her because her whole life's frame of reference got jerked from under her and it turned her life upside down. She lost friends and public standing. I remember Lily tellin me this story and then tellin me in the next breath she was never going to give up doing what "her faith" tells her is the right thing.

Also remember a seventy-something White man, we'll call him Fred, tellin me he had been, more or less, raised to be prejudiced all his life, but now that he accepted the Bahá'í teachings on the oneness of humankind he was going to work on his prejudices till he got through them. Told me one day, "it's not easy to change when you've been raised a certain way." Only he and God know how far he has come, but I've seen him come a long way. As an aside, doing research on his family tree, Fred found out he had Negro kin folk back in the day. As far as he could tell, it came from a consensual union. He seemed happy and proud to find this out. He put this all down in a book and happily shared it with his relatives.

And there are many others. I think of a long-time friend of Jewish heritage who later became a Bahá'í. We'll call him Nat, because that's the name his friends called him, and he wouldn't mind me using it. He was a good friend to our family way back in Minnetonka. It was back in that day that he and his wife named their son after me. His name is Tod Rutstein. In the 1950s such a thing was almost unheard of, a man of Jewish background and his White wife naming their son after a Black person, and a child at that. Nat ended up working tire-lessly for the realization of racial unity and justice and for the oneness of the human family. He got grief from all quarters, but he made a difference. He hung tough and relied on spirit and faith. He passed away, leaving behind a tremendous and sacrificial legacy. Citing the Bahá'í Writings, he used to say to all who would listen, "Seek the realities underlying the one-ness of the world of humanity" ('Abdu'l-Bahá, 1982, p. 144). Tod remains proud to this day to be named after me and I share the same pride that he is my namesake. Like his father he too works for racial justice.

And then there is a young and brilliant White fella named Lex. Lex has spent the last several years of his life ensuring that deceased and unsung African American heroes received proper state and national recognition; that graveyards and gravestones of African American's were restored when they

262

otherwise would have been irretrievably lost or would have fallen into disrepair. One time he organized a family reunion, bringing together families from various parts of the country in celebration of one of their deceased and prominent African American relative. Some family members had no idea how prominent this relative was until Lex brought them together. Three years later, he assisted in bringing together 150 of their family members from France to Haiti to the US of America.

By the way, the relative was Louis George Gregory, a Bahá'í who worked fearlessly during his life to further the cause of racial unity. He traveled throughout the South during the 1910s and beyond, at great risk to himself, giving talks and promoting racial justice. His eloquence and spirit commanded attention from those in all walks of life. He also had an interracial marriage. He believed that interracial marriage, over time would be a key factor in obliterating racism.

Lex has spent countless hours and a lot of his own money planning these very meaningful and moving occasions. His sole reason for doing so is his belief, that White folk must play their part. His inspiration comes from the Bahá'í Scriptures, which unequivocally state the role White folk have to play in enhancing the honor and promoting the advancement of African Americans. Lex has taken, and continues to take, the spirit of this Scriptural direction to heart.

When I told another friend, Tony Joy, about my book and its title, he shared with me a compelling moment in his life. When he was sixteen years old, Dr. King was murdered. There were riots in Washington, DC, close to where he lived. Some of his friends were suggesting that they as Whites might need to get shotguns to protect themselves against Black folk. Tony told them that Whites were probably safer in the Black neighborhoods than Blacks would be in White neighborhoods. They challenged him to go into the riot areas if he was so sure of

263

himself. He did just that. He told me he went into the heart of the riots with the faith that if he tried to see God, "heaven," honor and dignity in the faces of this grief-stricken and angry Blacks folks, he'd be okay. He walked through those riot-torn streets receiving some hostile stares and long looks however experienced no physical violence. He did not stay long, but to him, the point was made. Some may find his behavior reckless and maybe it was, but it was also courageous for any age, but especially for a sixteen-year-old.

Another White female I know, whose name is Heather, chose to live with her boys in a very poor, rural and predominately Black area in the South and teach in the public schools. She lives and has taught there for virtually her whole career because she believes in the capacity of the children. Upon retirement, she had many choices but chose to develop a writing program entitled *Bump It Up* and deliver it in some of these same schools. Her program has dramatically increased the writing level as well as the self-esteem of scores of African American children. Though she cares about reaching children of all colors, she recognizes the unique challenges in certain African American communities and wants to make a difference. She's not trying to *save* anyone, she is simply trying to make sure these students are provided the best opportunities possible. I know she's faced tremendous obstacles, racial and otherwise, in her journey, but she's never given up. Her journey continues.

And finally there's my former White female business partner, Janice. Because of her passion for race unity and her disdain for racism, she *pressured* me into joining her in a consulting business. Her whole deal was for us, as a Black/White, male/female team, to address racism on a state and national level. I say pressured because when I left my job as Minority Affairs Director at the University in St. Cloud Minnesota, I was emotionally exhausted. I meant for my move to South Carolina to represent a clean break from this line of work. She convinced

264

me that we could make a difference and persistently insisted I could do this because of my faith. She was fearless in her efforts and at a time and in places that were often hostile to this kind of work. With no particular training in this field, she pushed herself until she gained the necessary skills and knowledge to be able to make a difference. We worked together for fifteen rewarding and challenging years. Without her, I may never have jumped back in to this noble struggle.

These are all every day folks who drew and draw on their faith to address these issues, in a spirit and in a manner both honorable and forthright, transcending the fear of rejection by Whites or Blacks, just putting themselves out there. They aren't trying to do anybody any favors, but simply doing what their "grace space" guided them, as human beings, to do.

Dr. King spoke of this "grace space" in his own way in a speech he gave outside a prison after visiting prisoner Joan Baez. Dr. King had begun speaking out against the Viet Nam war late in his life. Prior to that he had felt his struggle was solely that of civil rights. Eventually his conscience guided him otherwise. Soon after speaking out against the war, he was maligned and attacked from almost all quarters.

In this case a reporter asked him if he wasn't taking a chance of losing support if he spoke out against the war. After making it clear that he did not plan to cooperate with evil at any point, he stated the following:

> On some positions cowardice asks the question, 'Is it safe?!' Expediency asks the question, 'Is it politic?' Vanity asks the question, 'Is it popular?' But conscience must ask the question, 'Is it right?!' And there comes a time when one must take a stand that is neither safe, nor politic, nor popular. But one must take it because

it is right. And that is where I find myself today (King, 1968, "Role of the Behavioral Scientist")

I say to you all, from one of my favorite prayers, as I say to myself; have faith. "As ye have faith so shall your powers and blessings be" ('Abdu'l-Bahá as cited in Balyuzi, 1971, p. 73). I heard motivational speaker Les Brown say something like this: faith is not faith until it's all you got to hang onto.

The Rubber Meets the Road: Who Has to Do What?

My plea, oh brethren and sisters, is that we search our souls and imagine what we can be as individuals and as a nation. In the spirit of hope and learning, let's take this race thing on and participate in the joy of being a part of what this US of America experiment is all about. Is it possible to bring the diversity of humanity to one place and live in harmony? I stand up and say yes. What do you say? I also say it's gotta start with rooting out the rest of the deep seated vestiges of racism. Doesn't have to end there or only be there, but it sure has to focus there.

We also have to encourage and educate our young people in the kind of character development that will compel them to finish the job. To do that, we have to be changing ourselves. Said before, we can't just leave it to time and the younger generation without examples to follow. No one, and I mean no one, is absolved from this—no matter how far you think you've come, regardless if you're are young or old, grew up in this country or not. As the basketball coaches say, we need a full court press on this. To put it another way, it has been said, *we are the ones we are waiting for.*

I am truly gettin my last licks in here because my belief is it's gonna take all the wisdom, tact, love , patience, mature

266

understanding, initiative, humility and deliberate and persistent effort we can muster to get this resolved. Hopefully these last few pages have put you in a grace space because now comes the phi slamma jama quote. Bahá'í teachings are straight up about who has to do what to get this thing resolved. Says what I've been trying to say, only much better. This particular passage gives me chills when I read it because it is so right on. It uses the term *Negro* because it was written in 1937, when this was the appropriate terminology. Sit down, buckle up and read this. There's something in it for both Whites and Blacks.

Let the White make a supreme effort in their resolve to contribute their share to the solution of this problem, to abandon once for all their usually inherent and at times subconscious sense of superiority, to correct their tendency towards revealing a patronizing attitude towards the members of the other race, to persuade them through their intimate, spontaneous and informal association with them of the genuineness of their friendship and the sincerity of their intentions, and to master their impatience of any lack of responsiveness on the part of a people who have received, for so long a period, such grievous and slow-healing wounds. Let the Negroes, through a corresponding effort on their part, show by every means in their power the warmth of their response, their readiness to forget the past, and their ability to wipe out every trace of suspicion that may still linger in their hearts and minds. Let neither think that the solution of so vast a problem is a matter that exclusively concerns the other. Let neither think that such a problem can either easily or immediately be resolved. Let neither think that they can wait confidently for the solution of this problem until the initiative has been taken, and the favorable circumstances created, by agencies that stand outside the orbit of their Faith. Let neither think that anything short of genuine

267

love, extreme patience, true humility, consummate tact, sound initiative, mature wisdom, and deliberate, persistent, and prayerful effort, can succeed in blotting out the stain which this patent evil has left on the fair name of their common country. (Effendi, 1937, p. 40)

That is straight talk and something to really ponder. It takes deep reflection because some of it may go against your emotional grain but we have to step it up to another place. Again I'm asking you all to think spiritually and not emotionally. Don't think your emotions will allow you to wrap yourself around all of what this passage says. It's as true today as it was in 1937. Says to me, we're gonna sink or swim together, so get real!

As a young Bahá'í, I used to get excited about what this passage said White folk needed to do, almost ignoring what it said Black folk had to do, kind of blowin it off as if I was somehow automatically doing my part. One day I realized, "oh yeah, it says I got a piece to play in this as well. Part that I always struggled with was about forgetting the past till I realized it wasn't asking me to have amnesia but rather not to treat White folk based on the past. Hard as that is, I get it! But I can only do that from my high road self and that's a fact. My emotional low road self says, "No way."

So now, I guess it's clear that continuing progress toward racial unity and justice will not come about, as Ms. Tutu stated, *"oh by the way?"* Efforts must be intentional down to the micro level. Let me squeeze in this small example on that sort of micro-level. I'm part of a diverse team, in Washington, DC, who work with young people, ages ten to thirteen. Our goal is to collaborate with these young people in developing their moral, spiritual and intellectual and capacities. Because we are a diverse team, but all middle class and the kids we work with are all lower income and Black, we realize that race, culture and class can be issues that impact our interactions. So after each class our team reflects on three questions: How well did we meet our objectives? How well did we work together as a team? (The purpose of this question is to make sure that across age, race, and culture we all have a voice.) Finally, the third question is the following: did we sense that there were any racial, cultural or class factors that might have impacted our interactions with each other, with the kids and us and among the kids themselves? These questions are *intentional* and are designed to help us get through the surface level of our interactions to the deeper more subtle levels where a lot of the racial/cultural challenges resides. They represent a simple process that invites learning, and invites all team members of all backgrounds to address issues that might be sensitive. Without such a process, we leave it up to the courage of an individual to just sort of bring up a concern or issue they might wonder about. This can be very difficult. For example, say everyone else is happy about the way things went, but you felt like something needed to be said about a matter of consequence that involved race or class. You know you might be upsetting the apple cart, as everyone else was *on board*. Since racial issues are so loaded, who wants to upset the apple cart or go against the grain? It's easier to go along just to get along. However, having an intentional reflection process, with the focus on learning, not blaming, our group has benefited time and again from sensitive discussions that otherwise would not have come up. More importantly, in my view, these consultations and discussions have improved the quality of our service and strengthened our bonds and our capacity to talk about these issues. Is this type of process applicable in other settings for anyone to use? Absolutely!

Can you imagine if we as U.S. Americans committed ourselves to serving our communities and purposely sought ways to serve with diverse groups, what we could gain as a nation? Faith groups and organizations could find ways to work with other demographically diverse Faith groups or community organizations. Service clubs could do the same. Neighborhoods could choose projects seeking to collaborate with demographically diverse neighborhoods. Projects could range from efforts to work with youth and children to litter pick up to serving elders. The point is service can bring out the best in us and at the same time help us learn about each other.

Groups could use the type of consultative questions suggested above to make sure we are learning about each others perspectives. It is when we work together for a common purpose that the opportunity to learn about differences and similarities can be the greatest. So without working out all the details I say *seek diversity* in this way and learn to use it for good. I think at this point in history there are enough folk of good will that are ready to move in this direction.

There are so many demographically mixed environments at work, in communities, in schools and universities on councils and committees where race and culture are factors but there are no processes to examine them. Issues simply smolder, and folk get talked about instead of talked to and undercurrents, conscious and unconscious prevail. Equally important, there are so many such institutions and organizations that have no diversity, so these issues simply are not part of the dialogue. If we set up reflection processes—not for blaming but for learning—we can be proactive versus reactive. We can look for ways to learn, to be more vital and inclusive. Intentionality again is the key word. We leave things to chance that don't matter; this matters.

What racial/cultural implications might this decision have? Are there any racial/cultural factors we need to consider before we make a decision, implement a project, and engage in interactions across cultures? Are there racial and cultural factors I need to think about as I write this report, decide on this policy, craft language, decide on what pictures go on a promotional cover, or decide who will greet parents as they come to visit the school? Simply asking the question can trigger new thinking. Often folk think if they just say it's important to be open-minded, or express that to their employees or those in their families, communities, agencies or organization, somehow just saying it will magically translate into behavior. (Note, I did say families because that's where it starts) Too often that means we just assume things and, consciously or not, act as if everyone thinks, interacts and is impacted in the same fashion. Again, there's an assumption that everyone's life experiences are the same. So I say we need processes of all kinds if we want real progress and using questions is a simple and powerful tool.

Sometimes the results of having such processes can lead to difficult discussions or a prolongation of some task, project or goal you want to accomplish, but without unity, most things ultimately fail anyway. Unity is a most fundamental spiritual law of the universe. When folk feel excluded often, consciously or unconsciously, they withdraw their efforts anyway. At worst they will undermine whatever the project is by engaging in what is called, from my recollection of what I heard years ago at a talk, a *discount revenge cycle*. That basically means meaning since you excluded me, I'm going to find a way to undermine you. The human body comes to mind yet again. What if the human body is not working in harmony? Glossing over issues of prejudice or cultural dynamics because it's easier not to deal with them or because you have a deadline or because you don't slow down long enough to pay attention has always been a deadly strategy is like glossing over an infection in your body. Sooner or later it'll get you. Deal with it early, prevent the deeper infection and maintain the health of the body.

You might be thinkin how impractical that is. How can you have unity in every situation or circumstance before you proceed? When it comes to decisions that involve more than one person, it is critical that everyone have a voice. One thing racism and all the -isms take away is folk's ability to be heard. Opinions, perspectives and viewpoints of whole groups of people are dismissed or belittled based on who they are and or how they look. One of the greatest forms of acknowledgement is to really listen and invite "voice." So what my Faith teaches is me is that to maximize the possibly for unity in a discussion, it is important to create a warm environment, where those present are encouraged to be detached from their opinions but speak their minds, not clinging to their viewpoints or becoming estranged if others disagree. This takes a lot of getting centered first, so humans are being human instead of letting egos kick each other to pieces. I dare say all of us have experienced that.

I believe in this approach, but to get myself in the right space, I have to meditate and or pray and or take some deep breaths first, and then remind myself, though I may have part of the truth, I don't have it all. Sounds simple, but check yourself out and see how often you say things assuming that you are right, that your thinking represents the entirety of a situation, subject or challenge. See how many times you filter other people's ideas, concepts or suggestions through your experience and either negate or somehow dismiss them a bit too quickly. How often do you speak your truth as if it were from on *High*? Can you see how this might happen in discussions about race?

When a consulting environment is established, ideas are ex-changed with the goal of coming to a consensus. If consensus is not reached, a vote is taken. Whatever the majority decides becomes the will of the group because everyone has had a voice. The decision is carried out in unity without those who disagree railing against the decision, in or out of the meeting or discussion. That's part of the deal and most critical. With unified support of the decision, it all works out great. If not, it can be reevaluated and changed with full knowledge that the decision didn't go wrong because of disagreeing members tearing it down. The unity in support of the decision will ensure, if it doesn't work out, it was the decision itself that needed to be changed.

It takes a whole lot of discipline to act in this way. You have to admit though; it makes a whole lot of sense. So if you decide you want to use questions or some other process, so you can reflect on issues of race and culture with folk, you also need to create the right dynamics and energy to establish the environment for discussion as just described. It'll take folk adopting a new mind-set, heart-set and soul-set, willing to tap into their better selves before speaking and listening. It is this type of dialogue we need. I love this approach, and it demonstrates to me, yet again, the practicality of spirituality.

With that, I reiterate to my "heavenly"-faced Black brothers and sisters, my belief that all the suffering we've been and are going through can be transformed into measures of patience, wisdom and compassion for all people. When I say patience I realize we've been patient already. I'm not talking about the kind of patience that says we don't push the envelope at the same time. I am talking about the kind of patience that demonstrates our faith that rightness will prevail. Our community needs us and the world needs us. I say that without arrogance or apology. The bruises and broken hearts we suffer(ed) can, if we let them, transform us. Then we can carve out a new road of hope and offering new life where things are messed up including, but not limited to, racism. We not only can help Black folk and our communities, but all communities, if we use our gifts the way they were intended. That sort of vision of our suffering gives me hope, otherwise it would have been in vain. We simply can't let that be the case. These sentiments have been stated more clearly than I can in a letter to African Americans from the governing body of my Faith:

> There can be no doubt that Americans of African descent can find in themselves the capacity, so well developed as a result of their long encounter with injustice, to recognize and respond to the vision of love and justice..... Imbued with that vision, past and present sufferings are transformed into measures of patience, wisdom and compassion—qualities so essential to the effort to moderate the discordant ways of a confused world and aid the healing of its spiritual ills. What better than the transformed character of a bruised people to smooth the course, to offer perspectives for a new beginning. (Universal House of Justice, 1985)

How sweet it is!

I don't deny the cause of much of our suffering has been gross injustice. However, if we allow the suffering we've experienced to make us bitter and not better, we are losers twice! We'd have allowed that suffering to only make us bleed, instead of driving us to lead. We'd give new meaning to the term "two time losers." We'd have lost because we were unjustly treated and oppressed for so long, and we'd have lost because we would have tarnished our legacy and given away our future; a future in which we were intended to play a preponderating share in building a unified humanity. We as a people cannot allow that to happen!

When we, Black and White folk, get this right, we will show the whole world that what looks impossible can be done and divisions that appear intractable can be transformed into new-found possibilities. I affirm, this is the hope we will offer the world, so let's get on with it.

Last bit of preachin I'm gonna do, as far as I can tell. Here's where we all must start. It's very simple but very hard. We have to start with desire! I mean down home, hard core, serious business, no phoniness, heart-felt desire. We have to actually WANT to unite with other folk. WE have to desire it. Sounds simple, but the place to start is in our heart, and our heart has to want to unify with folks we have always seen as "other" or that we've grown suspicious of. With all our history and her story, that is the first step.

> If you desire with all your heart, friendship with every race on earth, your thought, spiritual and positive, will spread; it will become the desire of others, growing stronger and stronger, until it reaches the minds of all men. Do not despair! Work steadily. Sincerity and love will conquer hate. How many seemingly impossible events are coming to pass in these days! Set your faces steadily towards the Light of the World. Show love to all... Take courage! God never forsakes His children who strive and work and pray! Let your hearts be filled with the strenuous desire that tranquility and harmony may encircle all this warring world. So will success crown your efforts, and with the universal brotherhood will come the Kingdom of God in peace and goodwill. ('Abdu'l-Bahá, 1995, p. 29)

Sweet and powerful passage isn't it?

Next question I want to ask brings to mind a question Clint Eastwood asked in the tough guy movie *Dirty Harry*. Movie lines pop into my mind all the time when I'm talkin and writin so humor me. Clint (Dirty Harry) had just fired several shots at some run away bank robbers and one of the suspects was lying wounded on the ground with Clint pointing his gun at him. Suspect is deciding whether he should go for his gun to shoot Clint but he's not sure if Clint fired all six of his shots

275

or only five. Clint, still pointing his gun at suspect tells him he knows what the suspect is thinking, did he fire six shots or only five? Clint says in all this *excitement* he lost track of how many shots he'd fired. He goes on to say to the suspect, "So you gotta ask yourself a question. Do you feel lucky?" Then he emphatically stated, "Well do ya punk?" So let me say something similar to you. In all the craziness around race issues in the US of America have you lost track of a need to care about and desire friendship with every race on earth? "So you gotta ask yourself a question? Do you really desire friendship with every race on earth? Well do ya punk?" I'm not callin anyone a punk; I only said that because it's such a great testosterone line from the movie. However, rephrasing I'm asking you as pointedly as Clint did, "Well do you my brothers and sisters?"

Movie reference aside this is a deep and profound question. Do you really desire friendship with folks of other races; in this case White to Black and Black to White? Has all the crazy making racial dynamics in this country made you lose that desire or never find it? Without over stretching the *Dirty Harry* version, we all need to find that desire because we can metaphorically say a gun is pointing at us if we don't get this right. In the movie it's a White cop pointing a gun at a Black suspect and in that case they both lived. It can be that way for real. We, Black and White, can both live. If you don't desire friendship with every race on earth, pray about it, meditate about it, work with it till some desire comes and then it will build. Without desire things aren't gonna change.

Desire has helped me to develop a very simple daily strategy. I call it "lead with love." I may not know everyone's cultural background. I may have some deep hard feelings about racism, but when I get up in the morning, I focus myself, before I go out the door, to lead with love. Translation: I decide to

276

demonstrate a caring attitude to everyone I meet that day: a hello, a nod, a handshake, a hug, whatever it takes.

I myself get inspired by such talk, and I encourage you to look into your Scriptures for gems like the one I just shared about desire because they are there. We have to be inspired and driven by them if we are going to make a difference. You can look in my Scriptures too, if you'd like. We will all find a lot of truth, but the point is we can't just look. We have to look and leap!

If you're skeptical about the power of thought, of unity and of love, wondering if it can really make a difference, you can view all your effort as simply tryin it out as an experiment. You don't even have to commit to stickin to it. The following passage from the the Bahá'í Scriptures suggests as much:

> During these six thousand years there has been con-stant war, strife, bloodshed. We can see at a glance the results. Have we not a sufficient standard of ex-perience in this direction? Let us now try peace for a while. If good results follow, let us adhere to it. If not let us throw it away and fight again. Nothing will be lost by the experiment. ('Abdu'l-Bahá as cited in Gail, 1976, p. 189)

I say the same to my White brothers and sisters as well as to my Black brothers and sisters. Why not try? If it doesn't work, it won't be hard to go back to racism, hostility, distrust and suspicion. As Rev. Jesse once said when he was runnin for President, though I am changing it a bit: if we try we might succeed, if we don't try we won't succeed for sure.

Whatever religion you profess to or whatever spirituality you use, I say it's time to take stock, time to *check in* for a *check-up*. That's right; we'd all better get a spiritual check-up; just like we get a maintenance check for our car before embarking on a long journey. Need to make sure your mind, body and spirit are tuned in and tuned up. Might find you need a spiritual oil change because it's been far too long. Maybe the thickness in your thinkin is gummin up everything. You may need a spiritually rebuilt engine because there's some misfiring in your brain because you focused on *otherness* instead of *oneness* too long. A spiritual tire check may also be necessary. Your willpower needs to get pumped up to drive this whole thing. In fact you probably need a front-end spiritual alignment because you might've been running from this thing for so long your equilibrium is out of whack. Need an alignment to stay on track. Don't forget the spiritual radiator flush because over time and through neglect, there might be rust up in that heart. Or you might need to flush out the poison in your heart, accumulated from long suffering and pain. You're gonna need room for the new blood. I say it's time. It's time we all check in and check up on our body, mind, soul, spirit and heart and make sure we didn't get out of balance somewhere. Thinkin we are mostly out of tune when it comes to applying our higher selves to this race issue.

That's the truth as I see it. By the way, if you don't believe in God, I'm surely not leavin you out; a lot of folk who don't necessarily believe in God, just believe in doin the right thing, and they get out and do it. I say keep on and thank you! Believers in God or not, remember what a good *Texan* friend of mine once told me. He said: "If you're out in front taking the lead, you may get shot in the back but that's what makes you HOLY." Brought a smile to my face though I hope I can get holy another way. He's a guy who I once referred to as a European American. He stopped me in my tracks and said emphatically, "I'm not a European American. I'm Texan."

My brothers and sisters of all hues, this has been quite a day we've spent together. To think it all started with me sharing coffee with you and reading my newspaper, which I did finally finish at some point. Thinkin back, I didn't offer you any coffee, did I? That's okay; it's a bad habit anyway. So, as the sun sets on this story and I bid you a good day and a good night. I will say these last words for the last time. Oh, by the way, I sold my Corolla to a Japanese guy—that was a story in itself that'll wait for another time.

To my darker-hued brothers and sisters I say, keep the faith, fight the good fight, remember and keep the sacred spirit of your ancestors' crusade of justice; that spirit that Dr. King so eloquently worded this way: "I may not get there with you. But I want you to know tonight, that we, as a people, will get to the Promised Land" (King, 1968, "I've Been to the Mountain Top").

To my lighter-hued brothers and sisters I say, keep the faith, fight the good fight, remember and keep the sacred spirit of your ancestors' crusade of justice; that spirit that Dr. King so eloquently worded this way: "I may not get there with you. But I want you to know tonight, that we, as a people, will get to the Promised Land" (King, 1968, "I've Been to the Mountain Top").

Let it matter to you that wakin up Black in the US of America makes me tired. Most importantly, when things get tough and you get hurt, discouraged, angry or sad, don't say the "coffee break" is over. Instead, stick around and keep drinkin; the whole cup, however hot it is and however long it takes to finish.

Chapter 21

Seein Heaven in the Face of a Black Man

The US of America that I want to be part of shapin, makin and creatin is one that expects to see heaven in the face of a Black man. What a vision that is for this fifty-something African American: coming to a time when US of Americans, White and Black, figuratively and literally, expect to, want to and see heaven in the face of Black men. I pray for the day when we don't feel fear, anxiety, distrust, resentment or indifference when we see a Black man; but rather we look for, expect to see, have an image in our head of heaven in that face; when we show enough regard for each other that not only White folk see heaven in the face of Black men, but more Black men and women see heaven in their own faces. When we get to that day, I will know "America the Beautiful" includes my Colored, Negro, Black, Afro-American, African American, Person of Color, African Descent self.

Epilogue: NEWS FLASH

Shortly after I completed this book, Barack Hussein Obama was elected the 44th President of the United States of America. The world rejoiced and tears of joy were shed by masses of humanity worldwide. It seemed that the ability of the US of America to elect an African American President touched a chord in the hearts, that in many cases, transcended political parties and preferences. (I am not a member of any political party, but vote my conscience.)

On Election Day, shortly after voting, I felt, deep down, I wanted and needed to honor this momentous day in some manner. It struck me that I wanted to go to a place that had significance related to the sacrifice of my enslaved ancestors. I wanted to pay tribute to them and to humbly thank them for the opportunity that was now before the United States of America. I found the perfect place, near the White House, where slaves had once been sold and marched down Pennsylvania Avenue. How appropriate it was. As a misty rain came down, I spent over an hour in reflection, prayer and meditation. It was a profound experience as I felt the spirit of the slaves seep into my veins and calm my heart.

I went home at peace, open to whatever happened. At 11:00 pm eastern time, Tuesday November 4, 2008, I listened to news anchor, Charlie Gibson, announce that the 44th president of the United States was Barack Hussein Obama. I cried and screamed a primal scream. At the end of, and as I part of that scream, I shouted to the Almighty with incredulity, joy and awe, "What have you done? What have you done?" I shouted it over and over as my wife rejoiced with me.

This was not just a victory for Democrats. Politics is not why so many in the world rejoiced. Barack Obama's election tapped

281

something profound and deep. It resonated with hope for so many. Hope for what? I'm not sure anyone could exactly define it at that moment, but surely it was hope for something better, something good, something connecting, safe and unifying. Regardless of party preference or feelings about the United States or a particular world view, there was something right about this, something just about this, something moral, ethical even spiritual about this. Something good just happened and a significant portion of the world responded.

Conversely hate groups grew in membership. Guns were sold at an astounding rate, in part because of the view that Mr. Obama would beef up gun control laws and in part because some were worried about the economy and wanted to "protect" themselves and in part, I fear, as a knee-jerk reaction. Mr. Obama's security detail is unprecedented in size while the threats on his life are unprecedented in number. Though many voted for him because of their belief in his policies and in his goodness, regardless of race, many could not vote for him because of his race. Though we heard overwhelmingly positive reactions to his election; throughout the country, from high schools to work places to churches, despicable acts of protest occurred. Not just protest springing from the natural disappointment of a candidate of choice loosing, but protest that was ugly and vicious. In some cases, protests advocating violence against Mr. Obama. At work the next day, some folks would not sit down by Black folk, reacted to them angrily or were standoffish. Voices from certain parts of the world trickled in that made clear President Obama's color mattered and not in a good way.

All that said, I have a choice and I choose to let my soul thoroughly rejoice in this major step for our country and consequently for the world. I rejoice, not as a member of a political party but as a member of the human family. I choose to reflect on the irony of how a man with heritage from Kenya to Kansas, with White and Black blood running through his veins, with a name like Barack Hussein Obama, who spent early years in Indonesia and Hawaii and who, at one point, was too Black for some and not Black enough for others, was elected the first "Black" President of the United States of America. I choose to be thrilled from head to toe, to see a "brown-skinned" proud, beautiful, intelligent and fine African American sister become the first lady of the US of America. I am thrilled for myself, for my African American sisters and especially for the dark-skinned ones, and in general for all of us. I choose to let my soul take all of this in and to feel intensely grateful.

I also choose to caution myself, while not dampening my exhilaration, remembering what President Obama said in his acceptance speech. In essence he made clear that his election was not the end goal, but represented a chance. I say, it is a chance to do all I've said in this book and to be wise, insistent, loving and intentional about it. It is a chance to prayerfully reflect and dig deeper till we come to that point of discovering or rediscovering our profoundly spiritual humanity. It is a chance to find opportunities to serve our communities together across racial/cultural/class barriers so we can learn about each other in service to the common good. It is a chance to create a fairer and more just America based on the understanding of our essential oneness. It is a chance to come together across communities in prayer that the US of America will become "glorious in spiritual degrees even as it has aspired to material degrees" ('Abdu'l-Bahá, 1991, p. 24). It is a chance to bring our children and young people together and say, "look what we can be, look what we can do if we work together, look what the US of America can be."

It is not the time to rest, but to rejoice while simultaneously and intentionally, pushing the envelope to the point of no return, knowing the last push on this mountain will perhaps be the most difficult. Some will dig their heels in, knowing that once the mountain crumbles, the system of advantage, based upon race, is over. So let us all push with the spirit that if we do it with love and compassion and fortitude, the forces of the universe will conspire with us to win the victory. This story of a man becoming discouraged and wanting to give up, because he could not move the mountain he was instructed to push on by the Creator, best illustrates my point.

> The Creator responded compassionately (to the discouraged man), "My friend, when I asked you to serve me and you accepted, I told you that your task was to push against the rock with all your strength, which you have done. Never once (mountain) did I mention to you that I expected you to move it. Your task was to push.

> "Now you come to me with your strength spent, thinking that you have failed. But is that really so? Look at yourself. Your arms are strong and muscled, your back is sinewy and brown, your hands are callused from constant pressure, and your legs have become massive and hard. Through opposition you have grown much, and your abilities now surpass that which you used to have. Yet you haven't moved the rock. But your calling was to be obedient and to push and to exercise your faith in My wisdom. This you have done. I, my friend, will now move the rock.

> …. By all means, exercise the faith that moves mountains, but know that it is still the Creator who moves the mountains." (Unknown, 2008)

And so it is.

NEWS FLASH OVER

Bibliography

'Abdu'l-Bahá. (1991). O thou kind Lord. In Bahá'í Publishing Trust, *Bahá'í Prayers* (p. 24). Wilmette: Bahá'í Publishing Trust.

'Abdu'l-Bahá. (1991). O God refresh. In Bahá'í Publishing Trust, *Bahá'í Prayers* (p. 151). Wilmette: Bahá'í Publishing Trust.

'Abdu'l-Bahá. (1995). *Paris talks.* London: Bahá'í Publishing Trust.

'Abdu'l-Baha'. (1982). *Promulgation of universal peace.* Wilmette: Bahá'í Publishing Trust.

Amenta, P. (Director). (1987). *True colors* [News Show]. Australia: 7 Network.

Amersbach, G. (2002, Winter). Through the lens of race: Unequal health care in America. *Harvard Public Health Review.* Retrieved September 4, 2008, from http://www.hsph.harvard.edu/review/ review_winter_02/featurerace.html

Arntz, W. & Chasse, B. (Director). (2004). *What the bleep do we know?* [Motion Picture]. United States: Captured Light.

Bahá'u'lláh. (1983). *Gleanings from the writings of Bahá'u'lláh.* Wilmette: Bahá'í Publishing Trust.

Bahá'u'lláh. (1954). *The hidden words of Bahá'u'lláh.* Wilmette: Bahá'í Publishing Trust.

Bahá'u'lláh. (1988). *Tablets of Bahá'u'lláh.* Wilmette: Bahá'í Publishing Trust.

Bahá'u'lláh. (1991). Praise be to thee. In Bahá'í Publishing Trust, *Bahá'í Prayers* (p. 127–28). Wilmette: Bahá'í Publishing Trust.

Balyuzi, H. (1971). *'Abdu'l-Bahá.* London: George Ronald.

Blackmon, D. A. (2008). *Slavery by another name.* New York: Doubleday.

Borris-Dunchunstang, E. R. (2009, January 19). Martin Luther King on forgiveness. *Finding Forgiveness.* Retrieved July 21, 2009, from http://findingforgiveness.blogspot.com/2009/01/martin-luther-king-on-forgiveness.html

Bowden, T. (2005, June 30). Uneven playing field. *Yahoo Sports.* Retrieved September 3, 2008, from http://rivals.yahoo.com/ncaa/

football/ws?slug=tb-minoritycoaches062905&prov=yhoo&type=lgns

Brinson, C. S. (2001, March 24). States past on collision course with the future. *State Newspaper (South Carolina)*, p. A1.

Brown, J. (Composer). (1968). Say it loud: I'm black and I'm proud. On *Say tt loud.* [J. Brown, Performer]. Los Angeles: Polydor.

Brown, S. (2007, January 11). Rooney rule helping minority coaching candidates. *TribLIVE*. Retrieved December 24, 2008, from http://www.pittsburghlive.com

Brunner, B. (n.d.). The Tuskegee syphilis experiment. *The Tuskegee University*. Retrieved September 5, 2008, from http://www.tuskegee.edu/global/story.asp?s=1207586&ClientType=Printable

Bush, G. (2003, July 8). *President Bush speaks at Goree Island in Senegal*. Retrieved September 5, 2008, from http://georgewbushwhitehouse.archives.gov/news/releases/2003/07/20030708-1.html

Butterworth, E. (1992). *Discover the power within you.* New York: Harper Collins.

Cobb, R. (2001, August 23). Tulsa 1921. *The Nation*. Retrieved July 21, 2009, from http://www.thenation.com/doc/20010820/1921tulsa

Commission on Children at Risk. (2003). *Hardwired to connect.* New York: Institute for American Values.

Duncan, C. (2000 June 2). Remembering the night Tulsa burned. *The Guardian*. Retrieved May 5, 2009 from http://www.guardian.co.uk/world/2000/jun/02/duncancampbell

Duster, T. (Summer 2006). Explaining differential trust of DNA technology: Grounded in assessment or inexplicable paranoia. *Journal of Law, 34*(2): 293-300.

Dyer, W. (2004). *The power of intention.* Carlsbad: Hay House.

Effendi, S. (1937). *The advent of divine justice.* Wilmette: Bahá'í Publishing Trust.

Gail, M. (1976). *Dawn over Mount Hira.* Oxford: George Ronald.

Hacker, A. (1995). *Two nations: Black and white, separate, hostile and unequal.* New York: Ballentine Books.

Harris, J. F. (2001, September 14). God gave us what we deserve, Falwell says. *Washington Post*, p. C03.

Hughes, L. (1967). *Simple's Uncle Sam.* New York: Hill and Wang.

Johansson, F. (2006). *The Medici effect.* Boston: Harvard.

Johnson, R. E. (1993, July 26). Arthur Ashe's new book, 'Days of Grace,' tells of his three burdens: race, AIDS and Davis Cup. *BNET.* Retrieved September 3, 2008, from http://findarticles.com/p/articles/mi_m1355/is_n13_v84/ai_14086943

Jones, S. (2001, March 18). Serena Williams wins as the boos pour down. *New York Times.* Retrieved September 5, 2008, from http://nytimes.com

King, M. L. (1962, April 16). Letter from Birmingham Jail. Retrieved September 4, 2008, from http://www.mlkonline.net

King, M. L. (1957, May 17). Give us the ballot. Retrieved September 4, 2008, from http://www.mlkonline.net

King, M. L. (1968, April 3). I've Been to the Mountain Top. Retrieved July 21, 2009, from http://www.americanrhetoric.com/speeches/mlkivebeentothemountaintop.htm

King, M. L. (1968, January). The Role of the Behavioral Scientiest in the Civil Rights Movement. *APA Monitor Online, 30*(1). Retrieved July 22, 2009, from http://www.apa.org/monitor/jan99/king.html.

King, M. L. (1967). Why I oppose the Viet Nam war. Retrieved July 21, 2009, from http://www.lib.berkeley.edu/MRC/pacificaviet/riversidetranscript.html

Leonhardt, D., & Fessenden, F. (2005, March 22). Black coaches in NBA have shorter tenures. *New York Times.* Retrieved December 24, 2008, from http://www.nytimes.com

Lischer, R. (1997). *The preacher king: Martin Luther King Jr. and the word that moved America.* Oxford: Oxford University Press.

McCarthy, M. (2007, April 5). The fight game: NHL's rules of engagement. *USA Today.* Retrieved January 4, 2009, from www.usatoday.com/sports/hockey/nhl/2007-04-04-fighting_N.htm

McIntosh, P. (1988). Unpacking the invisible knapsack. *Seamonkey.* Retrieved September 5, 2008, from http://seamonkey.esu.asu/~mcisaac/emc598ge/Unpacking.html

Michaels, C. (2007, November). Hundreds march to support Megan Williams. *Black Press USA.* Retrieved January 6, 2009, from http://www.blackpressusa.com/News/Article.asp?SID=3&Title=Hot+Storie

s&NewsID=14570

Murchie, G. (1999). *The seven mysteries of life.* Boston: Mariner Books.

The My Hero Project. (2001, September 15). Peacemaker hero. Retrieved September 5, 2008, from http://www.myhero.com/myhero/hero. asp?hero=a_lookinghorse

The National Spiritual Assembly of the Bahá'ís of the United States. (1991). The vision of race unity: America's most challenging issue. Retrieved May 5, 2009 from http://www.bahai.com/Bahaullah/ raceunity2.htm

Nichols, J. (2008, April 29). Wright, Jefferson and the wrath of God. *The Nation.* Retrieved May 3, 2009 from http://www.thenation.com/ blogs/thebeat/316575

Oates, S. (1994). *Let the trumpet sound: A life of Martin Luther King, Jr.* New York: Harper Perennial.

Pager, D. (2003). The Mark of a Criminal Record. *American Journal of Sociology, 108*(5), 937–75.

Protest against negro family moving into Lake Minnetonka suburb. (1952, January 30). *St. Paul Recorder.*

Race prejudice blooms in our suburbs, Too. (1952). *Minneapolis Star and Tribune.*

Schwartz, L. (n.d.). Hank Aaron: Hammerin' Back at Racism. *ESPN.* Retrieved August 31, 2008. http://espn.go.com/classic/biography/s/ Aaron_Hank.html

Smith, M. D. (2008, July 5). Floyd Mayweather rips HBO, says "I've seen Jim Lampley in the same strip club as me." *AOL Sports.* Retrieved September 3, 2008, from http://mma.fanhouse.com

Solomon, J. (1994, October 30). Skin deep: Reliving "black like me": My own journey into the Heart of race consciousness. *Washington Post,* p. C01.

Tatum, B. D. (2003). *Why do all the black kids sit together in the cafeteria.* New York: Basic Books.

Tutu, M. (2007, Dec 4). Conflict resolution through forgiveness and reconciliation. Montgomery College, Rockville, Maryland, United States.

The Universal House of Justice. (2007, June 3). Letter. Haifa, Israel: The Universal House of Justice.

The Universal House of Justice Justice. (1985). *The Promise of World Peace.* Wilmette: Bahá'í Publishing Trust.

Unknown. (n.d.). *God calling earth.* Retrieved December 31, 2008, from http://www.godcallingearth.com

Wah, L. M. (Producer). (1994). *The Color of Fear.* United States: Stir Fry Productions.

Washington, D. (Actor). (1992). In Lee, S., *Malcolm X* [Motion picture]. United States: 40 Acres and a Mule Filmworks.

Wise, T. (2001, March). School shootings and white denial. *Alter Net.* Retrieved September 3, 2008, from http://www.alternet.org/story/10560/